JACOBEAN AND CAROLINE POETRY
AN ANTHOLOGY

JACOBEAN AND CAROLINE POETRY

AN ANTHOLOGY

EDITED BY

T. G. S. Cain

METHUEN

LONDON & NEW YORK

First published in 1981 by
Methuen & Co. Ltd
11 *New Fetter Lane, London* EC4P 4EE
Published in the USA by
Methuen & Co.
in association with Methuen, Inc.
733 *Third Avenue, New York,* NY 10017
© 1981 *T. G. S. Cain (selection and editorial matter)*
Typeset by Nene Phototypesetters Ltd
Printed in Great Britain by
Richard Clay (The Chaucer Press) Ltd,
Bungay, Suffolk.

British Library Cataloguing in Publication Data

Jacobean and Caroline poetry.
1. *English poetry – Early modern,* 1500–1700
I. Cain, T. G. S.
821'.3'08   PR1209   80–42217
ISBN 0–416–31060–5
ISBN 0–416–31070–2 *Pbk*

CONTENTS

ROBERT HERRICK

PART TWO: MISCELLANY

PREFACE

The primary aim of this anthology is to offer an annotated selection substantial enough for it to be used as the only primary text in a course on early seventeenth-century poetry at university, college or school level. At the same time it sets out to fulfil three other common functions of an anthology: to give a selection of the best poems of the period, to introduce readers to poets who deserve to be better known and to give an accurate impression of the general contours of poetic activity during the period. In order to fulfil these aims, and to facilitate use, the anthology is divided into two sections, both arranged in chronological order. The first consists of substantial selections from ten leading poets of the period. Here I have tried to give enough of the work of each poet for the reader to take away an adequate sense of the character of his *oeuvre* as a whole; the necessary exception to this is Milton, who poses insuperable problems for the anthologist, and whose long poems I have not attempted to represent by extracts.

The second section is a miscellany in which poems have been chosen either for intrinsic merit or in a very few cases for the light they shed on the intellectual attitudes of the period. I hope that this arrangement, instead of intensifying the already damaging division of poets of the period into minor and major figures, will have the opposite effect by encouraging readers to look more closely at the less well-known poets and poems included here.

I have tried to avoid the simple acceptance of established reputations, and instead to look at each poet afresh. Hence the appearance of Drayton and Carew, and (by modern standards) the large selection of Herrick in Part One. The amount of space devoted to Donne is likewise not so much a reflection of his current reputation as the result of rereading him with as few preconceptions about his relative status as possible. In Part Two I have tried to read and select in the same spirit; I have had to exclude a number of minor poets with some regret, because their inclusion would have meant the exclusion of someone else. Others, like Campion at one end and Cotton at the other, are excluded on chronological grounds. I have given less space than usual to Denham and Cleveland, and none at all to Quarles. Their continued modern reputations seem to rest on inflated reputations gained in their own time, while the converse is true of such writers as Sir John Beaumont, Godolphin, Hammond, Strode and Philipott. It is obviously part of the business of the anthologist to suggest such revaluations as are implied here; on the other hand, he does not seek originality of selection for its own sake, and I have tried to avoid temptations in that direction.

The texts are not authoritative, but are based wherever possible on the earliest printed or manuscript sources, with orthography and punctuation modernized except where rhyme, scansion or some other element depends on an obsolete form. At the end of a poem, or a group of poems, the source of the text is given.

INTRODUCTION

For all its acknowledged importance, the poetry of the period 1600–60 is still too often described in simple and distorting formulas. The picture commonly presented is of two schools of poets, 'Metaphysical' and 'Cavalier', differing clearly from each other and both reacting sharply against the supposed Petrarchism of Elizabethan poetry and against the wider values of the Elizabethan world. The Metaphysical group – Donne, the Herberts, Vaughan, Crashaw, Cowley, Marvell – has engaged the attention and esteem of modern readers a great deal more than has the other group, usually thought of as including Ben Jonson, Herrick, Carew, Suckling, Lovelace and others. Milton, a figure who clearly fits into neither group and who, since he cannot be ignored, tends to spoil the pattern, is usually seen with some puzzlement as the inheritor of the values of the third and most minor grouping, that of the 'Spenserians' – Drayton, Browne, the Fletchers, Sir John Beaumont – a group of writers who seem on the whole to be inconveniently late Elizabethans, and who are thus given very short shrift by most modern critics.

The currency of these divisions may be seen in the titles of many anthologies and works of criticism; and of course like most generalizations about literary history, they do contain a substantial element of truth. But the time has surely come when we should question whether they do not now do as much harm as good, whether instead of offering the usefully clarifying perspective on the period which they undoubtedly did in the 1920s, they have not hardened into an orthodoxy which prevents us from looking with any degree of freshness at the whole body of poetry written during these years.

The primary difficulty in taking such a fresh look is that it must avoid abandoning those aspects of the currently received picture which remain true. No one can deny that some poets did indeed commit themselves to one set of literary principles, one way of writing, rather than another. This is most strikingly true of the least discussed 'school' of the seventeenth century, that of George Herbert; but the 'Sons of Ben' also clearly saw themselves as guided (to widely varying extents) by Jonson's principles, while others did indeed feel that they were maintaining the traditions of Spenser. It is, curiously, those poets most discussed by modern critics, the 'Metaphysicals', whom it is most difficult to see as forming any kind of coherent group. Certainly it is difficult to take T. S. Eliot's notion of a 'School of Donne' at all literally, as Eliot himself seems to have been aware. No poet of any real substance is committed to Donne in the way that Vaughan is to Herbert, Herrick to Jonson, or Drayton to Spenser. His most distinguished imitators are Herbert of Cherbury and Habington, but even they are different enough from Donne to emphasize that he had, in the strict sense, no disciples. This is not to say that his influence is not important and pervasive, though less so than that of Jonson or George Herbert. Jonson, Herrick and even Milton, as well as Marvell, George Herbert or Carew, all learn a great deal from him. This fact alone, however, should alert us to the danger of seeing seventeenth-century poetry primarily in terms of schools and movements. For just as Donne's influence is to be found in unexpected areas, so is that of Jonson or Spenser. Milton, in turning to all three (and to Shakespeare), is not an exception: he is typical. Few poets can be adequately characterized by terms like 'Metaphysical' or 'Cavalier'; even when they saw themselves as members of a particular literary group, all but the most minor and derivative poets of these years are more distinctively individual than those of preceding or later periods, turning to many models, classical and contemporary, European and English, but using them to articulate their own personal response to a common predicament.

It is when we look at the individual poets in this way, as distinctive voices speaking out of a broadly common spiritual, social, intellectual and political background, that the distortions of critical judgement imposed by the conventional view of literary history become most obvious. In that conventional view, Donne and the 'Metaphysicals' dominate, and it is they who seem most obviously troubled by the many dilemmas of a troubled age. In fact, Drayton's preoccupation with an ideal pastoral world in opposition to the corrupt and uncertain one he saw around him, Herrick's preoccupation with the transience and flux of life, and the rich variety of means he explores to counter them, and Jonson's concern with an Augustan civic and individual morality are all profound poetic responses to similar dilemmas. It is partly because we no longer take pastoral seriously, because Herrickian lyric grace seems to us 'merely' delightful and because the Augustan ideal has lost so much of its force that this is not obvious. But Drayton is normally damned with faint praise, Herrick's poetry is read as a light relief from weightier things and Jonson is seen primarily as a playwright in large measure also because they are patently not members of the 'School of Donne', and thus receive less than their due of serious and sympathetic attention.

To speak of a common predicament, of a shared background against which we should set these poets, is inevitably to generalize at least as largely as in grouping the poets in the conventional manner. If generalizations about the background of the period are open to the same sort of objections, however, they too contain important elements of truth, which in this case continue to be more useful than harmful in understanding the poetry of these years. Primary amongst them is the argument that during this time we witness a decisive break (of which the Civil Wars and the execution of the king are both the result and the symbol) with the values of the previous century. Though we may now recognize more clearly the Elizabethan heritage of Donne, Herbert, Herrick and Marvell, as well as that of Drayton and Milton, it remains the case that in the larger view the elements of change over these years are more important than those of continuity. The often repeated claim that the period 1600–60 sees the death of a world still recognizably medieval, and the birth of one that is recognizably modern, remains substantially true. All of the poets in this anthology are caught up in the tensions of that transition, reacting in their various ways to a predicament broadly similar for all of them, so that poets as different as Donne, Drayton, Herbert and Herrick are all related by the problems they face, and at times by the strategies they adopt to cope with them.

It is only possible here to give the broadest account of the nature of that common predicament and of the responses to it. The change which takes place during these years in the way in which men look at the moral and physical universe around them cannot be traced to any single decisive blow which shook faith in the old order in the way in which Darwin shook the faith of some Victorians. Some, seeking an analogy with the latter, have linked the sense of doubt and disillusionment we see amongst many writers at the beginning of the century with Copernicus's discovery, confirmed by Galileo, Kepler and others, that the earth was not the centre of the universe. Some relate the changes in attitude to the rise of Protestantism, with its tendency to faction and anti-authoritarianism, and its growing emphasis on eschatology and the coming of the millennium. Others simply to

the course of political and economic events in England, with the dis-
illusionment of the troubled final years of Elizabeth's reign increas-
ing rather than subsiding under the Stuarts. All of these and more are
partial causes, none by itself sufficient; but what they all have in
common is the calling into question of received authority, whether
intellectual, spiritual or political; and by focusing on the question of
authority, we can best understand the nature of those changes which
take place in England during the early seventeenth century.

The most momentous difference of all between the England of
1600 and the England of 1660 is that between a political, religious and
intellectual consensus that is largely based on received authority and
a much more uncertain one that is based on inductive reasoning and a
pragmatic approach to political problems. It is during this period
that Bacon and Descartes both insist, in their different ways, that
truth is subject to reason, that traditional teachings should be
approached with doubt and tested for their veracity either by logic or
by physical experiment and observation. In the troubled 1650s the
third great philosopher of the period, Thomas Hobbes, applies
similar principles to the study of human society in *Leviathan*, and by
the 1660s the supremacy of the new attitudes was signalled, on the
one hand, by the restoration of the monarchy with more limited
powers, and, on the other, by the founding of the Royal Society
which approached knowledge 'the Baconian way'. For the poets of
the pre-Restoration period, however, it is the challenge to authority,
the introduction of doubt in most spheres of activity, that is
important. In many ways their philosophical spokesman is not
Bacon, Descartes or Hobbes but the great sceptic Montaigne:

> In few, *there is no constant existence, neither of our being, nor of the
> objects*. And we, and our judgement, and all mortall things else do
> uncessantly rowle, turne, and passe away. Thus can nothing be
> certainely established, nor of the one, nor of the other; both the
> judgeing and the judged being in continuall alteration and motion.
> We have no communication with being; for every humane nature
> is ever in the middle between being borne and dying; giving
> nothing of it selfe but an obscure apparence and shadow, and an
> uncertaine and weake opinion. And if perhaps you fix your
> thought to take its being; it would be even, as if one should go
> about to grasp the water: for, how much the more he shal close and
> presse that, which by its owne nature is ever gliding, so much the
> more he shall loose what he would hold and fasten. Thus, seeing
> all things are subject to passe from one change to another; reason,

which therein seeketh a reall subsistence, findes herself deceived as unable to apprehend any thing subsistent and permanent.

('An Apologie of *Raymond Sebond*', *Essayes*, trans. Florio, Book II, Chapter 12)

Such a sense of uncertainty and of the meaningless flux of human experience is clearly apparent in Donne's 'Anniveraries' and in many of his love poems. But it is present also, if less obviously, in the work of many other poets represented here. Even those who are most strongly aware of an all-guiding Providence at work in the world are frequently at a loss as to the significance of their own experience, as Herbert shows in 'Affliction [1]' or 'The Flower', while a poet like Herrick might well be described as one who 'goes about to grasp the water' of transient experience by pinning it down decisively in the brief lyric or epigram.

Closely related to this sense of the shapeless flux of human experience, its disordered transience, was the belief, also apparently shared by many, that the close and complex interrelationship between heaven and earth posited by Renaissance philosophers and celebrated by Renaissance poets was in disarray. That interrelationship depended on a universe that was above all an ordered, harmonious and hierarchic one, every particle of it an aspect of God's creative love, and as such related back to the God who was at the centre of it. It was a universe of coherence and of multiplied relationships, a cosmic system in which everything had its place and purpose. Social and moral order, as well as the medieval and Renaissance sciences of astrology and alchemy, found their sanction in its harmonious structure. Donne's famous lines in 'The First Anniversary'

'Tis all in pieces, all coherence gone
All just supply, and all relation

refer to the breakdown, for him at least, of that structure. Coherence, relationship, unity – the major identifying characteristics of the universe of Sidney, Spenser and Shakespeare – have lost their force.

For Donne the explanation was that the world was in a state of decay, 'in her decrepit wane' ('Satire 3'): it was not that the universe of coherence and order had never existed, but that it had gradually ceased to function harmoniously. Donne's style, particularly his use of the conceit, his liking, in Dr Johnson's famous phrase, for yoking heterogeneous ideas by violence together, is partly the product of advanced literary fashions, of a liking for the extravagantly witty paradox; but on a more profound level the conceit involves the forging of new relationships, of a new harmony, between things apparently unlike. In a world increasingly bereft of relationships, the poet discovers new ones and proves them by logical argument. At the same time Donne's poems as wholes create new, complex and paradoxical harmonies through that same witty but convincing logic. The poems are in part microcosmic reflections of Donne's disordered world, in part answers to the problems it posed.

Donne's is the most immediately striking response to this predicament, but there are other responses which can produce poetry of a similar stature to his. One is that advised by Donne himself in 'The First Anniversary': 'thou hast but one way not to admit/ The world's infection, to be none of it'. The obvious strategy of turning one's back on the corrupt world of man to look only towards God is clearest, as one would expect, in the great devotional poets, Herbert, Vaughan, Crashaw and Donne himself. But we see it also in 'Lycidas' and 'Il Penseroso', in Marvell's love for nature and solitude, in Greville's increasingly sombre Calvinism, in Drayton's bitter nostalgia for an England that is lost or in Jonson's 'To the World'.

Normally, however, Jonson was characteristically unwilling to turn his back on the world or to accept that mankind was in a state of inevitable decline, and his poetry usually takes a quite different course. Jonson continued, like Milton after him, to believe in the ability of man to cope with his moral experience, but like Donne he felt that the moral and social world around him was under threat; and his plays and poems represent a heroic and sustained effort to create a new moral order out of the chaos. Jonson, like Donne, was less than ten years younger than Shakespeare, but, as in Donne's case, those years seem to have been crucial ones. We tend to lump Shakespeare and Jonson together as contemporaries, but though both were friends and though Shakespeare acted in Jonson's plays, the plays themselves are a long way apart. In every one of Shakespeare's plays, even in the cosmic chaos of *Lear* or *Macbeth*, we are in a setting whose terms of reference are universal. Underlying the plays is that world of order which Ulysses describes in a famous speech in *Troilus and Cressida*. In all the plays, and particularly in *Troilus*, that order is under threat, and the result, whether in comedy or tragedy, is described by Ulysses: 'Take but degree away, untune that string, And hark what discord follows!' (I.iii.109–10). Macbeth's murder of Duncan, Lear's denial of the duties of kingship and fatherhood, his daughters' denial of their filial duty are the untunings of strings in the great hierarchy whose commonest symbol is a musical instrument. They are worldly acts, but they lead to a disorder that is more than worldly. Heaven responds to them, because for Shakespeare that active interrelationship between heaven and earth is still a profound reality. For Jonson, this is no longer true; like Donne, he seems acutely aware of a distancing between heaven and earth, and his poems as well as his plays focus almost exclusively on the realities of man's earthly state, presenting it without reference to anything beyond the human world itself. The moral positives Jonson presents are not those of a divine order, but the more earthly, pragmatic ones of moderation, balance, urbanity, stoicism. He turns to the non-Christian society of Augustan Rome for his ethical and poetic models, and his eyes rest, for all his unquestionable Christian belief, on an essentially human scene.

Jonson is one of the first to cultivate what may be seen as another poetic response to a world of disorder, that of the self-consciously graceful lyric which aims to delight the reader by creating its own set of brief but resonant harmonies. Again, many poets take up this strategy, but the one who takes it furthest is Robert Herrick. Herrick's lyrics have seemed delightful but essentially trivial to many modern readers, but to a contemporary their assertion of harmony, their creation of a small world of grace and order in the midst of one apparently bereft of those qualities, would have given even the slightest of them a profundity and a poignancy which, though we may find it difficult to account for, is still not wholly lost to the twentieth-century reader. It is significant that the sense of completeness which marks the end of the graceful lyric by Jonson, Herrick or Carew is similar to that achieved by the witty logic of one of Donne's love poems: each is creating an experience of order in response to a disordered world.

Herrick's *Hesperides* was published in 1648, the year before the execution of Charles I; some of its poems are in fact directly concerned with the Civil Wars. Both the wars and the execution, events almost unthinkable in 1600, mark an obvious intensification in the process of the breakdown of the old order, and also the recognition that a new order must be built. Of the slightly younger generation of poets, Milton and, later, Marvell are deeply engaged during the 1640s and 1650s in political affairs, with the vision of a truly Christian Commonwealth, heralding the millennium, opening up before both men. The response of many, however – and Marvell is amongst these also – is to see the world of man and that of God as still more clearly separated from each other than they had been even for Donne. As a consequence the world of nature, which for the man of the sixteenth century had not been at variance with human society and institutions, which were themselves 'natural', is seen more and more only in contrast to the corrupt world of man. Marvell and Vaughan turn to nature for solitude and truth in a way that is significantly similar to the Romantic poets of the late eighteenth century. Others, like Cowley and the much younger Dryden, accommodate their poetry to the new rational consensus. For Dryden in particular it is a fruitful and creative compromise; but as the new Augustanism, cool and rational rather than impassioned, public rather than private, emerges in the post-Restoration period, it is clear that much has been lost to poetry, especially in its disavowal of what Cowley and others call 'the Fancy'. 'Fancy' was not simply fantasy; it was the creative imagination at work in areas of experience where truth cannot be verified by logic or experiment, where it can only draw on intuitive knowledge or on the sanction of inherited systems of ideas which were themselves the products of the creative imagination. It is the unique strength of the poets of the early seventeenth century that, whatever their doubts about the old order, they were still able to draw on the rich store of image and metaphor that it offered. Marvell and Cowley both wrote poems called 'The Garden', but they are very different in scope. Marvell's poem reaches a magnificent visionary climax in which the body lies beneath a tree while the disembodied soul sits like a bird above it:

> And, till prepared for longer flight
> Waves in its plumes the various light.

This is very clearly an example of what Cowley, in his ode 'To the Royal Society' dismisses from the proper range of the artist as merely an image which lies 'in his own fancy or his memory' (see p. 304). Cowley's garden is, as one would expect, an altogether more prosaic and earthbound place, a pleasant country retreat. Neither he nor Dryden, Pope or Dr Johnson would have attempted such a climax as Marvell's because it would have seemed to them patently untrue, a private and extravagant fantasy which neither reason nor observation could possibly support. It is, in fact, neither private nor extravagant, but one of the last products of a long tradition which recognized different avenues to the truth from those approved by the new Age of Reason.

PART ONE
TEN POETS

MICHAEL DRAYTON
(1563–1631)

Though he was forty when James I became king and though his literary allegiances make him seem very much an Elizabethan, nearly all Drayton's best work was done in the years after 1603. This is only partly because he is one of the most thorough and creative revisers of his work amongst English poets, turning, for example, the vapidly fashionable sonnet sequence of 1594, *Idea's Mirror*, into the larger and altogether finer sequences of 1616, and enlarging *The Shepherd's Garland* of 1593 into the more embracing pastoral vision of the 1606 *Eclogues*. Perhaps more important than this habit of revision in explaining the late and sustained flowering of Drayton's genius is his growing alienation from the age of James I, an alienation at first based on purely personal disappointments as his hopes of royal preferment remained unrealized, and as his most ambitious work, *Poly-Olbion*, a massive geographical–historical poem about Great Britain, 'met with barbarous ignorance and base detraction'. The acute personal disappointment of the neglected poet is the subject of 'The Tenth Eclogue'; but in Drayton's later work it modulates into a larger, more disinterested disapproval of things Jacobean, as he came to see himself, and was seen by others, as the guardian of the values of an England that seemed lost or fast disappearing. From this standpoint he developed new strengths as a satirist and pastoral poet; the freshness of his fairy poem, 'Nymphidia' (1627), and of *The Muse's Elysium*, written in his late sixties, owes much to this strong sense of the corruption of the real world, to which fairyland and Elysium are the simpler pastoral alternatives.

Drayton saw his own poems through four revised editions, with a posthumous one appearing in 1637; thereafter he attracted relatively little attention until J. W. Hebel, Kathleen Tillotson and B. H. Newdigate edited the *Works* (5 volumes, Oxford, 1931–41). There is a good selection by John Buxton, *Poems* (2 volumes, London, 1953), a biography, *Michael Drayton and His Circle*, by Newdigate (Oxford, 1941) and a critical study, *Drayton*, by J. A. Berthelot (New York, 1967).

From IDEA

Sonnet 9

As other men, so I myself do muse
Why in this sort I wrest invention so,
And why these giddy metaphors I use,
Leaving the path the greater part do go.
I will resolve you; I am lunatic,   5
And ever this in madmen you shall find:
What they last thought of, when the brain grew sick,
In most distraction they keep that in mind.
Thus talking idly in this bedlam fit,
Reason and I, you must conceive, are twain;   10
'Tis nine years now since first I lost my wit,
Bear with me, then, though troubled be my brain.
With diet and correction, men distraught
(Not too far past) may to their wits be brought.

Sonnet 61

Since there's no help, come, let us kiss and part.
Nay, I have done: you get no more of me,
And I am glad, yea, glad with all my heart
That thus so cleanly I myself can free.
Shake hands for ever, cancel all our vows,   5
And when we meet at any time again
Be it not seen in either of our brows
That we one jot of former love retain.
Now at the last gasp of Love's latest breath,
When, his pulse failing, Passion speechless lies,   10
When Faith is kneeling by his bed of death,
And Innocence is closing up his eyes,
    Now if thou wouldst, when all have given him over,
    From death to life thou mightst him yet recover.

PASTORALS

The Tenth Eclogue

What time the weary weather-beaten sheep,
To get them fodder, hie them to the fold,
And the poor herds that lately did them keep,
Shuddered with keenness of the winter's cold:
    The groves of their late summer pride forlorn,   5
    In mossy mantles sadly seemed to mourn.

That silent time, about the upper world,
Phoebus had forced his fiery-footed team,
And down again the steep Olympus whirled,
To wash his chariot in the western stream,   10
    In night's black shade, when Rowland all alone,
    Thus him complains, his fellow shepherds gone:

'You flames,' quoth he, 'wherewith thou heaven art dight,
That me (alive) the woefull'st creature view,
You, whose aspects have wrought me this despite,   15
And me with hate, yet ceaselessly pursue,
    For whom too long I tarried for relief,
    Now ask but death, that only ends my grief.

Yearly my vows, O heavens, have I not paid,
Of the best fruits, and firstlings of my flock?   20
And oftentimes have bitterly inveighed,
'Gainst them that you profanely dared to mock?
    O, who shall ever give what is your due,
    If mortal man be uprighter than you?

If the deep sighs of an afflicted breast,   25
O'erwhelmed with sorrow, or th'erected eyes
Of a poor wretch with miseries oppressed
For whose complaints, tears never could suffice,
    Have not the power your deities to move,
    Who shall e'er look for succour from above?   30

O night, how still obsequious have I been,
To thy slow silence whispering in thine ear,
That thy pale sovereign often hath been seen,
Stay to behold me sadly from her sphere,
  Whilst the slow minutes duly I have told,   35
  With watchful eyes attending on my fold.

How oft by thee the solitary swain,
Breathing his passion to the early spring,
Hath left to hear the nightingale complain,
Pleasing his thoughts alone, to hear me sing!   40
  The nymphs forsook their places of abode,
  To hear the sounds that from my music flowed.

To purge their springs and sanctify their grounds,
The simple shepherds learned I the mean,
And sovereign simples to their use I found,   45
Their teeming ewes to help when they did yean:
  Which when again in summer time they share,
  Their wealthy fleece my cunning did declare.

In their warm cots whilst they have soundly slept,
And passed the night in many a pleasant bower,   50
On the bleak mountains I their flocks have kept,
And bid the brunt of many a cruel shower,
  Warring with beasts in safety mine to keep;
  So true was I, and careful of my sheep.

Fortune and time, why tempted you me forth,   55
With those your flattering promises of grace,
Fickle, so falsely to abuse my worth,
And now to fly me, whom I did embrace?
  Both that at first encouraged my desire,
  Lastly against me lewdly do conspire.   60

Or nature, didst thou prodigally waste
Thy gifts on me, unfortunatest swain,
Only thereby to have thy self disgraced?
Virtue in me why was thou placed in vain?
  If to the world predestined a prey,   65
  Thou wert too good to have been cast away.

There's not a grove that wondereth not my woe,
Nor not a river weeps not at my tale,
I hear the echoes (wandering to and fro)
Resound my grief through every hill and dale,   70
    The birds and beasts yet in their simple kind,
    Lament for me, no pity else that find.

None else there is gives comfort to my grief,
Nor my mishaps amended with my moan,
When heaven and earth have shut up all relief,   75
Nor care avails what cureless now is grown:
    And tears I find do bring no other good,
    But as new showers increase the rising flood.'

When on an old tree, under which ere now,
He many a merry roundelay had sung,   80
Upon a leafless canker-eaten bough,
His well-tuned bag-pipe carelessly he hung:
    And by the same, his sheep-hook, once of price,
    That had been carved with many a rare device.

He called his dog, (that sometime had the praise)   85
Whitefoot, well known to all that kept the plain,
That many a wolf had worried in his days;
A better cur, there never followed swain:
    Which, though as he his master's sorrows knew,
    Wagged his cut tail, his wretched plight to rue.   90

'Poor cur,' quoth he, and him therewith did stroke,
'Go, to our cot, and there thyself repose,
Thou with thine age, my heart with sorrow broke:
Be gone, ere death my restless eyes do close;
    The time is come, thou must thy master leave,   95
    Whom the vile world shall never more deceive.'

With folded arms thus hanging down his head,
He gave a groan, his heart in sunder cleft,
And as a stone, already seemed dead,
Before his breath was fully him bereft: 100
    The faithful swain here lastly made an end,
    Whom all good shepherds ever shall defend.
                                    (*Poems*, 1619)

The Tenth Nymphal

NAIIS, CLAIA, CORBILUS, SATYR
A Satyr on Elysium lights,
Whose ugly shape the nymphs affrights;
Yet when they hear his just complaint
They make him an Elysian saint.

CORBILUS

What, breathless, nymphs? Bright virgins let me know   5
What sudden cause constrains ye to this haste?
What have ye seen that should affright ye so?
What might it be from which ye fly so fast?
I see your faces full of pallid fear,
As though some peril followed on your flight;   10
Take breath awhile, and quickly let me hear
Into what danger ye have lately light.

NAIIS

Never were poor distressed girls so glad
As when kind, loved Corbilus we saw,
When our much haste us so much weakened had   15
That scarcely we our wearied breaths could draw.
In this next grove, under an aged tree,
So fell a monster lying there we found
As till this day our eyes did never see,
Nor ever came on the Elysian ground.   20
Half man, half goat he seemed to us in show:
His upper parts our human shape doth bear,
But he's a very perfect goat below,
His crooked cambrels armed with hoof and hair.

CLAIA

Through his lean chops a chattering he doth make   25
Which stirs his staring, beastly, drivelled beard,
And his sharp horns he seemed at us to shake;
Canst thou then blame us though we were afeared?

CORBILUS

Surely it seems some satyr this should be.
Come, and go back and guide me to the place;   30
Be not afraid, ye are safe enough with me;
Silly and harmless be their sylvan race.

CLAIA

How, Corbilus? A satyr, do you say?
How should he over high Parnassus hit,
Since to these fields there's none can find the way,   35
But only those the Muses will permit?

CORBILUS

'Tis true: but oft the sacred sisters grace
The silly satyr, by whose plainness they
Are taught the world's enormities to trace,
By beastly men's abominable way.   40
Beside, he may be banished his own home
By this base time, or be so much distressed
That he the craggy bi-cliffed hill hath clomb
To find out these more pleasant fields of rest.

NAIIS

Yonder he sits, and seems himself to bow   45
At our approach. What, doth our presence awe him?
Me thinks he seems not half so ugly now
As at the first, when I and Claia saw him.

CORBILUS

'Tis an old satyr, nymph, I now discern;
Sadly he sits, as he were sick or lame.   50
His looks would say that we may eas'ly learn
How, and from whence, he to Elysium came.
Satyr, these fields how came thou first to find?
What fate first showed thee this most happy shore,
When never any of the sylvan kind   55
Set foot on the Elysian earth before?

SATYR

O never ask how I came to this place.
What cannot strong necessity find out?
Rather bemoan my miserable case,
Constrained to wander the wide world about.   60
With wild Sylvanus and his woody crew,
In forests I, at liberty and free
Lived in such pleasure as the world ne'er knew,
Nor any rightly can conceive but we.

This jocund life we many a day enjoyed,   65
Till this last age those beastly men forth brought,
That all those great and goodly woods destroyed,
Whose growth their grandsires with such sufferance sought.
That fair Felicia, which was but of late
Earth's paradise, that never had her peer,   70
Stands now in that most lamentable state
That not a sylvan will inhabit there.
Where in the soft and most delicious shade
In heat of summer we were wont to play,
When the long day too short for us we made,   75
The sliding hours so slyly stole away.
By Cynthia's light, and on the pleasant lawn,
The wanton fairy we were wont to chase,
Which to the nimble cloven-footed fawn
Upon the plain durst boldly bid the base.   80
The sportive nymphs with shouts and laughter shook
The hills and valleys in their wanton play,
Waking the echoes, their last words that took,
Till at the last they louder were than they.
The lofty high wood, and the lower spring,   85
Shelt'ring the deer in many a sudden shower,
Where choirs of birds oft wonted were to sing,
The flaming furnace wholly doth devour.
Once fair Felicia, but now quite defaced,
Those braveries gone wherein she did abound   90
With dainty groves, when she was highly graced
With goodly oak, ash, elm and beeches crowned.
But that from heaven their judgement blinded is,
In human reason it could never be
But that they might have clearly seen by this   95
Those plagues their next posterity shall see.
The little infant on the mother's lap
For want of fire shall be so sore distressed
That whilst it draws the lank and empty pap,
The tender lips shall freeze unto the breast.   100
The quaking cattle which their warmstall want,
And with bleak winter's northern wind oppressed,
Their browse and stover waxing thin and scant
The hungry crows shall with their carrion feast.
Men wanting timber wherewith they should build,   105
And not a forest in Felicia found,

Shall be enforced upon the open field
To dig them caves, for houses, in the ground.
The land thus robbed of all her rich attire
Naked and bare herself to heaven doth show,   110
Begging from thence that Jove would dart his fire
Upon those wretches that disrobed her so.
This beastly brood by no means may abide
The name of their brave ancestors to hear,
By whom their sordid slavery is described,   115
So unlike them as though not theirs they were;
Nor yet they sense, nor understanding have,
Of those brave Muses that their country sung,
But with false lips ignobly do deprave
The right and honour that to them belong.   120
This cruel kind thus viper-like devour
That fruitful soil which them too fully fed;
The earth doth curse the age, and every hour
Again, that it these vip'rous monsters bred.
I, seeing the plagues that shortly are to come   125
Upon this people, clearly them forsook,
And thus am light into Elysium,
To whose straight search I wholly me betook.

NAIIS

Poor silly creature, come along with us;
Thou shalt be free of the Elysian fields.   130
Be not dismayed, nor inly grieved thus,
This place content in all abundance yields.
We to the cheerful presence will thee bring
Of Jove's dear daughters, where in shades they sit,
Where thou shalt hear those sacred sisters sing   135
Most heavenly hymns, the strength and life of wit.

CLAIA

Where to the Delphian god upon their lyres
His priests seem ravished in his height of praise,
Whilst he is crowning his harmonious choirs
With circling garlands of immortal bays.   140

CORBILUS

Here live in bliss till thou shalt see those slaves,
Who thus set virtue and desert at naught,
Some sacrificed upon their grandsires graves,
And some like beasts in markets sold and bought.
Of fools and madmen leave thou then the care,   145
That have no understanding of their state:
For whom high heaven doth so just plagues prepare,
That they to pity shall convert thy hate.
And to Elysium be thou welcome then,
Until those base Felicians thou shalt hear   150
By that vile nation captived again,
That many a glorious age their captives were.

(*The Muses Elysium*, 1630)

JOHN DONNE
(1572–1631)

Donne grew up in a strongly Roman Catholic family, and ended his life as one of the most celebrated preachers of the Anglican church. He was thus no stranger to controversy or paradox; indeed he saw God's word and His creation as essentially 'witty' and paradoxical, and his own characteristic mode would not therefore have seemed to him, or to the relatively small group who read his poems in manuscript, to have involved quite such a radical break with the old ideal of the harmony of the well-wrought lyric which echoed God's harmonious Creation as modern readers often assume. His poems work typically towards the establishment of a surprising but convincing harmony wrought out of heterogeneous material, his wit serving not merely to surprise and impress, but to convince the reader of a truth of feeling that is inseparable in Donne from the truth of his logic. It has long been recognized that it is a mistake to assign Donne's love poetry and his religious poetry to different periods of his life, or even to different facets of his personality. The erotic imagery of his religious poetry and the religious imagery of his love poetry indicate how close were the two areas of experience for him. One of the most significant factors uniting this poetry is its tendency to turn its back on 'the world's infection, to be none of it'. In a way that would have been highly improbable in a poet of the previous generation, Donne turns away from what now seems a corrupt and decaying world to the more stable private world of the two lovers, or to the other world offered him by Christ. That heavenly world is seen in Donne as far more remote from the earthly world than was the case for Spenser or even Shakespeare.

Donne was very much a coterie poet, his work circulating in manuscript until two years after his death, when *Poems by J.D.* appeared. The major modern editions are by H. J. C. Grierson, *Poetical Works* (2 volumes, Oxford, 1912); Helen Gardner, *The Divine Poems* (Oxford, 1952) and *The Elegies and the Songs and*

Sonnets (Oxford, 1965); and W. Milgate, *The Satires, Epigrams and Verse Letters* (Oxford, 1967). The standard biography is R. C. Bald's *John Donne: A Life* (Oxford, 1970). Amongst a very large number of critical studies, Samuel Johnson's life of Cowley in his *Lives of the Poets* (1779) is essential reading, while good modern introductions are provided by J. B. Leishman, *The Monarch of Wit* (London, 1951), K. W. Gransden, *John Donne* (London, 1954), Frank Kermode, *John Donne* (2nd edn, London, 1961) and Wilbur Sanders, *John Donne's Poetry* (Cambridge, 1971).

SONGS AND SONNETS

The Good-Morrow

I wonder, by my troth, what thou and I
Did, till we loved? were we not weaned till then?
But sucked on country pleasures, childishly?
Or snorted we in the Seven Sleepers' den?
'Twas so; but this, all pleasures fancies be.   5
If ever any beauty I did see
Which I desired, and got, 'twas but a dream of thee.

And now good-morrow to our waking souls,
Which watch not one another out of fear;
For love, all love of other sights controls,   10
And makes one little room an everywhere.
Let sea-discoverers to new worlds have gone,
Let maps to others, worlds on worlds have shown,
Let us possess one world, each hath one, and is one.

My face in thine eye, thine in mine appears,   15
And true plain hearts do in the faces rest;
Where can we find two better hemispheres,
Without sharp north, without declining west?
Whatever dies was not mixed equally:
If our two loves be one, or, thou and I   20
Love so alike that none do slacken, none can die.

Song

Go and catch a falling star,
  Get with child a mandrake root,
Tell me where all past years are,
  Or who cleft the Devil's foot,
Teach me to hear mermaids singing,   5
  Or to keep off envy's stinging,
    And find
    What wind
Serves to advance an honest mind.

If thou be'st born to strange sights,   10
  Things invisible to see,
Ride ten thousand days and nights,
  Till age snow white hairs on thee,
Thou, when thou return'st, wilt tell me
  All strange wonders that befell thee,   15
    And swear
    Nowhere
Lives a woman true, and fair.

If thou findst one, let me know,
  Such a pilgrimage were sweet.   20
Yet do not; I would not go,
  Though at next door we might meet;
Though she were true, when you met her,
  And last, till you write your letter,
    Yet she   25
    Will be
False, ere I come, to two, or three.

The Sun Rising

Busy old fool, unruly sun,
  Why dost thou thus,
Through windows, and through curtains, call on us?
Must to thy motions lovers' seasons run?
    Saucy pedantic wretch, go chide   5
    Late schoolboys, and sour prentices,

Go tell court-huntsmen that the King will ride,
Call country ants to harvest offices;
Love, all alike, no season knows, nor clime,
Nor hours, days, months, which are the rags of time.   10

Thy beams, so reverend and strong
Why shouldst thou think?
I could eclipse and cloud them with a wink,
But that I would not lose her sight so long:
If her eyes have not blinded thine,   15
Look, and tomorrow late, tell me
Whether both the Indias of spice and mine
Be where thou leftst them, or lie here with me.
Ask for those kings whom thou saw'st yesterday,
And thou shalt hear, All here in one bed lay.   20

She's all states, and all princes I,
Nothing else is.
Princes do but play us; compared to this,
All honour's mimic, all wealth alchemy.
Thou, sun, art half as happy as we,   25
In that the world's contracted thus;
Thine age asks ease, and since thy duties be
To warm the world, that's done in warming us.
Shine here to us, and thou art everywhere;
This bed thy centre is, these walls thy sphere.   30

The Canonization

For God's sake, hold your tongue, and let me love,
Or chide my palsy, or my gout,
My five grey hairs, or ruined fortune flout,
With wealth your state, your mind with arts improve,
Take you a course, get you a place,   5
Observe his honour, or his grace,
Or the King's real, or his stamped face
Contemplate; what you will, approve,
So you will let me love.

Alas, alas, who's injured by my love?   10
What merchant's ships have my sighs drowned?
Who says my tears have overflowed his ground?
When did my colds a forward spring remove?

When did the heats which my veins fill
   Add one more to the plaguey bill?   15
Soldiers find wars, and lawyers find out still
   Litigious men, which quarrels move,
   Though she and I do love.

Call us what you will, we are made such by love;
   Call her one, me another fly,   20
We're tapers too, and at our own cost die,
   And we in us find the eagle and the dove.
     The phoenix riddle hath more wit
     By us; we two being one, are it.
So, to one neutral thing both sexes fit: 25
   We die and rise the same, and prove
   Mysterious by this love.

We can die by it, if not live by love,
   And if unfit for tombs and hearse
Our legend be, it will be fit for verse;   30
   And if no piece of chronicle we prove,
     We'll build in sonnets pretty rooms;
     As well a well-wrought urn becomes
The greatest ashes, as half-acre tombs,
   And by these hymns, all shall approve   35
   Us *canonized* for Love.

And thus invoke us: 'You, whom reverend love
   Made one another's hermitage;
You, to whom love was peace, that now is rage;
    Who did the whole world's soul extract, and drove   40
    Into the glasses of your eyes
    (So made such mirrors, and such spies,
That they did all to you epitomize)
   Countries, towns, courts: beg from above
   A pattern of your love!'   45

Song

Sweetest love, I do not go
   For weariness of thee,
Nor in hope the world can show
   A fitter love for me:

          But since that I   5
Must die at last, 'tis best
To use myself in jest,
          Thus by feigned deaths to die.

Yesternight the sun went hence,
          And yet is here today;   10
He hath no desire nor sense,
          Nor half so short a way:
          Then fear not me,
But believe that I shall make
Speedier journeys, since I take   15
          More wings and spurs than he.

O how feeble is man's power,
          That if good fortune fall,
Cannot add another hour,
          Nor a lost hour recall!   20
          But come bad chance,
And we join to it our strength,
And we teach it art and length,
          Itself o'er us to advance.

When thou sigh'st, thou sigh'st not wind,   25
          But sigh'st my soul away;
When thou weep'st, unkindly kind,
          My life's blood doth decay.
          It cannot be
That thou lov'st me, as thou say'st,   30
If in thine my life thou waste;
          Thou art the best of me.

Let not thy divining heart
          Forethink me any ill;
Destiny may take thy part,   35
          And may thy fears fulfil;
          But think that we
Are but turned aside to sleep;
They who one another keep
          Alive, ne'er parted be.   40

Air and Angels

Twice or thrice had I loved thee,
Before I knew thy face or name;
So in a voice, so in a shapeless flame
Angels affect us oft, and worshipped be;
   Still when to where thou wert I came,   5
Some lovely glorious nothing I did see.
  But since my soul, whose child love is,
Takes limbs of flesh, and else could nothing do,
   More subtle than the parent is
Love must not be, but take a body too;   10
   And therefore what thou wert, and who,
     I bid Love ask, and now
That it assume thy body, I allow,
And fix itself in thy lip, eye, and brow.

Whilst thus to ballast love, I thought,   15
And so more steadily to have gone,
With wares which would sink admiration,
I saw I had love's pinnace overfraught;
   Every thy hair for love to work upon
Is much too much, some fitter must be sought;   20
   For, nor in nothing, nor in things
Extreme, and scatt'ring bright, can love inhere;
   Then as an angel, face, and wings
Of air, not pure as it, yet pure doth wear,
   So thy love may be my love's sphere;   25
     Just such disparity
As is 'twixt air and angels' purity,
'Twixt women's love and men's will ever be.

The Anniversary

   All kings, and all their favourites,
     All glory of honours, beauties, wits,
The sun itself, which makes times, as they pass,
Is elder by a year, now, than it was
When thou and I first one another saw: 5
All other things to their destruction draw,

Only our love hath no decay;
This, no tomorrow hath, nor yesterday;
Running it never runs from us away,
But truly keeps his first, last, everlasting day.   10

    Two graves must hide thine and my corse;
If one might, death were no divorce:
Alas, as well as other princes, we
(Who prince enough in one another be)
Must leave at last in death, these eyes, and ears,   15
Oft fed with true oaths, and with sweet salt tears;
    But souls where nothing dwells but love
(All other thoughts being inmates) then shall prove
This, or a love increased there above,
When bodies to their graves, souls from their graves remove.   20

    And then we shall be thoroughly blest,
    But we no more than all the rest;
Here upon earth, we're kings, and none but we
Can be such kings, nor of such subjects be;
Who is so safe as we, where none can do   25
Treason to us, except one of us two?
    True and false fears let us refrain,
Let us love nobly, and live, and add again
Years and years unto years, till we attain
To write threescore; this is the second of our reign.   30

Love's Growth

    I scarce believe my love to be so pure
        As I had thought it was,
        Because it doth endure
Vicissitude, and season, as the grass;
Methinks I lied all winter, when I swore   5
My love was infinite, if spring make it more.
But if this medicine, love, which cures all sorrow
With more, not only be no quintessence,
But mixed of all stuffs paining soul or sense,
And of the sun his working vigour borrow,   10
Love's not so pure, and abstract, as they use
To say, which have no mistress but their muse,
But as all else, being elemented too,
Love sometimes would contemplate, sometimes do.

And yet no greater, but more eminent,   15
    Love by the spring is grown,
      As, in the firmament,
Stars by the sun are not enlarged, but shown;
Gentle love deeds, as blossoms on a bough,
From love's awakened root do bud out now.   20
If, as in water stirred more circles be
Produced by one, love such additions take,
Those, like so many spheres, but one heaven make,
For they are all concentric unto thee;
And though each spring do add to love new heat,   25
As princes do in times of action get
New taxes, and remit them not in peace,
No winter shall abate the spring's increase.

The Flea

Mark but this flea, and mark in this
How little that which thou deny'st me is;
It sucked me first, and now sucks thee,
And in this flea our two bloods mingled be;
Thou know'st that this cannot be said   5
A sin, nor shame, nor loss of maidenhead,
    Yet this enjoys before it woo,
    And pampered swells with one blood made of two,
    And this, alas, is more than we would do.

Oh stay, three lives in one flea spare,   10
Where we almost, yea more than married are.
This flea is you and I, and this
Our marriage bed, and marriage temple is;
Though parents grudge, and you, we're met
And cloistered in these living walls of jet.   15
    Though use make you apt to kill me,
    Let not to that, self-murder added be,
    And sacrilege, three sins in killing three.

Cruel and sudden, hast thou since
Purpled thy nail in blood of innocence?   20
Wherein could this flea guilty be,
Except in that drop which it sucked from thee?

Yet thou triumph'st, and say'st that thou
Find'st not thyself, nor me, the weaker now;
   'Tis true; then learn how false, fears be;   25
   Just so much honour, when thou yield'st to me,
   Will waste, as this flea's death took life from thee.

A Nocturnal upon St Lucy's Day; Being the Shortest Day

'Tis the year's midnight, and it is the day's,
Lucy's, who scarce seven hours herself unmasks;
   The sun is spent, and now his flasks
   Send forth light squibs, no constant rays;
      The world's whole sap is sunk;   5
The general balm the hydroptic earth hath drunk,
Whither, as to the bed's feet, life is shrunk,
Dead and interred; yet all these seem to laugh,
Compared with me, who am their epitaph.

Study me then, you who shall lovers be   10
At the next world, that is, at the next spring:
   For I am every dead thing,
   In whom love wrought new alchemy.
      For his art did express
A quintessence even from nothingness,   15
From dull privations, and lean emptiness;
He ruined me, and I am re-begot
Of absence, darkness, death; things which are not.

All others, from all things, draw all that's good,
Life, soul, form, spirit, whence they being have;   20
   I, by love's limbeck, am the grave
   Of all that's nothing. Oft a flood
      Have we two wept, and so
Drowned the whole world, us two; oft did we grow
To be two chaoses, when we did show   25
Care to aught else; and often absences
Withdrew our souls, and made us carcasses.

But I am by her death (which word wrongs her)
Of the first nothing the elixir grown;
   Were I a man, that I were one   30
    I needs must know; I should prefer,
      If I were any beast,
Some ends, some means; yea plants, yea stones detest,
And love; all, all some properties invest;
If I an ordinary nothing were,   35
As shadow, a light and body must be here.

But I am none; nor will my Sun renew.
You lovers, for whose sake the lesser sun
   At this time to the Goat is run
   To fetch new lust, and give it you,   40
    Enjoy your summer all;
Since she enjoys her long night's festival,
Let me prepare towards her, and let me call
This hour her Vigil, and her Eve, since this
Both the year's, and the day's deep midnight is.   45

A Valediction: Forbidding Mourning

   As virtuous men pass mildly away,
    And whisper to their souls to go,
   Whilst some of their sad friends do say,
    'The breath goes now,' and some say, 'No,'

   So let us melt, and make no noise,   5
    No tear-floods, nor sigh-tempests move;
   'Twere profanation of our joys
    To tell the laity our love.

   Moving of the earth brings harms and fears,
    Men reckon what it did and meant;   10
   But trepidation of the spheres,
    Though greater far, is innocent.

   Dull sublunary lovers' love
    (Whose soul is sense) cannot admit
   Absence, because it doth remove   15
    Those things which elemented it.

But we, by a love so much refined
    That our selves know not what it is,
Inter-assured of the mind,
    Care less, eyes, lips, and hands to miss.   20

Our two souls therefore, which are one,
    Though I must go, endure not yet
A breach, but an expansion,
    Like gold to airy thinness beat.

If they be two, they are two so   25
    As stiff twin compasses are two:
Thy soul, the fixed foot, makes no show
    To move, but doth, if the other do;

And though it in the centre sit,
    Yet when the other far doth roam,   30
It leans, and hearkens after it,
    And grows erect, as that comes home.

Such wilt thou be to me, who must,
    Like the other foot, obliquely run;
Thy firmness makes my circle just,   35
    And makes me end where I begun.

The Ecstasy

Where, like a pillow on a bed,
    A pregnant bank swelled up, to rest
The violet's reclining head,
    Sat we two, one another's best.

Our hands were firmly cemented   5
    With a fast balm, which thence did spring;
Our eye-beams twisted, and did thread
    Our eyes, upon one double string;

So to intergraft our hands, as yet
    Was all the means to make us one,   10
And pictures in our eyes to get
    Was all our propagation.

As, 'twixt two equal armies, Fate
   Suspends uncertain victory,
Our souls (which to advance their state   15
   Were gone out) hung 'twixt her and me.

And whilst our souls negotiate there,
   We like sepulchral statues lay;
All day, the same our postures were,
   And we said nothing, all the day.   20

If any, so by love refined
   That he souls' language understood,
And by good love were grown all mind,
   Within convenient distance stood,

He (though he knew not which soul spake,   25
   Because both meant, both spake the same)
Might thence a new concoction take,
   And part far purer than he came.

This Ecstasy doth unperplex,
   We said, and tell us what we love;   30
We see by this it was not sex;
   We see we saw not what did move:

But as all several souls contain
   Mixture of things, they know not what,
Love these mixed souls doth mix again,   35
   And makes both one, each this and that.

A single violet transplant,
   The strength, the colour, and the size,
(All which before was poor, and scant)
   Redoubles still, and multiplies.   40

When love, with one another so
   Interinanimates two souls,
That abler soul, which thence doth flow,
   Defects of loneliness controls.

We then, who are this new soul, know   45
    Of what we are composed, and made,
For the atomies of which we grow
    Are souls, whom no change can invade.

But oh, alas, so long, so far
    Our bodies why do we forbear?   50
They're ours, though they're not we, we are
    The intelligences, they the sphere.

We owe them thanks because they thus
    Did us to us at first convey,
Yielded their forces, sense, to us,   55
    Nor are dross to us, but allay.

On man heaven's influence works not so,
    But that it first imprints the air,
So soul into the soul may flow,
    Though it to body first repair.   60

As our blood labours to beget
    Spirits as like souls as it can,
Because such fingers need to knit
    That subtle knot which makes us man:

So must pure lovers' souls descend   65
    To affections, and to faculties,
That sense may reach and apprehend,
    Else a great Prince in prison lies.

To our bodies turn we then, that so
    Weak men on love revealed may look;   70
Love's mysteries in souls do grow,
    But yet the body is his book.

And if some lover, such as we,
    Have heard this dialogue of one,
Let him still mark us, he shall see   75
    Small change, when we're to bodies gone.

ELEGIES

(9) The Autumnal

No spring, nor summer beauty hath such grace,
    As I have seen in one autumnal face.
Young beauties force our love, and that's a rape,
    This doth but counsel, yet you cannot 'scape.
If 'twere a shame to love, here 'twere no shame,   5
    Affection here takes reverence's name.
Were her first years the Golden Age? That's true,
    But now she's gold oft tried, and ever new.
That was her torrid and inflaming time,
    This is her tolerable tropic clime.   10
Fair eyes, who asks more heat than comes from hence,
    He in a fever wishes pestilence.
Call not these wrinkles, graves; if graves they were,
    They were Love's graves; for else he is nowhere.
Yet lies not Love dead here, but here doth sit   15
    Vowed to this trench, like an anachorit.
And here, till hers, which must be his death, come,
    He doth not dig a grave, but build a tomb.
Here dwells he, though he sojourn ev'rywhere;
    In progress, yet his standing house is here.   20
Here, where still evening is; not noon, nor night;
    Where no voluptuousness, yet all delight.
In all her words, unto all hearers fit,
    You may at revels, you at council, sit.
This is love's timber, youth his underwood;   25
    There he, as wine in June, enrages blood,
Which then comes seasonabliest, when our taste
    And appetite to other things is past.
Xerxes' strange Lydian love, the platane tree,
    Was loved for age, none being so large as she,   30
Or else because, being young, nature did bless
    Her youth with age's glory, barrenness.
If we love things long sought, age is a thing
    Which we are fifty years in compassing;
If transitory things, which soon decay,   35
    Age must be loveliest at the latest day.
But name not winter-faces, whose skin's slack,
    Lank, as an unthrift's purse, but a soul's sack;

Whose eyes seek light within, for all here's shade;
  Whose mouths are holes, rather worn out, than made;   40
Whose every tooth to a several place is gone,
  To vex their souls at Resurrection.
Name not these living death's-heads unto me,
  For these not ancient, but antique be.
I hate extremes; yet I had rather stay   45
  With tombs than cradles, to wear out a day.
Since such love's natural lation is, may still
  My love descend and journey down the hill,
Not panting after growing beauties, so,
  I shall ebb on with them who homeward go.   50

(19) To His Mistress Going to Bed

Come, madam, come, all rest my powers defy,
Until I labour, I in labour lie.
The foe oft-times having the foe in sight,
Is tired with standing though he never fight.
Off with that girdle, like heaven's zone glistering,   5
But a far fairer world encompassing.
Unpin that spangled breastplate which you wear,
That the eyes of busy fools may be stopped there.
Unlace yourself, for that harmonious chime
Tells me from you that now 'tis your bed time.   10
Off with that happy busk, which I envy,
That still can be, and still can stand so nigh.
Your gown, going off, such beauteous state reveals,
As when from flow'ry meads the hill's shadow steals.
Off with that wiry coronet, and show   15
The hairy diadem which on you doth grow:
Now off with those shoes, and then safely tread
In this love's hallowed temple, this soft bed.
In such white robes, heaven's angels used to be
Received by men; thou, Angel, bring'st with thee   20
A heaven like Mahomet's Paradise; and though
Ill spirits walk in white, we easily know
By this these angels from an evil sprite:
Those set our hairs, but these our flesh upright.
  License my roving hands, and let them go   25
Before, behind, between, above, below.

O my America! my new-found-land,
My kingdom, safeliest when with one man manned,
My mine of precious stones, my empery,
How blest am I in this discovering thee!   30
To enter in these bonds is to be free;
Then where my hand is set, my seal shall be.
    Full nakedness! All joys are due to thee,
As souls unbodied, bodies unclothed must be
To taste whole joys. Gems which you women use   35
Are like Atlanta's balls, cast in men's views,
That when a fool's eye lighteth on a gem,
His earthly soul may covet theirs, not them.
Like pictures, or like books' gay coverings made
For laymen, are all women thus arrayed;   40
Themselves are mystic books, which only we
(Whom their imputed grace will dignify)
Must see revealed. Then, since that I may know,
As liberally as to a midwife, show
Thyself: cast all, yea, this white linen hence,   45
Here is no penance, much less innocence.
    To teach thee, I am naked first; why than,
What needst thou have more covering than a man.

SATIRES

Satire 3

Kind pity chokes my spleen; brave scorn forbids
Those tears to issue which swell my eyelids;
I must not laugh, nor weep sins, and be wise,
Can railing then cure these worn maladies?
Is not our mistress, fair Religion,   5
As worthy of all our soul's devotion,
As virtue was to the first blinded age?
Are not heaven's joys as valiant to assuage
Lusts, as earth's honour was to them? Alas,
As we do them in means, shall they surpass   10
Us in the end, and shall thy father's spirit
Meet blind philosophers in heaven, whose merit
Of strict life may be imputed faith, and hear
Thee, whom he taught so easy ways and near

To follow, damned? O if thou dar'st, fear this;   15
This fear great courage and high valour is.
Dar'st thou aid mutinous Dutch, and dar'st thou lay
Thee in ships, wooden sepulchres, a prey
To leaders' rage, to storms, to shot, to dearth?
Dar'st thou dive seas and dungeons of the earth?   20
Hast thou courageous fire to thaw the ice
Of frozen North discoveries? And thrice
Colder than salamanders, like divine
Children in the oven, fires of Spain, and the line,
Whose countries limbecks to our bodies be,   25
Canst thou for gain bear? And must every he
Which cries not 'Goddess!' to thy mistress, draw,
Or eat thy poisonous words? Courage of straw!
O desperate coward, wilt thou seem bold, and
To thy foes and His (Who made thee to stand   30
Sentinel in His world's garrison) thus yield,
And for forbidden wars, leave the appointed field?
Know thy foes: the foul Devil, whom thou
Strivest to please, for hate, not love, would allow
Thee fain his whole realm to be quit; and as   35
The world's all parts wither away and pass,
So the world's self, thy other loved foe, is
In her decrepit wane, and thou, loving this,
Dost love a withered and worn strumpet; last,
Flesh (itself's death) and joys which flesh can taste,   40
Thou lovest; and thy fair goodly soul, which doth
Give this flesh power to taste joy, thou dost loathe.
Seek true religion. O where? Mirreus,
Thinking her unhoused here, and fled from us,
Seeks her at Rome; there, because he doth know   45
That she was there a thousand years ago;
He loves her rags so, as we here obey
The statecloth where the Prince sat yesterday.
Crantz to such brave Loves will not be enthralled,
But loves her only, who at Geneva is called   50
Religion: plain, simple, sullen, young,
Contemptuous, yet unhandsome; as among
Lecherous humours, there is one that judges
No wenches wholesome but coarse country drudges.
Graius stays still at home here, and because   55
Some preachers, vile ambitious bawds, and laws,

Still new like fashions, bid him think that she
Which dwells with us is only perfect, he
Embraceth her whom his godfathers will
Tender to him, being tender, as wards still   60
Take such wives as their guardians offer, or
Pay values. Careless Phrygius doth abhor
All, because all cannot be good, as one,
Knowing some women whores, dares marry none.
Gracchus loves all as one, and thinks that so   65
As women do in diverse countries go
In divers habits, yet are still one kind,
So doth, so is Religion; and this blind-
ness too much light breeds; but unmoved thou
Of force must one, and forced but one allow,   70
And the right; ask thy father which is she,
Let him ask his; though Truth and Falsehood be
Near twins, yet Truth a little elder is;
Be busy to seek her, believe me this,
He's not of none, nor worst, that seeks the best.   75
To adore, or scorn an image, or protest,
May all be bad; doubt wisely; in strange way
To stand inquiring right is not to stray;
To sleep, or run wrong is. On a huge hill,
Cragged and steep, Truth stands, and he that will   80
Reach her, about must, and about must go;
And what the hill's suddenness resists, win so.
Yet strive so, that before age, death's twilight,
Thy soul rest, for none can work in that night.
To will implies delay, therefore now do.   85
Hard deeds, the body's pains; hard knowledge to
The mind's endeavours reach, and mysteries
Are like the sun, dazzling, yet plain to all eyes.
Keep the truth which thou hast found; men do not stand
In so ill case here that God hath with His hand   90
Signed kings blank charters to kill whom they hate,
Nor are they vicars, but hangmen to fate.
Fool and wretch, wilt thou lét thy soul be tied
To man's laws, by which she shall not be tried
At the last day? Will it then boot thee   95
To say a Philip, or a Gregory,
A Harry, or a Martin taught thee this?
Is not this excuse for mere contraries

Equally strong? Cannot both sides say so?
That thou mayest rightly obey power, her bounds know;   100
Those passed, her nature, and name is changed; to be
Then humble to her is idolatry.
As streams are, power is; those blest flowers that dwell
At the rough stream's calm head, thrive and do well,
But having left their roots, and themselves given   105
To the stream's tyrannous rage, alas, are driven
Through mills, and rocks, and woods, and at last, almost
Consumed in going, in the sea are lost:
So perish souls, which more choose men's unjust
Power from God claimed, than God Himself to trust.   110

From AN ANATOMY OF THE WORLD.
THE FIRST ANNIVERSARY

¶

She, she is dead; she's dead: when thou knowest this,
Thou knowest how poor a trifling thing man is.
And learn'st thus much by our anatomy,   185
The heart being perished, no part can be free.
And that except thou feed (not banquet) on
The supernatural food, religion,
Thy better growth grows withered and scant;
Be more than man, or thou art less than an ant.   190
Then, as mankind, so is the world's whole frame
Quite out of joint, almost created lame:
For, before God had made up all the rest,
Corruption entered and depraved the best.
It seized the angels, and then first of all   195
The world did in her cradle take a fall,
And turned her brains, and took a general maim,
Wronging each joint of the universal frame.
The noblest part, man, felt it first; and then

Decay of nature   Both beasts and plants, cursed in the curse of man.   200
in other parts.   So did the world from the first hour decay,
That evening was beginning of the day,
And now the springs and summers which we see,
Like sons of women after fifty be.
And new philosophy calls all in doubt,   205
The element of fire is quite put out,

The sun is lost, and the earth, and no man's wit
Can well direct him where to look for it.
And freely men confess that this world's spent,
When in the planets and the firmament   210
They seek so many new; they see that this
Is crumbled out again to his atomies.
'Tis all in pieces, all coherence gone;
All just supply, and all relation:
Prince, subject, father, son, are things forgot,   215
For every man alone thinks he hath got
To be a phoenix, and that there can be
None of that kind, of which he is, but he.
This is the world's condition now, and now
She that should all parts to reunion bow,   220
She that had all magnetic force alone,
To draw, and fasten sundered parts in one;
She whom wise nature had invented then
When she observed that every sort of men
Did in their voyage in this world's sea stray.   225
And needed a new compass for their way;
She that was best, and first original
Of all fair copies, and the general
Steward to Fate; she whose rich eyes and breast
Gilt the West Indies, and perfumed the East;   230
Whose having breathed in this world did bestow
Spice on those Isles, and bade them still smell so,
And that rich Indy which doth gold inter,
Is but as single money, coined from her:
She to whom this world must itself refer,   235
As suburbs, or the microcosm of her,
She, she is dead; she's dead: when thou know'st this,
Thou know'st how lame a cripple this world is.
And learn'st thus much by our anatomy,
That this world's general sickness doth not lie   240
In any humour, or one certain part;
But, as thou sawest it rotten at the heart,
Thou seest a hectic fever hath got hold
Of the whole substance, not to be controlled,
And that thou hast but one way not to admit   245
The world's infection, to be none of it.
For the world's subtlest immaterial parts
Feel this consuming wound, and age's darts.

Disformity
of parts.

For the world's beauty is decayed or gone;
Beauty, that's colour and proportion.   250
We think the heavens enjoy their spherical,
Their round proportion embracing all.
But yet their various and perplexed course,
Observed in divers ages, doth enforce
Men to find out so many eccentric parts,   255
Such divers down-right lines, such overthwarts,
As disproportion that pure form. It tears
The firmament in eight and forty shares,
And in those constellations there arise
New stars, and old do vanish from our eyes: 260
As though heav'n suffered earthquakes, peace or war,
When new towns rise, and old demolished are.
They have impaled within a zodiac
The free-born sun, and keep twelve signs awake
To watch his steps; the Goat and Crab control.   265
And fright him back, who else to either pole
(Did not these tropics fetter him) might run:
For his course is not round; nor can the sun
Perfect a circle, or maintain his way
One inch direct; but where he rose today   270
He comes no more, but with a cozening line,
Steals by that point, and so is serpentine:
And seeming weary with his reeling thus,
He means to sleep, being now fall'n nearer us.
So, of the stars which boast that they do run   275
In circle still, none ends where he begun.
All their proportion's lame, it sinks, it swells.
For of meridians and parallels,
Man hath weaved out a net and this net thrown
Upon the heavens, and now they are his own.   280
Loath to go up the hill, or labour thus
To go to heaven, we make heaven come to us.

[. . .]

She, she is dead; she's dead: when thou know'st this,
Thou know'st how wan a ghost this our world is: 370
And learn'st thus much by our anatomy,
That it should more affright than pleasure thee.
And that, since all fair colour then did sink,
'Tis now but wicked vanity to think

To colour vicious deeds with good pretence,   375
Or with bought colours to illude men's sense.   *Weakness in*
Nor in aught more this world's decay appears,   *the want of*
Than that her influence the heav'n forbears,   *correspondence*
Or that the elements do not feel this;   *of heaven and*
The father or the mother barren is.   *earth.*
                                                     380
The clouds conceive not rain, or do not pour
In the due birth time, down the balmy shower;
The air doth not motherly sit on the earth,
To hatch her seasons and give all things birth;
Springtimes were common cradles, but are tombs;   385
And false conceptions fill the general wombs.
The air shows such meteors as none can see,
Not only what they mean, but what they be;
Earth such new worms, as would have troubled much
The Egyptian Mages to have made more such.   390
What artist now dares boast that he can bring
Heaven hither, or constellate anything,
So as the influence of those stars may be
Imprisoned in an herb, or charm, or tree,
And do by touch all which those stars could do?   395
The art is lost, and correspondence too.
For heaven gives little, and the earth takes less,
And man least knows their trade and purposes.
If this commerce 'twixt heaven and earth were not
Embarred, and all this traffic quite forgot,   400
She, for whose loss we have lamented thus,
Would work more fully and pow'rfully on us.
Since herbs and roots by dying lose not all,
But they, yea ashes too, are medicinal,
Death could not quench her virtue so, but that   405
It would be (if not followed) wondered at:
And all the world would be one dying swan,
To sing her funeral praise, and vanish then.

EPICEDES AND OBSEQUIES

Elegy on Mistress Boulstred

Death I recant, and say, unsaid by me
    Whate'er hath slipped, that might diminish thee.

Spiritual treason, atheism 'tis, to say,
   That any can thy summons disobey.
Th' earth's race is but thy table; there are set   5
   Plants, cattle, men, dishes for Death to eat.
In a rude hunger now he millions draws
   Into his bloody, or plaguey, or starved jaws.
Now he will seem to spare, and doth more waste,
   Eating the best first, well preserved to last.   10
Now wantonly he spoils, and eats us not,
   But breaks off friends, and lets us piecemeal rot.
Nor will this earth serve him; he sinks the deep
   Where harmless fish monastic silence keep,
Who (were Death dead) by roes of living sand,   15
   Might sponge that element, and make it land.
He rounds the air, and breaks the hymnic notes
   In birds', heaven's choristers, organic throats,
Which (if they did not die) might seem to be
   A tenth rank in the heavenly hierarchy.   20
O strong and long-lived death, how cam'st thou in?
   And how without creation didst begin?
Thou hast, and shalt see dead, before thou diest,
   All the four monarchies, and antichrist.
How could I think thee nothing, that see now   25
   In all this all, nothing else is, but thou.
Our births and lives, vices, and virtues, be
   Wasteful consumptions, and degrees of thee.
For, we to live, our bellows wear, and breath,
   Nor are we mortal, dying, dead, but death.   30
And though thou be'st, O mighty bird of prey,
   So much reclaimed by God, that thou must lay
All that thou kill'st at his feet, yet doth he
   Reserve but few, and leaves the most to thee.
And of those few, now thou hast overthrown   35
   One whom thy blow makes, not ours, nor thine own.
She was more storeys high: hopeless to come
   To her soul, thou hast offered at her lower room.
Her soul and body was a king and court:
   But thou hast both of captain missed and fort.   40
As houses fall not, though the king remove,
   Bodies of saints rest for their souls above.
Death gets 'twixt souls and bodies such a place
   As sin insinuates 'twixt just men and grace,

Both work a separation, no divorce.   45
　　Her soul is gone to usher up her corse,
Which shall be almost another soul, for there
　　Bodies are purer, than best souls are here.
Because in her, her virtues did outgo
　　Her years, wouldst thou, O emulous death, do so?   50
And kill her young to thy loss? must the cost
　　Of beauty, and wit, apt to do harm, be lost?
What though thou found'st her proof 'gainst sins of youth?
　　Oh, every age a diverse sin pursueth.
Thou shouldst have stayed, and taken better hold,   55
　　Shortly ambitious, covetous, when old,
She might have proved: and such devotion
　　Might once have strayed to superstition.
If all her virtues must have grown, yet might
　　Abundant virtue have bred a proud delight.   60
Had she persevered just, there would have been
　　Some that would sin, mis-thinking she did sin.
Such as would call her friendship, love, and feign
　　To sociableness, a name profane;
Or sin, by tempting, or, not daring that,   65
　　By wishing, though they never told her what.
Thus mightst thou have slain more souls, hadst thou not crossed
　　Thyself, and to triumph, thine army lost.
Yet though these ways be lost, thou hast left one,
　　Which is, immoderate grief that she is gone.   70
But we may 'scape that sin, yet weep as much,
　　Our tears are due, because we are not such.
Some tears, that knot of friends, her death must cost,
　　Because the chain is broke, though no link lost.

DIVINE POEMS

Holy Sonnets

I

　　As due by many titles I resign
　　Myself to Thee, O God, first I was made
　　By Thee, and for Thee, and when I was decayed
　　Thy blood bought that the which before was Thine;
　　I am Thy son, made with Thyself to shine,   5

Thy servant, whose pains Thou hast still repaid,
Thy sheep, Thine Image, and, till I betrayed
Myself, a temple of Thy Spirit divine;
Why doth the devil then usurp on me?
Why doth he steal, nay ravish that's Thy right?   10
Except Thou rise and for Thine own work fight,
Oh I shall soon despair, when I do see
That Thou lov'st mankind well, yet wilt not choose me,
And Satan hates me, yet is loath to lose me.

2

Oh my black soul! now thou art summoned
By sickness, death's herald, and champion;
Thou art like a pilgrim, which abroad hath done
Treason, and durst not turn to whence he is fled,
Or like a thief, which till death's doom be read,   5
Wisheth himself delivered from prison;
But damned and haled to execution,
Wisheth that still he might be imprisoned.
Yet grace, if thou repent, thou canst not lack;
But who shall give thee that grace to begin?   10
Oh make thyself with holy mourning black,
And red with blushing, as thou art with sin;
Or wash thee in Christ's blood, which hath this might
That being red, it dyes red souls to white.

3

This is my play's last scene, here heavens appoint
My pilgrimage's last mile; and my race,
Idly yet quickly run, hath this last pace,
My span's last inch, my minute's last point,
And gluttonous death will instantly unjoint   5
My body and soul, and I shall sleep a space,
But my ever-waking part shall see that face
Whose fear already shakes my every joint:
Then, as my soul to heaven, her first seat, takes flight,
And earth-born body in the earth shall dwell,   10
So, fall my sins, that all may have their right,
To where they're bred, and would press me, to hell.
Impute me righteous, thus purged of evil,
For thus I leave the world, the flesh, the devil.

4

At the round earth's imagined corners, blow
Your trumpets, angels, and arise, arise
From death, you numberless infinities
Of souls, and to your scattered bodies go,
All whom the flood did, and fire shall o'erthrow,   5
All whom war, dearth, age, agues, tyrannies,
Despair, law, chance, hath slain, and you whose eyes
Shall behold God and never taste death's woe.
But let them sleep, Lord, and me mourn a space;
For if above all these my sins abound,   10
'Tis late to ask abundance of Thy grace
When we are there; here, on this lowly ground,
Teach me how to repent; for that's as good
As if Thou hadst sealed my pardon with Thy blood.

5

If poisonous minerals, and if that tree
Whose fruit threw death on else immortal us,
If lecherous goats, if serpents envious
Cannot be damned, alas, why should I be?
Why should intent or reason, born in me,   5
Make sins, else equal, in me more heinous?
And mercy being easy, and glorious
To God, in His stern wrath why threatens He?
But who am I that dare dispute with Thee?
O God, oh! of Thine only worthy blood,   10
And my tears, make a heavenly Lethean flood,
And drown in it my sin's black memory.
That Thou remember them, some claim as debt,
I think it mercy, if Thou wilt forget.

6

Death be not proud, though some have called thee
Mighty and dreadful, for thou art not so;
For those whom thou think'st thou dost overthrow
Die not, poor death, nor yet canst thou kill me.
From rest and sleep, which but thy pictures be,   5
Much pleasure; then from thee much more must flow;
And soonest our best men with thee do go,

Rest of their bones, and soul's delivery.
Thou art slave to fate, chance, kings, and desperate men,
And dost with poison, war, and sickness dwell;   10
And poppy or charms can make us sleep as well,
And better than thy stroke; why swell'st thou then?
One short sleep past, we wake eternally,
And death shall be no more; death, thou shalt die.

7

Spit in my face you Jews, and pierce my side,
Buffet, and scoff, scourge, and crucify me,
For I have sinned, and sinned, and only He
Who could do no iniquity hath died:
But by my death cannot be satisfied   5
My sins, which pass the Jews' impiety:
They killed once an inglorious man, but I
Crucify Him daily, being now glorified.
Oh let me then His strange love still admire:
Kings pardon, but He bore our punishment.   10
And Jacob came clothed in vile harsh attire
But to supplant, and with gainful intent;
God clothed himself in vile man's flesh that so
He might be weak enough to suffer woe.

8

Why are we by all creatures waited on?
Why do the prodigal elements supply
Life and food to me, being more pure than I,
Simple, and further from corruption?
Why brook'st thou, ignorant horse, subjection?   5
Why dost thou, bull and boar, so sillily
Dissemble weakness, and by one man's stroke die,
Whose whole kind you might swallow and feed upon?
Weaker I am, woe is me, and worse than you,
You have not sinned, nor need be timorous.   10
But wonder at a greater wonder, for to us
Created nature doth these things subdue,
But their Creator, whom sin nor nature tied,
For us, His creatures, and His foes, hath died.

9

What if this present were the world's last night?
Mark in my heart, O soul, where thou dost dwell,
The picture of Christ crucified, and tell
Whether that countenance can thee affright,
Tears in His eyes quench the amazing light,   5
Blood fills His frowns, which from His pierced head fell.
And can that tongue adjudge thee unto hell,
Which prayed forgiveness for His foes' fierce spite?
No, no, but as in my idolatry
I said to all my profane mistresses,   10
Beauty, of pity, foulness only is
A sign of rigour: so I say to thee,
To wicked spirits are horrid shapes assigned,
This beauteous form assures a piteous mind.

10

Batter my heart, three-personed God; for You
As yet but knock, breathe, shine, and seek to mend;
That I may rise and stand, o'erthrow me, and bend
Your force, to break, blow, burn, and make me new.
I, like an usurped town, to another due,   5
Labour to admit You, but Oh, to no end!
Reason, Your viceroy in me, me should defend,
But is captived, and proves weak or untrue.
Yet dearly I love You, and would be loved fain,
But am betrothed unto Your enemy: 10
Divorce me, untie or break that knot again,
Take me to You, imprison me, for I,
Except You enthrall me, never shall be free,
Nor ever chaste, except You ravish me.

11

Wilt thou love God, as He thee? then digest,
My soul, this wholesome meditation,
How God the Spirit, by angels waited on
In heaven, doth make His Temple in thy breast.
The Father, having begot a Son most blest,   5

And still begetting (for he ne'er begun),
Hath deigned to choose thee, by adoption,
Coheir to His glory and sabbath's endless rest;
And as a robbed man which by search doth find
His stol'n stuff sold must lose or buy it again,   10
The Son of glory came down, and was slain,
Us whom He had made, and Satan stol'n, to unbind.
'Twas much that man was made like God before,
But that God should be made like man, much more.

12

Father, part of His double interest
Unto Thy kingdom, Thy Son gives to me;
His jointure in the knotty Trinity
He keeps, and gives to me His death's conquest.
This Lamb, whose death with life the world hath blest,   5
Was from the world's beginning slain, and He
Hath made two wills, which with the legacy
Of His and Thy kingdom do Thy sons invest.
Yet such are those laws that men argue yet
Whether a man those statutes can fulfill;   10
None doth; but all-healing grace and spirit
Revive again what law and letter kill.
Thy law's abridgment and Thy last command
Is all but love; oh let that last will stand!

                                        (*Poems*, 1633)

¶

Since she whom I loved hath paid her last debt
To nature, and to hers, and my good is dead,
And her soul early into heaven ravished,
Wholly in heavenly things my mind is set.
Here the admiring her my mind did whet   5
To seek Thee, God; so streams do show the head;
But though I have found Thee, and Thou my thirst hast fed,
A holy thirsty dropsy melts me yet.

But why should I beg more love, when as Thou
Dost woo my soul, for hers off'ring all Thine: 10
And dost not only fear lest I allow
My love to saints and angels, things divine,
But in Thy tender jealousy dost doubt
Lest the world, flesh, yea devil put Thee out.

(Westmoreland MS)

Good Friday, 1613. Riding Westward

Let man's soul be a sphere, and then, in this,
The intelligence that moves, devotion is,
And as the other spheres, by being grown
Subject to foreign motions, lose their own,
And being by others hurried every day,   5
Scarce in a year their natural form obey,
Pleasure or business, so our souls admit
For their first mover, and are whirled by it.
Hence is 't that I am carried towards the West
This day, when my soul's form bends toward the East.   10
There I should see a Sun, by rising, set,
And by that setting endless day beget;
But that Christ on this cross did rise and fall,
Sin had eternally benighted all.
Yet dare I almost be glad I do not see   15
That spectacle of too much weight for me.
Who sees God's face, that is self life, must die;
What a death were it then to see God die?
It made His own lieutenant, Nature, shrink;
It made His footstool crack, and the sun wink.   20
Could I behold those hands which span the poles,
And turn all spheres at once, pierced with those holes?
Could I behold that endless height which is
Zenith to us, and our antipodes,
Humbled below us? or that blood which is   25
The seat of all our souls, if not of His,
Make dirt of dust, or that flesh which was worn
By God, for His apparel, ragg'd and torn?
If on these things I durst not look, durst I
Upon his miserable mother cast mine eye,   30
Who was God's partner here, and furnished thus
Half of that sacrifice which ransomed us?

Though these things, as I ride, be from mine eye,
They're present yet unto my memory,
For that looks towards them; and Thou look'st towards me, 35
O Saviour, as Thou hang'st upon the tree;
I turn my back to Thee but to receive
Corrections, till Thy mercies bid Thee leave.
O think me worth Thine anger, punish me,
Burn off my rusts and my deformity,   40
Restore Thine image so much, by Thy grace,
That Thou may'st know me, and I'll turn my face.

A Hymn to Christ,
at the Author's Last Going into Germany

In what torn ship soever I embark,
That ship shall be my emblem of Thy ark;
What sea soever swallow me, that flood
Shall be to me an emblem of Thy blood;
Though Thou with clouds of anger do disguise   5
Thy face, yet through that mask I know those eyes,
    Which, though they turn away sometimes,·
        They never will despise.

I sacrifice this island unto Thee,
And all whom I loved there, and who loved me;   10
When I have put our seas 'twixt them and me,
Put thou Thy sea betwixt my sins and Thee.
As the tree's sap doth seek the root below
In winter, in my winter now I go
    Where none but Thee, the eternal root   15
        Of true love, I may know.

Nor Thou nor Thy religion dost control
The amorousness of an harmonious soul,
But Thou would'st have that love Thyself; as Thou
Art jealous, Lord, so I am jealous now;   20
Thou lov'st not, till from loving more, Thou free
My soul: whoever gives, takes liberty:
    O, if Thou car'st not whom I love,
        Alas, Thou lov'st not me.

Seal then this bill of my divorce to all   25
On whom those fainter beams of love did fall;
Marry those loves which in youth scattered be
On fame, wit, hopes (false mistresses) to Thee.
Churches are best for prayer that have least light:
To see God only, I go out of sight;   30
    And to 'scape stormy days, I choose
      An everlasting night.

A Hymn to God the Father

Wilt Thou forgive that sin where I begun,
   Which is my sin, though it were done before?
Wilt Thou forgive those sins through which I run,
   And do them still, though still I do deplore?
     When Thou hast done, Thou hast not done,   5
      For I have more.

Wilt Thou forgive that sin by which I won
   Others to sin? and made my sin their door?
Wilt Thou forgive that sin which I did shun
   A year or two, but wallowed in a score?   10
     When Thou hast done, Thou hast not done,
      For I have more.

I have a sin of fear, that when I have spun
   My last thread, I shall perish on the shore;
Swear by Thyself that at my death Thy Sun   15
   Shall shine as it shines now, and heretofore;
     And, having done that, Thou hast done,
      I have no more.

(Poems, 1633)

BEN JONSON
(1572/3–1637)

Jonson was the dominant figure in the world of letters during the age of Shakespeare and of Donne, his robustly assertive personality, his impressive learning and his undoubted commitment to his art ensuring the respect, if not always the love of his contemporaries. The author of two of the greatest satirical comedies in any language, of numerous court masques, of some of the most discerning criticism of the period, it was nevertheless his poems which he valued most highly, and which drew to him the large number of younger writers – amongst them Herrick, Carew, Suckling, Clarendon and Falkland – who called themselves the 'Sons of Ben'. Jonson offered them a high humanist sense of the importance of the poet as the 'interpreter and arbiter of nature', and, more significantly, an example of a successful attempt to align English vernacular poetry with classical poetry for the first time. Jonson's own work is filled with echoes of that classical poetry, without ever forfeiting its Englishness or its originality; by following his example, his 'sons' could aspire to entry into a classical tradition, and thus to a status and permanence which, it was felt, was by no means guaranteed to earlier English writers. Randolph's 'Gratulatory' (see p. 253) makes this feeling very clear.

The flexible couplet form which Jonson made his own, and which Marvell inherited, embodied many of the 'classical' virtues for which he stood – virtues of balance, urbanity and restraint, championed in his poetry, but notably absent from his eventful life. In his commitment to his classical ideals, in the graceful delicacy of his lyric voice, the stoic dignity of his most serious verse, the bitter sting of his satirical epigrams, and in the primarily social orientation of his work as a whole, he is the first and arguably the greatest Augustan writer in English.

Jonson published his own collected *Works* in 1616 – an unprecedented step for a popular dramatist – and an enlarged edition appeared in 1640–1. The great modern edition by C. H. Herford and Percy and Evelyn Simpson, *Ben Jonson* (11 volumes, Oxford, 1925–52) contains a long introduction and biography. There are separate editions of the poems by Ian Donaldson (London, 1975) and George Parfitt (Harmondsworth, 1975), and good studies of the poetry by Wesley Trimpi, *Ben Jonson's Poems* (Stanford, 1962), and by Parfitt, *Ben Jonson: Public Poet and Private Man* (London, 1976).

EPIGRAMS

To William Camden

Camden, most reverend head, to whom I owe
   All that I am in arts, all that I know,
(How nothing's that?) to whom my country owes
   The great renown and name wherewith she goes;
Than thee the age sees not that thing more grave,   5
   More high, more holy, that she more would crave.
What name, what skill, what faith hast thou in things!
   What sight in searching the most antique springs!
What weight, and what authority in thy speech!
   Man scarce can make that doubt, but thou canst teach.   10
Pardon free truth, and let thy modesty,
   Which conquers all, be once overcome by thee.
Many of thine this better could than I;
   But for their powers accept my piety.

On My First Daughter

Here lies, to each her parents' ruth,
Mary, the daughter of their youth;
Yet, all heaven's gifts being heaven's due,
It makes the father less to rue.
At six months' end she parted hence   5
With safety of her innocence;
Whose soul heaven's Queen (whose name she bears),
In comfort of her mother's tears,
Hath placed amongst her virgin train;
Where, while that severed doth remain,   10
This grave partakes the fleshly birth;
Which cover lightly, gentle earth.

On My First Son

Farewell, thou child of my right hand, and joy;
   My sin was too much hope of thee, loved boy.
Seven years thou wert lent to me, and I thee pay,
   Exacted by thy fate, on the just day.
Oh, could I lose all father now! For why   5
   Will man lament the state he should envy?
To have so soon 'scaped world's and flesh's rage,
   And, if no other misery, yet age?
Rest in soft peace, and, asked, say here doth lie
   Ben Jonson his best piece of poetry;   10
For whose sake, henceforth, all his vows be such,
   As what he loves may never like too much.

To Fine Lady Would-Be

Fine Madam Would-Be, wherefore should you fear,
   That love to make so well, a child to bear?
The world reputes you barren; but I know
   Your 'pothecary, and his drug says no.
Is it the pain affrights? That's soon forgot.   5
   Or your complexion's loss? You have a pot
That can restore that. Will it hurt your feature?
   To make amends, you're thought a wholesome creature.
What should the cause be? Oh, you live at court:
   And there's both loss of time and loss of sport   10
In a great belly. Write, then, on thy womb:
   'Of the not born, yet buried, here's the tomb.'

To Pertinax Cob

Cob, thou nor soldier, thief, nor fencer art,
Yet by thy weapon liv'st! Thou hast one good part.

To Fine Grand

What is't, fine Grand, makes thee my friendship fly,
   Or take an epigram so fearfully,
As 'twere a challenge, or a borrower's letter?
   The world must know your greatness is my debtor.
In primis, Grand, you owe me for a jest   5
   I lent you, on mere acquaintance, at a feast;
Item, a tale or two some fortnight after,
   That yet maintains you and your house in laughter;
Item, the Babylonian song you sing;
   Item, a fair Greek posy for a ring,   10
With which a learned madam you belie.
   Item, a charm surrounding fearfully
Your *partie-per-pale* picture, one half drawn
   In solemn cypress, the other cobweb-lawn;
Item, a gulling imprese for you, at tilt;   15
   Item, your mistress' anagram, i' your hilt;
Item, your own, sewed in your mistress' smock;
   Item, an epitaph on my lord's cock,
In most vile verses, and cost me more pain
   Than had I made 'em good, to fit your vain.   20
Forty things more, dear Grand, which you know true:
   For which or pay me quickly or I'll pay you.

To John Donne

Who shall doubt, Donne, whe'er I a poet be,
   When I dare send my epigrams to thee?
That so alone canst judge, so alone dost make;
   And in thy censures, evenly dost take
As free simplicity to disavow   5
   As thou hast best authority to allow.
Read all I send; and if I find but one
   Marked by thy hand, and with the better stone,
My title's sealed. Those that for claps do write,
   Let puisnes', porters', players' praise delight,   10
And till they burst, their backs like asses' load:
   A man should seek great glory, and not broad.

Inviting a Friend to Supper

Tonight, grave sir, both my poor house and I
    Do equally desire your company;
Not that we think us worthy such a guest,
    But that your worth will dignify our feast
With those that come; whose grace may make that seem   5
    Something, which else could hope for no esteem.
It is the fair acceptance, sir, creates
    The entertainment perfect, not the cates.
Yet shall you have, to rectify your palate,
    An olive, capers, or some better salad   10
Ushering the mutton; with a short-legged hen,
    If we can get her, full of eggs, and then
Lemons, and wine for sauce; to these, a coney
    Is not to be despaired of, for our money;
And though fowl now be scarce, yet there are clerks,   15
    The sky not falling, think we may have larks.
I'll tell you of more, and lie, so you will come:
    Of partridge, pheasant, woodcock, of which some
May yet be there; and godwit, if we can;
    Knat, rail and ruff, too. Howsoe'er, my man   20
Shall read a piece of Virgil, Tacitus,
    Livy, or of some better book to us,
Of which we'll speak our minds, amidst our meat;
    And I'll profess no verses to repeat;
To this, if aught appear which I not know of,   25
    That will the pastry, not my paper, show of.
Digestive cheese and fruit there sure will be;
    But that which most doth take my muse and me
Is a pure cup of rich Canary wine,
    Which is the Mermaid's now, but shall be mine;   30
Of which had Horace or Anacreon tasted,
    Their lives, as do their lines, till now had lasted.
Tobacco, nectar, or the Thespian spring
    Are all but Luther's beer to this I sing.
Of this we will sup free, but moderately;   35
    And we will have no Poley or Parrot by;
Nor shall our cups make any guilty men,
    But at our parting we will be as when
We innocently met. No simple word
    That shall be uttered at our mirthful board   40

Shall make us sad next morning, or affright
The liberty that we'll enjoy tonight.

To a Weak Gamester in Poetry

With thy small stock, why art thou venturing still
  At this so subtle sport, and play'st so ill?
Think'st thou it is mere fortune that can win?
  Or thy rank setting? That thou dar'st put in
Thy all, at all; and whatsoe'er I do,   5
  Art still at that, and think'st to blow me up too?
I cannot for the stage a drama lay,
  Tragic or comic, but thou writ'st the play.
I leave thee there, and, giving way, intend
  An epic poem: thou hast the same end.   10
I modestly quit that, and think to write,
  Next morn, an ode: thou mak'st a song ere night.
I pass to elegies: thou meet'st me there;
  To satires: and thou dost pursue me. Where,
Where shall I 'scape thee? in an epigram?   15
  Oh, (thou criest out) that is thy proper game.
Troth, if it be, I pity thy ill luck,
  That both for wit and sense so oft dost pluck,
And never art encountered, I confess;
  Nor scarce dost colour for it, which is less.   20
Prithee yet save thy rest; give o'er in time:
  There's no vexation that can make thee prime.

On Gut

Gut eats all day, and lechers all the night;
  So all his meat he tasteth over, twice;
And striving so to double his delight,
  He makes himself a thoroughfare of vice.
Thus in his belly can he change a sin: 5
  Lust it comes out, that gluttony went in.

Epitaph on Salomon Pavy,
a Child of Queen Elizabeth's Chapel

Weep with me all you that read
    This little story,
And know, for whom a tear you shed,
    Death's self is sorry.
'Twas a child that so did thrive   5
    In grace and feature,
As heaven and nature seemed to strive
    Which owned the creature.
Years he numbered scarce thirteen
    When fates turned cruel,   10
Yet three filled zodiacs had he been
    The stage's jewel,
And did act (what now we moan)
    Old men so duly
As, sooth, the Parcae thought him one,   15
    He played so truly.
So, by error, to his fate
    They all consented,
But viewing him since (alas, too late)
    They have repented;   20
And have sought, to give new birth,
    In baths to steep him;
But being so much too good for earth,
    Heaven vows to keep him.

THE FOREST

To Penshurst

Thou art not, Penshurst, built to envious show
    Of touch or marble, nor canst boast a row
Of polished pillars, or a roof of gold;
    Thou hast no lantern whereof tales are told,
Or stair, or courts; but stand'st an ancient pile,   5
    And these grudged at, art reverenced the while.
Thou joy'st in better marks, of soil, of air,
    Of wood, of water, therein thou art fair.

Thou hast thy walks for health as well as sport:
   Thy Mount, to which the dryads do resort,   10
Where Pan and Bacchus their high feasts have made,
   Beneath the broad beech and the chestnut shade;
That taller tree, which of a nut was set
   At his great birth, where all the muses met.
There, in the writhed bark, are cut the names   15
   Of many a sylvan taken with his flames;
And thence the ruddy satyrs oft provoke
   The lighter fauns to reach thy lady's oak.
Thy copse, too, named of Gamage, thou hast there,
   That never fails to serve thee seasoned deer   20
When thou wouldst feast or exercise thy friends.
   The lower land, that to the river bends,
Thy sheep, thy bullocks, kine and calves do feed;
   The middle grounds thy mares and horses breed.
Each bank doth yield thee conies, and the tops,   25
   Fertile of wood, Ashour and Sidney's copse,
To crown thy open table, doth provide
   The purpled pheasant with the speckled side;
The painted partridge lies in every field,
   And for thy mess is willing to be killed.   30
And if the high-swoll'n Medway fail thy dish,
   Thou hast thy ponds that pay thee tribute fish:
Fat, aged carps, that run into thy net;
   And pikes, now weary their own kind to eat,
As loath the second draught or cast to stay,   35
   Officiously, at first, themselves betray;
Bright eels, that emulate them, and leap on land
   Before the fisher, or into his hand.
Then hath thy orchard fruit, thy garden flowers,
   Fresh as the air and new as are the hours: 40
The early cherry, with the later plum,
   Fig, grape and quince, each in his time doth come;
The blushing apricot and woolly peach
   Hang on thy walls, that every child may reach.
And though thy walls be of the country stone,   45
   They're reared with no man's ruin, no man's groan;
There's none that dwell about them wish them down,
   But all come in, the farmer and the clown,
And no one empty-handed, to salute
   Thy lord and lady, though they have no suit.   50

Some bring a capon, some a rural cake,
   Some nuts, some apples; some that think they make
The better cheeses, bring 'em; or else send
   By their ripe daughters, whom they would commend
This way to husbands; and whose baskets bear   55
   An emblem of themselves, in plum or pear.
But what can this (more than express their love)
   Add to thy free provisions, far above
The need of such? whose liberal board doth flow
   With all that hospitality doth know!   60
Where comes no guest but is allowed to eat
   Without his fear, and of thy lord's own meat;
Where the same beer and bread and self-same wine
   That is his lordship's shall be also mine;
And I not fain to sit, as some this day   65
   At great men's tables, and yet dine away.
Here no man tells my cups, nor, standing by,
   A waiter, doth my gluttony envy,
But gives me what I call, and lets me eat;
   He knows below he shall find plenty of meat: 70
Thy tables hoard not up for the next day.
   Nor, when I take my lodging, need I pray
For fire or lights or livery: all is there,
   As if thou then wert mine, or I reigned here;
There's nothing I can wish, for which I stay.   75
   That found King James, when, hunting late this way
With his brave son, the Prince, they saw thy fires
   Shine bright on every hearth as the desires
Of thy Penates had been set on flame
   To entertain them; or the country came   80
With all their zeal to warm their welcome here.
   What (great, I will not say, but) sudden cheer
Didst thou then make 'em! and what praise was heaped
   On thy good lady then! who therein reaped
The just reward of her high housewifery: 85
   To have her linen, plate, and all things nigh
When she was far; and not a room but dressed
   As if it had expected such a guest!
These, Penshurst, are thy praise, and yet not all.
   Thy lady's noble, fruitful, chaste withal;   90
His children thy great lord may call his own,
   A fortune in this age but rarely known.

They are and have been taught religion; thence
  Their gentler spirits have sucked innocence.
Each morn and even they are taught to pray   95
  With the whole household, and may every day
Read in their virtuous parents' noble parts
  The mysteries of manners, arms and arts.
Now, Penshurst, they that will proportion thee
  With other edifices, when they see   100
Those proud, ambitious heaps, and nothing else,
  May say, their lords have built, but thy lord dwells.

To the World: A Farewell for a Gentlewoman, Virtuous and Noble

False world, good night. Since thou hast brought
  That hour upon my morn of age,
Henceforth I quit thee from my thought;
  My part is ended on thy stage.
Do not once hope that thou canst tempt   5
  A spirit so resolved to tread
Upon thy throat and live exempt
  From all the nets that thou canst spread.
I know thy forms are studied arts,
  Thy subtle ways be narrow straits,   10
Thy courtesy but sudden starts,
  And what thou call'st thy gifts are baits.
I know too, though thou strut and paint,
  Yet art thou both shrunk up and old;
That only fools make thee a saint,   15
  And all thy good is to be sold.
I know thou whole art but a shop
  Of toys and trifles, traps and snares,
To take the weak, or make them stop;
  Yet art thou falser than thy wares.   20
And knowing this, should I yet stay,
  Like such as blow away their lives
And never will redeem a day,
  Enamoured of their golden gyves?
Or, having 'scaped, shall I return   25
  And thrust my neck into the noose
From whence so lately I did burn
  With all my powers myself to loose?

What bird or beast is known so dull
   That, fled his cage, or broke his chain,   30
And tasting air and freedom, wull
   Render his head in there again?
If these, who have but sense, can shun
   The engines that have them annoyed,
Little for me had reason done,   35
   If I could not thy gins avoid.
Yes, threaten, do. Alas, I fear
   As little as I hope from thee;
I know thou canst nor show nor bear
   More hatred than thou hast to me.   40
My tender, first, and simple years
   Thou didst abuse, and then betray;
Since stirredst up jealousies and fears,
   When all the causes were away.
Then in a soil hast planted me   45
   Where breathe the basest of thy fools,
Where envious arts professed be,
   And pride and ignorance the schools;
Where nothing is examined, weighed,
   But, as 'tis rumoured, so believed;   50
Where every freedom is betrayed,
   And every goodness taxed or grieved.
But what we're born for we must bear:
   Our frail condition it is such
That, what to all may happen here,   55
   If't chance to me, I must not grutch.
Else I my state should much mistake,
   To harbour a divided thought
From all my kind; that, for my sake,
   There should a miracle be wrought.   60
No, I do know that I was born
   To age, misfortune, sickness, grief;
But I will bear these with that scorn
   As shall not need thy false relief.
Nor for my peace will I go far,   65
   As wanderers do that still do roam,
But make my strengths, such as they are,
   Here in my bosom, and at home.

Song: To Celia

Come, my Celia, let us prove,
While we may, the sports of love;
Time will not be ours for ever;
He at length our good will sever.
Spend not then his gifts in vain.   5
Suns that set may rise again;
But if once we lose this light,
'Tis with us perpetual night.
Why should we defer our joys?
Fame and rumour are but toys.   10
Cannot we delude the eyes
Of a few poor household spies?
Or his easier ears beguile,
So removed by our wile?
'Tis no sin love's fruit to steal,   15
But the sweet theft to reveal:
To be taken, to be seen,
These have crimes accounted been.

To the Same

Kiss me, sweet: the wary lover
Can your favours keep and cover,
When the common courting jay
All your bounties will betray.
Kiss again: no creature comes.   5
Kiss, and score up wealthy sums
On my lips, thus hardly sundered,
While you breathe. First give a hundred,
Then a thousand, then another
Hundred, then unto the tother   10
Add a thousand, and so more,
Till you equal with the store
All the grass that Romney yields,
Or the sands in Chelsea fields,
Or the drops in silver Thames,   15
Or the stars that gild his streams

In the silent summer nights,
When youths ply their stol'n delights:
That the curious may not know
How to tell 'em as they flow,   20
And the envious, when they find
What their number is, be pined.

From *Epistle to Elizabeth, Countess of Rutland*

With you, I know, my offering will find grace.   30
For what a sin 'gainst your great father's spirit
    Were it to think that you should not inherit
His love unto the muses, when his skill
    Almost you have, or may have, when you will?
Wherein wise nature you a dowry gave   35
    Worth an estate treble to that you have.
Beauty, I know, is good, and blood is more;
    Riches thought most. But, madam, think what store
The world hath seen, which all these had in trust
    And now lie lost in their forgotten dust.   40
It is the muse alone can raise to heaven,
    And, at her strong arm's end, hold up and even
The souls she loves. Those other glorious notes,
    Inscribed in touch or marble, or the coats
Painted or carved upon our great men's tombs,   45
    Or in their windows, do but prove the wombs
That bred them graves; when they were born, they died
    That had no muse to make their fame abide.
How many equal with the Argive Queen
    Have beauty known, yet none so famous seen?   50
Achilles was not first that valiant was,
    Or, in an army's head, that locked in brass
Gave killing strokes. There were brave men before
    Ajax, or Idomen, or all the store
That Homer brought to Troy; yet none so live,   55
    Because they lacked the sacred pen could give
Like life unto 'em. Who heaved Hercules
    Unto the stars? or the Tyndarides?
Who placed Jason's Argo in the sky,
    Or set bright Ariadne's crown so high?   60

Who made a lamp of Berenice's hair,
  Or lifted Cassiopeia in her chair,
But only poets, rapt with rage divine?
  And such, or my hopes fail, shall make you shine.

To Heaven

Good and great God, can I not think of Thee,
  But it must straight my melancholy be?
Is it interpreted in me disease
  That, laden with my sins, I seek for ease?
Oh, be Thou witness, that the reins dost know   5
  And hearts of all, if I be sad for show;
And judge me after, if I dare pretend
  To aught but grace, or aim at other end.
As Thou art all, so be Thou all to me,
  First, midst, and last; converted one and three;   10
My faith, my hope, my love; and in this state,
  My judge, my witness, and my advocate.
Where have I been this while exiled from Thee?
  And whither rapt, now Thou but stoop'st to me?
Dwell, dwell here still: Oh, being everywhere,   15
  How can I doubt to find Thee ever here?
I know my state, both full of shame and scorn,
  Conceived in sin, and unto labour born,
Standing with fear, and must with horror fall,
  And destined unto judgement, after all.   20
I feel my griefs too, and there scarce is ground
  Upon my flesh to inflict another wound.
Yet dare I not complain, or wish for death
  With holy Paul, lest it be thought the breath
Of discontent; or that these prayers be   25
  For weariness of life, not love of Thee.
                              (*The Works*, 1616)

UNDERWOODS

A Celebration of Charis in
Ten Lyric Pieces

1   His Excuse for Loving

Let it not your wonder move,
Less your laughter, that I love.
Though I now write fifty years,
I have had, and have, my peers;
Poets, though divine, are men: 5
Some have loved as old again.
And it is not always face,
Clothes, or fortune gives the grace,
Or the feature, or the youth;
But the language, and the truth,   10
With the ardour and the passion,
Gives the lover weight and fashion.
If you will then read the story,
First prepare you to be sorry
That you never knew till now   15
Either whom to love, or how;
But be glad as soon with me,
When you know that this is she,
Of whose beauty it was sung,
She shall make the old man young,   20
Keep the middle age at stay,
And let nothing high decay,
Till she be the reason why
All the world for love may die.

4   Her Triumph

See the chariot at hand here of Love,
    Wherein my lady rideth!
Each that draws is a swan or a dove,
    And well the car Love guideth.
As she goes, all hearts do duty   5
        Unto her beauty;
And enamoured, do wish, so they might
        But enjoy such a sight,

That they still were to run by her side,
Through swords, through seas, whither she would ride.　10

Do but look on her eyes, they do light
　All that Love's world compriseth!
Do but look on her hair, it is bright
　As Love's star when it riseth!
Do but mark, her forehead's smoother　15
　　　Than words that soothe her!
And from her arched brows, such a grace
　　　Sheds itself through the face,
　As alone there triumphs to the life
All the gain, all the good, of the elements' strife.　20

Have you seen but a bright lily grow,
　Before rude hands have touched it?
Have you marked but the fall o' the snow,
　Before the soil hath smutched it?
Have you felt the wool o' the beaver?　25
　　　Or swan's down ever?
Or have smelled o' the bud o' the briar?
　　　Or the nard i' the fire?
　Or have tasted the bag o' the bee?
O so white! O so soft! O so sweet is she!　30

An Epitaph on Master Vincent Corbett

I have my piety too, which could
It vent itself but as it would,
　Would say as much as both have done
　Before me here, the friend and son;
For I both lost a friend and father,　5
Of him whose bones this grave doth gather:
　Dear Vincent Corbett, who so long
　Had wrestled with diseases strong
That though they did possess each limb,
Yet he broke them, ere they could him,　10
　With the just canon of his life;
　A life that knew nor noise nor strife,
But was, by sweetening so his will,
All order and disposure still.

His mind as pure, and neatly kept,   15
 As were his nurseries, and swept
So of uncleanness or offence,
That never came ill odour thence;
 And add his actions unto these,
 They were as specious as his trees.   20
'Tis true, he could not reprehend;
His very manners taught to amend,
 They were so even, grave, and holy;
 No stubbornness so stiff, nor folly
To license ever was so light   25
As twice to trespass in his sight;
 His looks would so correct it, when
 It chid the vice, yet not the men.
Much from him I profess I won,
And more and more I should have done,   30
 But that I understood him scant.
 Now I conceive him by my want,
And pray, who shall my sorrows read,
That they for me their tears will shed;
 For truly, since he left to be,   35
 I feel I'm rather dead than he!

Reader, whose life and name did e'er become
 An epitaph, deserved a tomb;
Nor wants it here, through penury or sloth;
 Who makes the one, so it be first, makes both.   40

From *An Epistle to a Friend, to Persuade Him to the Wars*

The whole world here, leavened with madness, swells,
And being a thing blown out of nought, rebels
Against his Maker; high alone with weeds
And impious rankness of all sects and seeds;
Not to be checked or frighted now with fate,   35
But more licentious made, and desperate!
Our delicacies are grown capital,
And even our sports are dangers; what we call

Friendship is now masked hatred; justice fled,
And shamefastness together; all laws dead   40
That kept man living; pleasures only sought;
Honour and honesty as poor things thought
As they are made; pride and stiff clownage mixed
To make up greatness! And man's whole good fixed
In bravery or gluttony, or coin,   45
All which he makes the servants of the groin:
Thither it flows! How much did Stallion spend
To have his court-bred filly there commend
His lace and starch, and fall upon her back
In admiration, stretched upon the rack   50
Of lust, to his rich suit and title, lord?
Aye, that's a charm and half! She must afford
That all respect; she must lie down – nay, more,
'Tis there civility to be a whore.
He's one of blood and fashion, and with these   55
The bravery makes; she can no honour leese.
To do 't with cloth, or stuffs, lust's name might merit;
With velvet, plush, and tissues, it is spirit.
Oh, these so ignorant monsters! light, as proud;
Who can behold their manners and not cloud-   60
Like upon them lighten? If nature could
Not make a verse, anger or laughter would,
To see 'em aye discoursing with their glass
How they may make someone that day an ass;
Planting their purls, and curls spread forth like net,   65
And every dressing for a pitfall set
To catch the flesh in, and to pound a prick.

An Ode. To Himself

Where dost thou careless lie,
    Buried in ease and sloth?
Knowledge that sleeps doth die;
And this security,
    It is the common moth   5
That eats on wits and arts, and oft destroys them both.

Are all the Aonian springs
   Dried up? Lies Thespia waste?
Doth Clarius' harp want strings,
That not a nymph now sings?   10
   Or droop they, as disgraced
To see their seats and bowers by chattering pies defaced?

If hence thy silence be,
   As 'tis too just a cause,
Let this thought quicken thee: 15
Minds that are great and free,
   Should not on fortune pause;
'Tis crown enough to virtue still, her own applause.

What though the greedy fry
   Be taken with false baits   20
Of worded balladry,
And think it poesie?
   They die with their conceits,
And only piteous scorn upon their folly waits.

Then take in hand thy lyre,   25
   Strike in thy proper strain;
With Japhet's line, aspire
Sol's chariot for new fire
   To give the world again;
Who aided him, will thee, the issue of Jove's brain.   30

And since our dainty age
   Cannot endure reproof,
Make not thyself a page
To that strumpet, the stage;
   But sing high and aloof,   35
Safe from the wolf's black jaw, and the dull ass's hoof.
                       (*The Works*, 1640–1)

To the Memory of My Beloved, The Author,
Mr William Shakespeare, And What He Hath Left Us

To draw no envy, Shakespeare, on thy name,
    Am I thus ample to thy book and fame;
While I confess thy writings to be such
    As neither man nor muse can praise too much;
'Tis true, and all men's suffrage. But these way   5
    Were not the paths I meant unto thy praise:
For silliest ignorance on these may light,
    Which, when it sounds at best, but echoes right;
Or blind affection, which doth ne'er advance
    The truth, but gropes, and urgeth all by chance;   10
Or crafty malice might pretend this praise,
    And think to ruin where it seemed to raise.
These are as some infamous bawd or whore
    Should praise a matron: what could hurt her more?
But thou art proof against them, and indeed   15
    Above the ill fortune of them, or the need.
I therefore will begin. Soul of the age!
    The applause, delight, the wonder of our stage!
My Shakespeare, rise: I will not lodge thee by
    Chaucer or Spenser, or bid Beaumont lie   20
A little further, to make thee a room;
    Thou art a monument without a tomb,
And art alive still while thy book doth live,
    And we have wits to read, and praise to give.
That I not mix thee so, my brain excuses: 25
    I mean with great, but disproportioned, muses;
For if I thought my judgement were of years
    I should commit thee surely with thy peers:
And tell how far thou didst our Lyly outshine,
    Or sporting Kyd, or Marlowe's mighty line.   30
And though thou hadst small Latin, and less Greek,
    From thence to honour thee I would not seek
For names, but call forth thundering Aeschylus,
    Euripides, and Sophocles to us,
Pacuvius, Accius, him of Cordova dead,   35
    To life again, to hear thy buskin tread
And shake a stage; or, when thy socks were on,
    Leave thee alone for the comparison
Of all that insolent Greece or haughty Rome
    Sent forth, or since did from their ashes come.   40

Triumph, my Britain, thou hast one to show
    To whom all scenes of Europe homage owe.
He was not of an age, but for all time!
    And all the muses still were in their prime
When like Apollo he came forth to warm   45
    Our ears, or like a Mercury to charm!
Nature herself was proud of his designs,
    And joyed to wear the dressing of his lines,
Which were so richly spun and woven so fit
    As, since, she will vouchsafe no other wit.   50
The merry Greek, tart Aristophanes,
    Neat Terence, witty Plautus, now not please,
But antiquated and deserted lie
    As they were not of nature's family.
Yet must I not give nature all: thy art,   55
    My gentle Shakespeare, must enjoy a part.
For though the poet's matter nature be,
    His art doth give the fashion. And that he
Who casts to write a living line must sweat
    (Such as thine are) and strike the second heat   60
Upon the muses' anvil: turn the same
    (And himself with it) that he thinks to frame;
Or for the laurel he may gain a scorn:
    For a good poet's made, as well as born;
And such wert thou. Look how the father's face   65
    Lives in his issue: even so, the race
Of Shakespeare's mind and manners brightly shines
    In his well-turned and true-filed lines:
In each of which he seems to shake a lance,
    As brandished at the eyes of ignorance.   70
Sweet swan of Avon! What a sight it were
    To see thee in our waters yet appear,
And make those flights upon the banks of Thames
    That so did take Eliza, and our James!
But stay, I see thee in the hemisphere   75
    Advanced, and made a constellation there!
Shine forth, thou star of poets, and with rage
    Or influence chide or cheer the drooping stage;
Which, since thy flight from hence, hath mourned like night,
    And despairs day, but for thy volume's light.   80
        (*Mr William Shakespeare's Comedies, Histories, and*
                      Tragedies, 1623)

[Echo's Song]

Slow, slow, fresh fount, keep time with my salt tears;
Yet slower yet, O faintly gentle springs;
List to the heavy part the music bears:
 Woe weeps out her division when she sings.
  Droop, herbs and flowers,   5
  Fall, grief, in showers;
  Our beauties are not ours:
   Oh, could I still
(Like melting snow upon some craggy hill)
  Drop, drop, drop, drop,   10
Since nature's pride is now a withered daffodil.

[Hesperus' Hymn to Cynthia]

Queen and huntress, chaste and fair,
Now the sun is laid to sleep,
Seated in thy silver chair,
State in wonted manner keep:
 Hesperus entreats thy light,   5
 Goddess excellently bright.

Earth, let not thy envious shade
Dare itself to interpose;
Cynthia's shining orb was made
Heaven to clear, when day did close: 10
 Bless us then with wished sight,
 Goddess excellently bright.

Lay thy bow of pearl apart,
And thy crystal-shining quiver;
Give unto the flying hart   15
Space to breathe, how short soever:
 Thou that mak'st a day of night,
 Goddess excellently bright.
      (*Cynthia's Revels*, 1600)

¶

Still to be neat, still to be dressed,
As you were going to a feast;
Still to be powdered, still perfumed:
Lady, it is to be presumed,
Though art's hid causes are not found,   5
All is not sweet, all is not sound.

Give me a look, give me a face,
That makes simplicity a grace;
Robes loosely flowing, hair as free:
Such sweet neglect more taketh me   10
Than all the adulteries of art:
They strike mine eyes, but not my heart.
                    (*Epicoene, or the Silent Woman*, 1609)

ROBERT HERRICK
(1591–1674)

Herrick has been undervalued by twentieth-century readers looking
more for what Eliot called 'tough reasonableness' than for delight in
the graceful, well-made lyric. For Herrick's earlier readers graceful-
ness was not a trivial virtue, and delight at the harmonious, well-
rounded artefact was recognized as a profound (but not solemn)
response. For readers of the 1630s and 1640s, Herrick's lyrics would
have had a special poignancy as microcosmic echoes of a larger, ideal
harmony that was more and more obviously lost to them. His
virtues, however, are not just those of the neatness and gracefulness
of the goldsmith's apprentice he once was: if so, he would merely
have been an earlier Waller. Herrick imbues his one collection,
Hesperides (1648), with a unity that is largely based on our strong
sense of the poet as a clear if paradoxical character in his poems, self-
mocking yet dedicated to his poetry, a pastoral poet who hates the
countryside, but who takes an anthropologist's delight in its
customs, a sensualist keenly aware of the transience of sensual
pleasure. It is this sense of transience and flux in all human ex-
perience that is Herrick's chief preoccupation: *Hesperides* is a rich and
various exploration of ways of coming to terms with what he calls
'times trans-shifting'. Always, however, he is aware that these
strategies can lead to only partial defeats of time and death, and his
finest poetry grows out of those moments – the last stanzas of
'Corinna's going a-Maying' or 'To Blossoms' – where he confronts
that fact most squarely.

Herrick published virtually nothing after *Hesperides*; his revival
began in the late eighteenth century, and he went through many
Victorian editions and selections. He has been well edited recently
by both L. C. Martin, *Poetical Works* (Oxford, 1956) and J. Max
Patrick, *Complete Poetry* (New York, 1963); but criticism has lagged
behind: there is an introductory study, *Robert Herrick*, by R. B.
Rollin (New York, 1966), and a collection of essays, *Trust to Good*

Verses: Herrick Tercentenary Essays, edited by Rollin and Patrick (Pittsburgh, 1978). The scant biography has been best covered by Marchette Chute in *Two Gentle Men* (New York, 1959).

HESPERIDES

The Argument of His Book

I sing of brooks, of blossoms, birds, and bowers,
Of April, May, of June, and July flowers;
I sing of Maypoles, hock-carts, wassails, wakes,
Of bridegrooms, brides, and of their bridal cakes.
I write of Youth, of Love, and have access   5
By these, to sing of cleanly wantonness;
I sing of dews, of rains, and, piece by piece,
Of balm, of oil, of spice, and ambergris;
I sing of times trans-shifting; and I write
How roses first came red, and lilies white;   10
I write of groves, of twilights, and I sing
The court of Mab, and of the Fairy King.
I write of Hell; I sing and ever shall,
Of Heaven, and hope to have it after all.

To His Book

Who with thy leaves shall wipe at need
The place where swelling piles do breed,
May every ill that bites or smarts
Perplex him in his hinder parts.

Upon Julia's Voice

So smooth, so sweet, so silv'ry is thy voice,
As, could they hear, the damned would make no noise,
But listen to thee, walking in thy chamber,
Melting melodious words to lutes of amber.

To the Reverend Shade of His Religious Father

That for seven lustres I did never come
To do the rites to thy religious tomb,
That neither hair was cut, or true tears shed
By me o'er thee (as justments to the dead),
Forgive, forgive me, since I did not know   5
Whether thy bones had here their rest or no.
But now 'tis known, behold, behold, I bring
Unto thy ghost the effused offering;
And look, what smallage, nightshade, cypress, yew,
Unto the shades have been, or now are due,   10
Here I devote; and something more than so:
I come to pay a debt of birth I owe.
Thou gav'st me life, but mortal; for that one
Favour I'll make full satisfaction:
For my life mortal, rise from out thy hearse,   15
And take a life immortal from my verse.

Delight in Disorder

A sweet disorder in the dress
Kindles in clothes a wantonness:
A lawn about the shoulders thrown
Into a fine distraction;
An erring lace, which here and there   5
Enthrals the crimson stomacher;
A cuff neglectful, and thereby
Ribbons to flow confusedly;
A winning wave, deserving note,
In the tempestuous petticoat;   10
A careless shoe-string, in whose tie
I see a wild civility;
Do more bewitch me, than when art
Is too precise in every part.

The Vision

Sitting alone, as one forsook,
Close by a silver-shedding brook,
With hands held up to love, I wept;
And after sorrows spent I slept:
Then in a vision I did see   5
A glorious form appear to me:
A virgin's face she had; her dress
Was like a sprightly Spartaness.
A silver bow, with green silk strung,
Down from her comely shoulders hung: 10
And as she stood, the wanton air
Dandled the ringlets of her hair.
Her legs were such Diana shows
When, tucked up, she a-hunting goes;
With buskins shortened to descry   15
The happy dawning of her thigh:
Which when I saw, I made access
To kiss that tempting nakedness:
But she forbade me with a wand
Of myrtle she had in her hand: 20
And, chiding me, said: Hence, remove,
Herrick, thou art too coarse to love.

To Dianeme

Sweet, be not proud of those two eyes,
Which, starlike, sparkle in their skies;
Nor be you proud that you can see
All hearts your captives, yours yet free;
Be you not proud of that rich hair,   5
Which wantons with the lovesick air:
Whenas that ruby which you wear,
Sunk from the tip of your soft ear,
Will last to be a precious stone,
When all your world of beauty's gone.   10

To a Gentlewoman,
Objecting to Him His Grey Hairs

Am I despised, because you say,
And I dare swear, that I am grey?
Know, lady, you have but your day:
And time will come when you shall wear
Such frost and snow upon your hair;   5
And when, though long it comes to pass,
You question with your looking-glass,
And in that sincere crystal seek
But find no rosebud in your cheek,
Nor any bed to give the show   10
Where such a rare carnation grew.
Ah! then too late, close in your chamber keeping,
      It will be told
      That you are old,
By those true tears y'are weeping.   15

Corinna's Going a-Maying

Get up, get up for shame, the blooming morn
Upon her wings presents the god unshorn.
    See how Aurora throws her fair
    Fresh-quilted colours through the air:
    Get up, sweet slug-a-bed, and see   5
    The dew bespangling herb and tree.
Each flower has wept, and bowed toward the east,
Above an hour since, yet you not dressed,
    Nay! not so much as out of bed;
    When all the birds have matins said,   10
    And sung their thankful hymns: 'tis sin,
    Nay, profanation to keep in,
Whenas a thousand virgins on this day
Spring, sooner than the lark, to fetch in May.

Rise, and put on your foliage, and be seen   15
To come forth, like the springtime, fresh and green,
    And sweet as Flora. Take no care
    For jewels for your gown or hair:
    Fear not, the leaves will strew
    Gems in abundance upon you: 20

Besides, the childhood of the day has kept
Against you come, some orient pearls unwept.
    Come, and receive them while the light
    Hangs on the dew-locks of the night,
    And Titan on the eastern hill   25
    Retires himself, or else stands still
Till you come forth. Wash, dress, be brief in praying:
Few beads are best, when once we go a-Maying.

Come, my Corinna, come; and coming, mark
How each field turns a street, each street a park   30
    Made green, and trimmed with trees: see how
    Devotion gives each house a bough
    Or branch; each porch, each door, ere this,
    An ark, a tabernacle is,
Made up of whitethorn neatly interwove,   35
As if here were those cooler shades of love.
    Can such delights be in the street
    And open fields, and we not see't?
    Come, we'll abroad, and let's obey
    The proclamation made for May: 40
And sin no more, as we have done, by staying;
But, my Corinna, come, let's go a-Maying.

There's not a budding boy or girl, this day,
But is got up and gone to bring in May.
    A deal of youth, ere this, is come   45
    Back, and with whitethorn laden home.
    Some have dispatched their cakes and cream
    Before that we have left to dream:
And some have wept, and wooed and plighted troth.
And chose their priest, ere we can cast off sloth: 50
    Many a green gown has been given;
    Many a kiss, both odd and even:
    Many a glance, too, has been sent
    From out the eye, love's firmament:
Many a jest told of the key's betraying   55
This night, and locks picked, yet we're not a-Maying.

Come, let us go, while we are in our prime,
And take the harmless folly of the time.
    We shall grow old apace and die
    Before we know our liberty.   60

Our life is short, and our days run
  As fast away as does the sun:
And as a vapour, or a drop of rain
Once lost, can ne'er be found again:
    So when or you or I are made   65
    A fable, song, or fleeting shade,
    All love, all liking, all delight,
    Lies drowned with us in endless night.
Then while time serves, and we are but decaying,
Come, my Corinna, come, let's go a-Maying.   70

To Violets

    Welcome, maids of honour,
        You do bring
        In the spring,
    And wait upon her.

    She has virgins many,   5
        Fresh and fair;
        Yet you are
    More sweet than any.

    Y'are the maiden posies,
        And so graced   10
        To be placed
    'Fore damask roses.

    Yet though thus respected,
        By-and-by
        Ye do lie,   15
    Poor girls, neglected.

To the Virgins, to Make Much of Time

Gather ye rosebuds while ye may,
  Old Time is still a-flying;
And this same flower that smiles today,
  Tomorrow will be dying.

The glorious lamp of heaven, the sun,   5
  The higher he's a-getting,
The sooner will his race be run,
  And nearer he's to setting.

That age is best which is the first,
  When youth and blood are warmer;   10
But being spent the worse and worst
  Times still succeed the former.

Then be not coy, but use your time,
  And while ye may, go marry;
For having lost but once your prime,   15
  You may for ever tarry.

His Poetry His Pillar

Only a little more
  I have to write,
    Then I'll give o'er,
And bid the world goodnight.

'Tis but a flying minute   5
  That I must stay,
    Or linger in it,
And then I must away.

O Time that cut'st down all!
  And scarce leav'st here   10
    Memorial
Of any men that were.

How many lie forgot
  In vaults beneath?
    And piecemeal rot   15
Without a fame in death?

Behold this living stone
  I rear for me,
    Ne'er to be thrown
Down, envious Time, by thee.   20

Pillars let some set up
    (If so they please);
Here is my hope
And my pyramides.

A Meditation for His Mistress

You are a Tulip seen today,
But, dearest, of so short a stay,
That where you grew, scarce man can say.

You are a lovely July-flower,
Yet one rude wind, or ruffling shower,   5
Will force you hence, and in an hour.

You are a sparkling Rose i' th' bud,
Yet lost, ere that chaste flesh and blood
Can show where you or grew, or stood.

You are a full-spread, fair-set Vine,   10
And can with tendrils love entwine,
Yet dried, ere you distil your wine.

You are like Balm, inclosed well
In amber, or some crystal shell,
Yet lost ere you transfuse your smell.   15

You are a dainty Violet
Yet withered, ere you can be set
Within the virgin's coronet.

You are the queen all flowers among,
But die you must, fair maid, ere long,   20
As he, the maker of this song.

Lyric for Legacies

Gold I've none, for use or show,
Neither silver to bestow
At my death; but thus much know,

That each lyric here shall be
Of my love a legacy,
Left to all posterity.   5
Gentle friends, then, do but please
To accept such coins as these
As my last remembrances.

The Changes to Corinna

Be not proud, but now incline
Your soft ear to discipline.
You have changes in your life,
Sometimes peace and sometimes strife;
You have ebbs of face and flows,   5
As your health or comes or goes;
You have hopes, and doubts, and fears
Numberless, as are your hairs.
You have pulses that do beat
High, and passions less of heat.   10
You are young, but must be old,
And, to these, ye must be told
Time ere long will come and plough
Loathed furrows in your brow:
And the dimness of your eye   15
Will no other thing imply
    But you must die
    As well as I.

The Coming of Good Luck

So good luck came, and on my roof did light,
Like noiseless snow, or as the dew of night:
Not all at once, but gently, as the trees
Are, by the sunbeams, tickled by degrees.

The Hock-Cart, or Harvest Home: to the
Right Honourable Mildmay, Earl of Westmorland

Come, sons of summer, by whose toil
We are the lords of wine and oil,
By whose tough labours and rough hands
We rip up first, then reap our lands;
Crowned with the ears of corn, now come,   5
And, to the pipe, sing harvest home.
Come, forth, my Lord, and see the cart
Dressed up with all the country art.
See here a maukin, there a sheet,
As spotless pure as it is sweet;   10
The horses, mares, and frisking fillies
Clad, all, in linen white as lilies.
The harvest swains and wenches bound
For joy to see the hock-cart crowned.
About the cart, hear how the rout   15
Of rural younglings raise the shout;
Pressing before, some coming after,
Those with a shout, and these with laughter.
Some bless the cart; some kiss the sheaves;
Some prank them up with oaken leaves;   20
Some cross the fill-horse; some, with great
Devotion, stroke the home-borne wheat;
While other rustics, less attent
To prayers than to merriment,
Run after with their breeches rent.   25
Well, on, brave boys, to your Lord's hearth,
Glitt'ring with fire, where, for your mirth,
Ye shall see first the large and chief
Foundation of your feast, fat beef,
With upper stories, mutton, veal,   30
And bacon, which makes full the meal,
With sev'ral dishes standing by,
As here a custard, there a pie,
And here all-tempting frumenty,
And for to make the merry cheer,   35
If smirking wine be wanting here,
There's that which drowns all care, stout beer;
Which freely drink to your Lord's health,
Then to the plough (the commonwealth),

Next to your flails, your fanes, your fats;   40
Then to the maids with wheaten hats;
To the rough sickle and crook'd scythe,
Drink, frolic boys, till all be blithe.
Feed, and grow fat; and as ye eat,
Be mindful that the lab'ring neat,   45
As you, may have their fill of meat.
And know, besides, ye must revoke
The patient ox unto the yoke,
And all go back unto the plough
And harrow (though they're hanged up now).   50
And, you must know, your Lord's word's true,
Feed him ye must, whose food fills you;
And that this pleasure is like rain,
Not sent ye for to drown your pain,
But for to make it spring again.   55

To Anthea,
Who May Command Him Anything

Bid me to live, and I will live
    Thy protestant to be,
Or bid me love, and I will give
    A loving heart to thee.

A heart as soft, a heart as kind,   5
    A heart as sound and free
As in the whole world thou canst find,
    That heart I'll give to thee.

Bid that heart stay, and it will stay
    To honour thy decree,   10
Or bid it languish quite away,
    And't shall do so for thee.

Bid me to weep, and I will weep
    While I have eyes to see,
And having none, yet I will keep   15
    A heart to weep for thee.

Bid me despair, and I'll despair
    Under that cypress tree,
Or bid me die, and I will dare
    E'en Death, to die for thee. 20

Thou art my life, my love, my heart,
    The very eyes of me,
And hast command of every part,
    To live and die for thee.

To Meadows

Ye have been fresh and green,
    Ye have been filled with flowers,
And ye the walks have been
    Where maids have spent their hours.

You have beheld how they 5
    With wicker arks did come
To kiss and bear away
    The richer cowslips home.

Y'ave heard them sweetly sing,
    And seen them in a round: 10
Each virgin, like a spring,
    With honeysuckles crowned.

But now we see none here
    Whose silv'ry feet did tread,
And with dishevelled hair 15
    Adorned this smoother mead.

Like unthrifts, having spent
    Your stock, and needy grown,
Y' are left here to lament
    Your poor estates, alone. 20

A Nuptial Song; or, Epithalamie on
Sir Clipseby Crew and His Lady

What's that we see from far? The spring of day
Bloomed from the east, or fair injewelled May
    Blown out of April; or some new
    Star filled with glory to our view,
        Reaching at heaven,   5
To add a nobler planet to the seven?
    Say, or do we not descry
Some goddess in a cloud of tiffany
      To move, or rather the
    Emergent Venus from the sea?   10

'Tis she! 'tis she! or else some more divine
Enlightened substance; mark how from the shrine
    Of holy saints she paces on,
    Treading upon vermilion
        And amber; spice-   15
ing the chafed air with fumes of Paradise.
    Then come on, come on, and yield
A savour like unto a blessed field,
      When the bedabbled morn
    Washes the golden ears of corn.   20

See where she comes, and smell how all the street
Breathes vineyards and pomegranates: O how sweet
    As a fired altar, is each stone,
    Perspiring pounded cinnamon.
        The phoenix nest,   25
Built up of odours, burneth in her breast.
    Who therein would not consume
His soul to ash-heaps in that rich perfume?
      Bestroking fate the while
    He burns to embers on the pile.   30

Hymen, O Hymen! tread the sacred ground;
Show thy white feet, and head with marjoram crowned:
    Mount up thy flames, and let thy torch
    Display the bridegroom in the porch,
        In his desires   35
More tow'ring, more disparkling than thy fires:

Show her how his eyes do turn
And roll about, and in their motions burn
    Their balls to cinders: haste,
    Or else to ashes he will waste. 40

Glide by the banks of virgins then, and pass
The showers of roses, lucky four-leaved grass:
    The while the cloud of younglings sing,
    And drown ye with a flowery spring:
        While some repeat 45
Your praise, and bless you, sprinkling you with wheat:
    While that others do divine,
'Blest is the bride, on whom the sun doth shine;'
        And thousands gladly wish
    You multiply, as doth a fish. 50

And beauteous bride, we do confess you're wise,
In dealing forth these bashful jealousies;
    In Love's name do so, and a price
    Set on yourself, by being nice:
        But yet take heed; 55
What now you seem, be not the same indeed,
    And turn apostate; Love will
Part of the way be met, or sit stone-still.
        On then, and though you slow-
    ly go; yet, howsoever, go. 60

And now you're entered; see the coddled cook,
Runs from his torrid zone, to pry and look,
    And bless his dainty mistress: see,
    The aged point out, 'This is she
        Who now must sway 65
The house (love shield her) with her Yea and Nay:'
    And the smirk butler thinks it
Sin, in's nap'ry, not to express his wit;
        Each striving to devise
    Some gin, wherewith to catch your eyes. 70

To bed, to bed, kind Turtles, now, and write
This the short'st day, and this the longest night;
    But yet too short for you: 'tis we
    Who count this night as long as three,

Lying alone,   75
Telling the clock strike ten, eleven, twelve, one.
    Quickly, quickly, then prepare;
And let the young men and the bridesmaids share
        Your garters; and their joints
        Encircle with the bridegroom's points.   80

By the bride's eyes, and by the teeming life
Of her green hopes, we charge ye, that no strife,
    Farther than gentleness tends, gets place
    Among ye, striving for her lace:
            Oh, do not fall   85
Foul in these noble pastimes, lest ye call
    Discord in, and so divide
The youthful bridegroom and the fragrant bride;
        Which love forefend; but spoken
        Be't to your praise, no peace was broken.   90

Strip her of springtime, tender-whimpering maids,
Now autumn's come when all those flow'ry aids
    Of her delays must end; dispose
    That lady-smock, that pansy, and that rose
            Neatly apart;   95
But for prick-madam, and for gentle-heart,
    And soft maiden's-blush, the bride
Makes holy these, all others lay aside:
        Then strip her, or unto her
        Let him come who dares undo her.   100

And to enchant ye more, see everywhere
About the roof a siren in a sphere,
    As we think, singing to the din
    Of many a warbling cherubin:
            O mark ye how   105
The soul of Nature melts in numbers; now
    See, a thousand Cupids fly,
To light their tapers at the bride's bright eye.
        To bed, or her they'll tire,
        Were she an element of fire.   110

And to your more bewitching, see, the proud
Plump bed bear up, and swelling like a cloud,

Tempting the two too modest; can
Ye see it brusle like a swan,
      And you be cold   115
To meet it, when it woos and seems to fold
The arms to hug you? Throw, throw
Yourselves into the mighty overflow
      Of that white pride, and drown
The night, with you, in floods of down.   120

The bed is ready, and the maze of love
Looks for the treaders; everywhere is wove
      Wit and new mystery; read, and
      Put in practice, to understand
          And know each wile,   125
Each hieroglyphic of a kiss or smile;
      And do it to the full; reach
High in your own conceit, and some way teach
      Nature and Art one more
Play than they ever knew before.   130

If needs we must for ceremony's sake
Bless a sack-posset; luck go with it; take
      The night-charm quickly; you have spells
      And magics for to end, and hells
          To pass, but such,   135
And of such torture, as no one would grutch
      To live therein for ever. Fry
And consume, and grow again to die
      And live, and in that case,
Love the confusion of the place.   140

But since it must be done, dispatch and sew
Up in a sheet your bride, and what if so
      It be with rock, or walls of brass,
      Ye tow'r her up as Danae was;
          Think you that this,   145
Or hell itself a powerful bulwark is?
      I tell ye no; but like a
Bold bolt of thunder he will make his way,
      And rend the cloud and throw
The sheet about, like flakes of snow.   150

All now is hushed in silence; midwife-moon,
With all her owl-eyed issue, begs a boon
   Which you must grant; that's entrance; with
   Which extract all we can call pith
      And quintessence   155
Of planetary bodies; so commence
   All fair constellations
Looking upon ye, that two nations
      Springing from two such fires,
May blaze the virtue of their sires.   160

Upon Prudence Baldwin Her Sickness

Prue, my dearest maid, is sick,
Almost to be lunatic;
Æsculapius! come and bring
Means for her recovering,
And a gallant cock shall be   5
Offered up by her to thee.

A Hymn to Bacchus

Bacchus, let me drink no more;
Wild are seas that want a shore.
When our drinking has no stint,
There is no one pleasure in't.
I have drank up, for to please   5
Thee, that great cup Hercules:
Urge no more, and there shall be
Daffodils given up to thee.

To Daffodils

Fair daffodils, we weep to see
   You haste away so soon;
As yet the early-rising sun
   Has not attained his noon.
     Stay, stay,   5
    Until the hasting day
     Has run

But to the evensong;
And, having prayed together, we
    Will go with you along.   10

We have short time to stay, as you;
    We have as short a spring;
As quick a growth to meet decay,
    As you, or any thing.
        We die,   15
    As your hours do, and dry
        Away
    Like to the summer's rain;
Or as the pearls of morning's dew,
    Ne'er to be found again.   20

Upon Glass: Epigram

Glass, out of deep and out of desperate want,
Turned from a papist here a predicant.
A vicarage at last Tom Glass got here,
Just upon five and thirty pounds a year.
Add to that thirty-five but five pounds more,   5
He'll turn a papist, ranker than before.

To Blossoms

Fair pledges of a fruitful tree,
    Why do ye fall so fast?
    Your date is not so past
But you may stay yet here a while,
    To blush and gently smile,   5
        And go at last.

What, were ye born to be
    An hour or half's delight,
    And so to bid good night?
'Twas pity nature brought ye forth   10
    Merely to show your worth,
        And lose you quite.

But you are lovely leaves, where we
May read how soon things have
Their end, though ne'er so brave;   15
And after they have shown their pride,
Like you a while, they glide
Into the grave.

His Prayer to Ben Jonson

When I a verse shall make,
Know I have prayed thee,
For old religion's sake,
Saint Ben, to aid me.

Make the way smooth for me,   5
When I, thy Herrick,
Honouring thee, on my knee
Offer my lyric.

Candles I'll give to thee,
And a new altar;   10
And thou, Saint Ben, shalt be
Writ in my psalter.

The Night-Piece, to Julia

Her eyes the glow-worm lend thee,
The shooting stars attend thee;
And the elves also
Whose little eyes glow
Like the sparks of fire, befriend thee.   5

No will-o'-the-wisp mislight thee,
Nor snake or slow-worm bite thee:
But on, on thy way,
Not making a stay,
Since ghost there's none to affright thee.   10

Let not the dark thee cumber;
What though the moon does slumber?
    The stars of the night
    Will lend thee their light,
Like tapers clear without number.   15

Then, Julia, let me woo thee,
Thus, thus to come unto me:
    And when I shall meet
    Thy silv'ry feet,
My soul I'll pour into thee.   20

Upon Julia's Clothes

Whenas in silks my Julia goes,
Then, then, methinks, how sweetly flows
That liquefaction of her clothes.

Next, when I cast mine eyes and see
That brave vibration each way free,   5
O how that glittering taketh me!

Upon Prue His Maid

In this little urn is laid
Prudence Baldwin (once my maid)
From whose happy spark here let
Spring the purple violet.

Ceremonies for Candlemas Eve

Down with the rosemary and bays,
    Down with the mistletoe;
Instead of holly, now upraise
    The greener box, for show.

The holly hitherto did sway;   5
    Let box now domineer
Until the dancing Easter Day
    Or Easter's eve appear.

Then youthful box, which now hath grace
   Your houses to renew,   10
Grown old, surrender must his place
   Unto the crisped yew.

When yew is out, then birch comes in,
   And many flowers beside,
Both of a fresh and fragrant kin,   15
   To honour Whitsuntide.

Green rushes then, and sweetest bents,
   With cooler oaken boughs,
Come in for comely ornaments,
   To readorn the house.   20
Thus times do shift, each thing his turn does hold;
New things succeed, as former things grow old.

The Pillar of Fame

Fame's pillar here at last we set,
Out-during marble, brass or jet;
   Charmed and enchanted so
   As to withstand the blow
      Of overthrow;   5
     Nor shall the seas,
     Or   outrages
     Of storms, o'erbear
     What we uprear;
     Tho' kingdoms fall,   10
   This pillar never shall
   Decline or waste at all;
But stand for ever by his own
Firm and well-fixed foundation.

To his book's end this last line he'd have placed:
Jocund his Muse was, but his life was chaste.

HIS NOBLE NUMBERS

His Litany to the Holy Spirit

In the hour of my distress,
When temptations me oppress,
And when I my sins confess,
  Sweet Spirit, comfort me!

When I lie within my bed, 5
Sick in heart and sick in head,
And with doubts discomforted,
  Sweet Spirit, comfort me!

When the house doth sigh and weep,
And the world is drowned in sleep, 10
Yet mine eyes the watch do keep,
  Sweet Spirit, comfort me!

When the artless doctor sees
No one hope, but of his fees,
And his skill runs on the lees, 15
  Sweet Spirit, comfort me!

When his potion and his pill
Has or none or little skill,
Meet for nothing but to kill,
  Sweet Spirit, comfort me! 20

When the passing bell doth toll,
And the furies in a shoal
Come to fright, a parting soul,
  Sweet Spirit, comfort me!

When the tapers now burn blue, 25
And the comforters are few,
And that number more than true,
  Sweet Spirit, comfort me!

When the priest his last hath prayed,
And I nod to what is said, 30
'Cause my speech is now decayed,
  Sweet Spirit, comfort me!

When, God knows, I'm tossed about,
Either with despair or doubt,
Yet, before the glass be out,   35
    Sweet Spirit, comfort me!

When the Tempter me pursu'th
With the sins of all my youth,
And half damns me with untruth,
    Sweet Spirit, comfort me!   40

When the flames and hellish cries
Fright mine ears and fright mine eyes,
And all terrors me surprise,
    Sweet Spirit, comfort me!

When the Judgement is revealed,   45
And that opened which was sealed,
When to Thee I have appealed,
    Sweet Spirit, comfort me!

The White Island, or Place of the Blest

In this world, the isle of dreams,
While we sit by sorrow's streams,
Tears and terrors are our themes
            Reciting:

But when once from hence we fly,   5
More and more approaching nigh
Unto young Eternity
                Uniting:

In that whiter island, where
Things are evermore sincere;   10
Candour here, and lustre there
                Delighting:

There no monstrous fancies shall
Out of hell an horror call,
To create, or cause at all,   15
                Affrighting.

There in calm and cooling sleep
We our eyes shall never steep;
But eternal watch shall keep,
          Attending   20

Pleasures, such as shall pursue
Me immortalized, and you;
And fresh joys, as never to
          Have ending.
(*Hesperides, or the Works both Human and Divine,* 1648)

GEORGE HERBERT
(1593–1633)

At the outset of his career, with his powerful family connections and
great abilities, Herbert does not seem to have intended to serve God
by turning his back on the world of court and politics in the same
way as he had, at the age of 17, promised his mother he would turn
his back on its poetry. He appeared set on a successful worldly career
when he became University Orator at Cambridge in 1620, but the
normal subsequent steps to power did not follow, and Herbert only
seems to have ended a period of great indecision with his firm
commitment to the life of a parish priest at the late age of 37. His
brother Edward Lord Herbert of Cherbury writes of him being 'litle
less than sainted' amongst the parishioners of Bemerton, but as
being subject also to 'passion and choler'. This suggestive juxta-
position may be usefully set against the more straightforwardly
saintly picture given in Walton's *Life* (1670). The tensions hinted at
by Edward Herbert are evident in many of George's poems of
spiritual struggle, poems which underline the accuracy of Herbert's
reported description of *The Temple* as 'a picture of the many
spiritual conflicts that have past betwixt God and my soul before I
could subject mine to the Will of Jesus my Master' (Walton). The
simplicity of statement found in his poetry can obscure these con-
flicts if it is confused with a spiritual simplicity, a quality Herbert
sought but which his complex character can never have fully
achieved. Herbert's simplicity, as seen in a poem like 'Redemption',
is the weapon of the sophisticated rhetorician: largely based on the
Bible, whose influence is everywhere, it is related to other rhetorical
devices such as the interweaving of 'A Wreath', or the similar inter-
weaving of one poem with another found in the opening pages of
'The Church'. 'The Church' itself, from which all the poems here
are taken, is the central and longest section of *The Temple*; it is
preceded there by a long homiletic poem, 'The Church Porch', and
followed by another long poem, of less obvious architectural
relevance, 'The Church Militant'.

The Temple appeared in 1633 and became extremely popular. The standard edition of Herbert's *Works* was edited by F. E. Hutchinson (2nd edn, Oxford, 1945), while there is a good edition of the *English Poems* by C. A. Patrides (London, 1974). The fullest biography is Amy Charles's *Life of George Herbert* (Ithaca and London, 1977), while amongst several critical studies Rosamond Tuve's *A Reading of George Herbert* (Chicago, 1952), Joseph H. Summers's *George Herbert: His Religion and Art* (London, 1954) and Helen Vendler's *The Poetry of George Herbert* (Cambridge, Mass. and London, 1975) stand out.

THE CHURCH

The Altar

A broken altar, Lord, Thy servant rears,
Made of a heart and cemented with tears;
   Whose parts are as Thy hand did frame;
   No workman's tool hath touched the same.
       A   h e a r t   a l o n e   5
       Is   such   a   stone
       As   nothing   but
       Thy power doth cut.
       Wherefore each part
       Of my hard heart
       Meets in this frame   10
       To praise Thy name;
That if I chance to hold my peace,
These stones to praise Thee may not cease.
Oh, let Thy blessed sacrifice be mine,
And sanctify this altar to be Thine.

The Agony

Philosophers have measured mountains,
Fathomed the depths of seas, of states, and kings,
Walked with a staff to heaven, and traced fountains;
   But there are two vast, spacious things,
The which to measure it doth more behove,   5
Yet few there are that sound them: Sin and Love.

Who would know Sin, let him repair
Unto Mount Olivet; there shall he see
A man so wrung with pains that all his hair,
    His skin, his garments bloody be.   10
Sin is that press and vice which forceth pain
To hunt his cruel food through every vein.

Who knows not love, let him assay
And taste that juice which on the cross a pike
Did set again abroach; then let him say   15
    If ever he did taste the like.
Love is that liquor sweet and most divine,
Which my God feels as blood, but I as wine.

Redemption

Having been tenant long to a rich lord,
    Not thriving, I resolved to' be bold,
    And make a suit unto him, to afford
A new small-rented lease and cancel th'old.
In heaven at his manor I him sought: 5
    They told·me there that he was lately gone
    About some land which he had dearly bought
Long since on earth, to take possession.
I straight returned, and knowing his great birth,
    Sought him accordingly in great resorts;   10
    In cities, theatres, gardens, parks, and courts:
At length I heard a ragged noise and mirth
    Of thieves and murderers; there I him espied,
    Who straight, 'Your suit is granted' said, and died.

Affliction [1]

When first Thou didst entice to Thee my heart,
    I thought the service brave;
So many joys I writ down for my part,
    Besides what I might have
Out of my stock of natural delights,   5
Augmented with Thy gracious benefits.

I looked on Thy furniture so fine,
   And made it fine to me;
Thy glorious household-stuff did me entwine,
   And 'tice me unto Thee.   10
Such stars I counted mine: both heav'n and earth
Paid me my wages in a world of mirth.

What pleasures could I want, whose King I served,
   Where joys my fellows were?
Thus argued into hopes, my thoughts reserved   15
   No place for grief or fear.
Therefore my sudden soul caught at the place,
And made her youth and fierceness seek Thy face.

At first Thou gav'st me milk and sweetnesses;
   I had my wish and way;   20
My days were strawed with flowers and happiness,
   There was no month but May.
But with my years, sorrows did twist and grow,
And made a party unawares for woe.

My flesh began unto my soul in pain: 25
   'Sicknesses cleave my bones;
Consuming agues dwell in ev'ry vein,
   And tune my breath to groans.'
Sorrow was all my soul; I scarce believed,
Till grief did tell me roundly, that I lived.   30

When I got health, Thou took'st away my life,
   And more, for my friends die.
My mirth and edge was lost; a blunted knife
   Was of more use than I.
Thus thin and lean, without a fence or friend,   35
I was blown through with ev'ry storm and wind.

Whereas my birth and spirit rather took
   The way that takes the town,
Thou didst betray me to a ling'ring book,
   And wrap me in a gown.   40
I was entangled in the world of strife
Before I had the power to change my life.

Yet, for I threatened oft the siege to raise,
   Not simp'ring all mine age,
Thou often didst with academic praise   45
   Melt and dissolve my rage.
I took the sweetened pill till I came where
I could not go away, nor persevere.

Yet lest perchance I should too happy be
   In my unhappiness,   50
Turning my purge to food, Thou throwest me
   Into more sicknesses.
Thus doth Thy power cross-bias me, not making
Thine own gift good, yet me from my ways taking.

Now I am here, what Thou wilt do with me   55
   None of my books will show.
I read and sigh and wish I were a tree,
   For sure then I should grow
To fruit or shade. At least some bird would trust
Her household to me, and I should be just.   60

Yet, though Thou troublest me, I must be meek;
   In weakness must be stout.
Well, I will change the service and go seek
   Some other master out.
Ah, my dear God! though I am clean forgot,   65
Let me not love Thee if I love Thee not.

Prayer [1]

Prayer, the church's banquet, angels' age,
   God's breath in man returning to his birth,
   The soul in paraphrase, heart in pilgrimage,
The Christian plummet sounding heaven and earth;
Engine against the Almighty, sinner's tower,   5
   Reversed thunder, Christ-side-piercing spear,
   The six days' world transposing in an hour,
A kind of tune, which all things hear and fear;

Softness, and peace, and joy, and love, and bliss,
   Exalted manna, gladness of the best,   10
   Heaven in ordinary, man well-dressed,
The Milky Way, the bird of Paradise,
   Church bells beyond the stars heard, the soul's
      blood,
   The land of spices, something understood.

Jordan [1]

Who says that fictions only and false hair
Become a verse? Is there in truth no beauty?
Is all good structure in a winding stair?
May no lines pass except they do their duty
   Not to a true, but painted chair?   5

Is it no verse except enchanted groves
And sudden arbours shadow coarse-spun lines?
Must purling streams refresh a lover's loves?
Must all be veiled, while he that reads, divines,
   Catching the sense at two removes?   10

Shepherds are honest people; let them sing.
Riddle who list for me, and pull for prime;
I envy no man's nightingale or spring,
Nor let them punish me with loss of rhyme,
   Who plainly say, My God, my King.   15

Grace

My stock lies dead, and no increase
Doth my dull husbandry improve.
O let Thy graces without cease
   Drop from above!

If still the sun should hide his face,   5
Thy house would but a dungeon prove,
Thy works night's captives. O let grace
   Drop from above!

The dew doth every morning fall,
And shall the dew outstrip Thy dove?   10
The dew, for which grass cannot call,
        Drop from above.

Death is still working like a mole,
And digs my grave at each remove.
Let grace work too, and on my soul   15
        Drop from above.

Sin is still hammering my heart
Unto a hardness, void of love.
Let suppling grace, to cross his art,
        Drop from above.   20

O come! for Thou dost know the way;
Or if to me Thou wilt not move,
Remove me where I need not say,
        Drop from above.

Church Monuments

While that my soul repairs to her devotion,
Here I entomb my flesh, that is betimes
May take acquaintance of this heap of dust,
To which the blast of Death's incessant motion,
Fed with the exhalation of our crimes,   5
Drives all at last. Therefore I gladly trust

My body to this school, that it may learn
To spell his elements, and find his birth
Written in dusty heraldry and lines;
Which dissolution sure doth best discern,   10
Comparing dust with dust, and earth with earth.
These laugh at jet and marble, put for signs,

To sever the good fellowship of dust,
And spoil the meeting: what shall point out them,
When they shall bow and kneel and fall down flat   15
To kiss those heaps which now they have in trust?
Dear flesh, while I do pray, learn here thy stem
And true descent, that, when thou shalt grow fat,

And wanton in thy cravings, thou mayst know
That flesh is but the glass which holds the dust   20
That measures all our time; which also shall
Be crumbled into dust. Mark here below
How tame these ashes are, how free from lust,
That thou mayst fit thyself against thy fall.

Employment [2]

He that is weary, let him sit.
    My soul would stir
And trade in courtesies and wit,
    Quitting the fur
To cold complexions needing it.   5

Man is no star, but a quick coal
    Of mortal fire;
Who blows it not, nor doth control
    A faint desire,
Lets his own ashes choke his soul.   10

When the elements did for place contest
    With Him, whose will
Ordained the highest to be best,
    The earth sat still,
And by the others is oppressed.   15

Life is a business, not good cheer;
    Ever in wars.
The sun still shineth there or here,
    Whereas the stars
Watch an advantage to appear.   20

Oh that I were an orange tree,
    That busy plant!
Then should I ever laden be,
    And never want
Some fruit for him that dressed me.   25

But we are still too young or old;
   The man is gone
Before we do our wares unfold:
   So we freeze on,
Until the grave increase our cold.   30

Denial

When my devotions could not pierce
   Thy silent ears,
Then was my heart broken, as was my verse;
   My breast was full of fears
     And disorder.   5

My bent thoughts, like a brittle bow,
   Did fly asunder.
Each took his way; some would to pleasures go,
   Some to the wars and thunder
     Of alarms.   10

As good go anywhere, they say,
   As to benumb
Both knees and heart, in crying night and day,
   'Come, come, my God, O come,'
     But no hearing.   15

Oh that Thou shouldst give dust a tongue
   To cry to Thee,
And then not hear it crying! All day long
   My heart was in my knee,
     But no hearing.   20

Therefore my soul lay out of sight,
   Untuned, unstrung;
My feeble spirit, unable to look right,
   Like a nipped blossom hung
     Discontented.   25

O cheer and tune my heartless breast,
   Defer no time;
That so Thy favours granting my request,
   They and my mind may chime,
     And mend my rhyme.   30

Virtue

Sweet day, so cool, so calm, so bright,
   The bridal of the earth and sky;
The dew shall weep thy fall tonight,
   For thou must die.

Sweet rose, whose hue, angry and brave,   5
   Bids the rash gazer wipe his eye;
Thy root is ever in its grave,
   And thou must die.

Sweet spring, full of sweet days and roses,
   A box where sweets compacted lie;   10
My music shows ye have your closes,
   And all must die.

Only a sweet and virtuous soul,
   Like seasoned timber, never gives;
But though the whole world turn to coal,   15
   Then chiefly lives.

The Pearl. Matthew 13

I know the ways of learning: both the head
And pipes that feed the press, and make it run;
What reason hath from nature borrowed,
Or of itself, like a good housewife, spun
In laws and policy; what the stars conspire;   5
What willing nature speaks, what forced by fire;
Both the old discoveries, and the new-found seas,
The stock and surplus, cause and history;
All these stand open, or I have the keys;
   Yet I love Thee.   10

I know the ways of honour: what maintains
The quick returns of courtesy and wit;
In vies of favours whether party gains,
When glory swells the heart, and mouldeth it
To all expressions both of hand and eye,   15
Which on the world a true-love-knot may tie,

And bear the bundle wheresoe'er it goes;
How many drams of spirit there must be
To sell my life unto my friends or foes;
    Yet I love Thee.   20

I know the ways of pleasure: the sweet strains,
The lullings and the relishes of it;
The propositions of hot blood and brains;
What mirth and music mean; what love and wit
Have done these twenty hundred years and more;   25
I know the projects of unbridled store;
My stuff is flesh, not brass; my senses live,
And grumble oft that they have more in me
Than he that curbs them, being but one to five;
    Yet I love Thee.   30

I know all these, and have them in my hand;
Therefore not seeled, but with open eyes
I fly to Thee, and fully understand
Both the main sale and the commodities;
And at what rate and price I have Thy love,   35
With all the circumstances that may move.
Yet through these labyrinths, not my grovelling wit,
But Thy silk twist let down from heaven to me
Did both conduct and teach me how by it
    To climb to Thee.   40

Affliction [4]

Broken in pieces all asunder,
    Lord, hunt me not,
    A thing forgot,
Once a poor creature, now a wonder,
  A wonder tortured in the space   5
    Betwixt this world and that of grace.

My thoughts are all a case of knives,
    Wounding my heart
    With scattered smart,
As watering pots give flowers their lives.   10
  Nothing their fury can control
    While they do wound and prick my soul.

All my attendants are at strife,
   Quitting their place
    Unto my face: 15
Nothing performs the task of life:
   The elements are let loose to fight,
   And while I live, try out their right.

O help, my God! let not their plot
   Kill them and me,   20
    And also Thee,
Who art my life: dissolve the knot,
   As the sun scatters by his light
   All the rebellions of the night.

Then shall those powers, which work for grief,   25
   Enter Thy pay,
    And day by day
Labour Thy praise and my relief,
   With care and courage building me
   Till I reach heaven and, much more, Thee.   30

Life

I made a posy while the day ran by:
'Here will I smell my remnant out, and tie
    My life within this band.'
But Time did beckon to the flowers, and they
By noon most cunningly did steal away,   5
    And withered in my hand.

My hand was next to them, and then my heart;
I took, without more thinking, in good part
    Time's gentle admonition;
Who did so sweetly death's sad taste convey,   10
Making my mind to smell my fatal day,
    Yet sug'ring the suspicion.

Farewell, dear flowers; sweetly your time ye spent,
Fit, while ye lived, for smell or ornament,
    And after death for cures.   15
I follow straight, without complaints or grief;
Since, if my scent be good, I care not if
    It be as short as yours.

Submission

But that Thou art my wisdom, Lord,
    And both mine eyes are Thine,
My mind would be extremely stirred
    For missing my design.

Were it not better to bestow   5
    Some place and power on me?
Then could Thy praises with me grow,
    And share in my degree.

But when I thus dispute and grieve,
    I do resume my sight,   10
And pilfering what I once did give,
    Disseize thee of Thy right.

How know I, if Thou shouldst me raise,
    That I should then raise Thee?
Perhaps great places and Thy praise   15
    Do not so well agree.

Wherefore unto my gift I stand;
    I will no more advise:
Only do Thou lend me a hand,
    Since thou hast both mine eyes.   20

The Quip

The merry World did on a day
With his trainbands and mates agree
To meet together where I lay,
And all in sport to jeer at me.

First, Beauty crept into a rose,   5
Which when I plucked not, 'Sir,' said she,
'Tell me, I pray, whose hands are those?'
But thou shalt answer, Lord, for me.

Then Money came and, chinking still,
'What tune is this, poor man?' said he;   10
'I heard in music you had skill.'
But thou shalt answer, Lord, for me.

Then came brave Glory puffing by
In silks that whistled, who but he?
He scarce allowed me half an eye.   15
But thou shalt answer, Lord, for me.

Then came quick Wit and Conversation,
And he would needs a comfort be,
And, to be short, make an oration.
But thou shalt answer, Lord, for me.   20

Yet when the hour of Thy design
To answer these fine things shall come,
Speak not at large: say I am thine,
And then they have their answer home.

Confession

Oh what a cunning guest
Is this same grief! Within my heart I made
        Closets; and in them many a chest;
        And like a master in my trade,
In those chests, boxes; in each box, a till: 5
Yet grief knows all, and enters when he will.

No screw, no piercer can
Into a piece of timber work and wind
        As God's afflictions into man,
        When he a torture hath designed.   10
They are too subtle for the subtlest hearts,
And fall, like rheums, upon the tenderest parts.

We are the earth; and they,
Like moles within us, heave and cast about:
        And till they foot and clutch their prey,   15
        They never cool, much less give out.
No smith can make such locks, but they have keys:
Closets are halls to them, and hearts, highways.

        Only an open breast
Doth shut them out, so that they cannot enter,   20
    Or, if they enter, cannot rest,
    But quickly seek some new adventure.
Smooth open hearts no fastening have, but fiction
Doth give a hold and handle to affliction.

      Wherefore my faults and sins,   25
Lord, I acknowledge; take thy plagues away:
    For since confession pardon wins,
     I challenge here the brightest day,
The clearest diamond: let them do their best,
They shall be thick and cloudy to my breast.   30

Love Unknown

Dear friend, sit down: the tale is long and sad,
And in my faintings I presume your love
Will more comply than help. A lord I had,
And have, of whom some grounds which may improve,
I hold for two lives, and both lives in me.   5
To him I brought a dish of fruit one day,
And in the middle placed my heart. But he
        (I sigh to say)
Looked on a servant, who did know his eye
Better than you know me, or (which is one)   10
Than I my self. The servant instantly
Quitting the fruit, seized on my heart alone,
And threw it in a font, wherein did fall
A stream of blood, which issued from the side
Of a great rock. I well remember all,   15
And have a good cause: there it was dipped and dyed,
And washed and wrung: the very wringing yet
Enforceth tears. *Your heart was foul, I fear.*
Indeed, 'tis true. I did and do commit
Many a fault more than my lease will bear,   20
Yet still asked pardon, and was not denied.
But you shall hear. After my heart was well,
And clean and fair, as I one eventide
        (I sigh to tell)

Walked by myself abroad, I saw a large 25
And spacious furnace flaming, and thereon
A boiling cauldron, round about whose verge
Was in great letters set *AFFLICTION*.
The greatness showed the owner. So I went
To fetch a sacrifice out of my fold, 30
Thinking with that, which I did thus present,
To warm his love, which I did fear grew cold.
But as my heart did tender it, the man
Who was to take it from me, slipped his hand,
And threw my heart into the scalding pan; 35
My heart that brought it (do you understand?)
The offerer's heart. *Your heart was hard, I fear.*
Indeed, 'tis true. I found a callous matter
Began to spread and to expatiate there.
But with a richer drug than scalding water 40
I bathed it often, even with holy blood,
Which at a board, while many drunk bare wine,
A friend did steal into my cup for good,
Even taken inwardly, and most divine
To supple hardnesses. But at the length 45
Out of the cauldron getting, soon I fled
Unto my house, where to repair the strength
Which I had lost, I hasted to my bed.
But when I thought to sleep out all these faults
        (I sigh to speak) 50
I found that some had stuffed the bed with thoughts,
I would say *thorns*. Dear, could my heart not break,
When with my pleasures even my rest was gone?
Full well I understood, who had been there:
For I had given the key to none but one: 55
It must be he. *Your heart was dull, I fear.*
Indeed, a slack and sleepy state of mind
Did oft possess me, so that when I prayed,
Though my lips went, my heart did stay behind.
But all my scores were by another paid, 60
Who took the debt upon him. *Truly, friend,*
For ought I hear, your master shows to you
More favour than you wot of. Mark the end:
The Font did only what was old, renew;
The Cauldron suppled what was grown too hard; 65
The Thorns did quicken what was grown too dull;

All did but strive to mend what you had marred.
Wherefore be cheered, and praise him to the full
Each day, each hour, each moment of the week,
Who fain would have to be new, tender, quick.   70

The Jews

Poor nation, whose sweet sap and juice
Our scions have purloined, and left you dry:
Whose streams we got by the Apostles' sluice,
And use in baptism, while ye pine and die:
Who by not keeping once, became a debtor,   5
   And now by keeping lose the letter.

Oh that my prayers! mine, alas!
Oh that some angel might a trumpet sound:
At which the Church falling upon her face
Should cry so loud, until the trump were drowned,   10
And by that cry of her dear Lord obtain
   That your sweet sap might come again.

The Collar

I struck the board, and cried, 'No more!
   I will abroad!
What? Shall I ever sigh and pine?
My lines and life are free, free as the road,
   Loose as the wind, as large as store.   5
      Shall I be still in suit?
Have I no harvest but a thorn
To let me blood, and not restore
What I have lost with cordial fruit?
      Sure there was wine   10
Before my sighs did try it. There was corn
      Before my tears did drown it.
Is the year only lost to me?
      Have I no bays to crown it?
No flowers, no garlands gay? All blasted?   15
      All wasted?

Not so, my heart! But there is fruit,
                And thou hast hands.
        Recover all thy sigh-blown age
On double pleasures. Leave thy cold dispute   20
Of what is fit and not. Forsake thy cage,
                Thy rope of sands,
Which petty thoughts have made, and made to thee
        Good cable, to enforce and draw,
                And be thy law,   25
        While thou didst wink and wouldst not see.
                Away! Take heed!
                I will abroad!
Call in thy death's head there! Tie up thy fears!
                He that forbears   30
            To suit and serve his need
                Deserves his load.'
But as I raved, and grew more fierce and wild
                At every word,
        Methoughts I heard one calling, 'Child!'   35
                And I replied, 'My Lord!'

The Flower

    How fresh, O Lord, how sweet and clean
Are Thy returns! Even as the flowers in spring,
    To which, besides their own demean,
The late-past frosts tributes of pleasure bring.
                Grief melts away   5
                Like snow in May,
        As if there were no such cold thing.

    Who would have thought my shrivelled heart
Could have recovered greenness? It was gone
        Quite underground, as flowers depart   10
To see their mother-root, when they have blown;
                Where they together
                All the hard weather,
        Dead to the world, keep house unknown.

These are Thy wonders, Lord of power,   15
Killing and quickening, bringing down to hell
And up to heaven in an hour;
Making a chiming of a passing bell.
    We say amiss
    This or that is;   20
Thy word is all, if we could spell.

Oh, that I once past changing were,
Fast in Thy paradise, where no flower can wither!
Many a spring I shoot up fair,
Offering at heav'n, growing and groaning thither;   25
    Nor doth my flower
    Want a spring shower,
My sins and I joining together.

But while I grow in a straight line,
Still upwards bent, as if heaven were mine own,   30
Thy anger comes, and I decline.
What frost to that? What pole is not the zone
    Where all things burn,
    When Thou dost turn,
And the least frown of Thine is shown?   35

And now in age I bud again;
After so many deaths I live and write;
I once more smell the dew and rain,
And relish versing. O my only Light,
    It cannot be   40
    That I am he
On whom Thy tempests fell all night.

These are Thy wonders, Lord of love,
To make us see we are but flowers that glide;
Which when we once can find and prove,   45
Thou hast a garden for us where to bide.
    Who would be more,
    Swelling through store,
Forfeit their paradise by their pride.

The Forerunners

The harbingers are come. See, see their mark;
White is their colour, and behold my head.
But must they have my brain? must they dispark
Those sparkling notions which therein were bred?
  Must dullness turn me to a clod?   5
Yet have they left me, 'Thou art still my God.'

Good men ye be to leave me my best room,
Ev'n all my heart, and what is lodged there;
I pass not, I, what of the rest become,
So 'Thou art still my God' be out of fear.   10
  He will be pleased with that ditty;
And if I please Him, I write fine and witty.

Farewell, sweet phrases, lovely metaphors.
But will ye leave me thus? when ye before
Of stews and brothels only knew the doors,   15
Then did I wash you with my tears, and more,
  Brought you to church well-dressed and clad:
My God must have my best, ev'n all I had.

Lovely enchanting language, sugar-cane,
Honey of roses, whither wilt thou fly?   20
Hath some fond lover 'ticed thee to thy bane?
And wilt thou leave the Church, and love a sty?
  Fie! thou wilt soil thy broidered coat,
And hurt thyself and him that sings the note.

Let foolish lovers, if they will love dung,   25
With canvas, not with arras, clothe their shame;
Let Folly speak in her own native tongue.
True Beauty dwells on high; ours is a flame
  But borrowed thence to light us thither.
Beauty and beauteous words should go together. 30

Yet if you go, I pass not; take your way.
For 'Thou art still my God' is all that ye
Perhaps with more embellishment can say.
Go, birds of spring; let winter have his fee;
  Let a bleak paleness chalk the door,   35
So all within be livelier than before.

A Wreath

A wreathed garland of deserved praise,
Of praise deserved, unto Thee I give,
I give to Thee, who knowest all my ways,
My crooked winding ways, wherein I live,
Wherein I die, not live: for life is straight,   5
Straight as a line, and ever tends to Thee,
To Thee, who art more far above deceit
Than deceit seems above simplicity.
Give me simplicity, that I may live,
So live and like, that I may know Thy ways,   10
Know them and practise them: then shall I give
For this poor wreath, give Thee a crown of praise.

Death

Death, thou wast once an uncouth, hideous thing,
                    Nothing but bones,
        The sad effect of sadder groans:
Thy mouth was open, but thou couldst not sing.

For we considered thee as at some six   5
                    Or ten years hence,
        After the loss of life and sense,
Flesh being turned to dust, and bones to sticks.

We looked on this side of thee, shooting short;
                    Where we did find   10
        The shells of fledge souls left behind,
Dry dust, which sheds no tears, but may extort.

But since our Saviour's death did put some blood
                    Into thy face,
        Thou art grown fair and full of grace,   15
Much in request, much sought for as a good.

For we do now behold thee gay and glad,
                    As at doomsday,
        When souls shall wear their new array,
And all thy bones with beauty shall be clad.   20

Therefore we can go die as sleep, and trust
                    Half that we have
           Unto an honest faithful grave,
Making our pillows either down or dust.

Doomsday

              Come away,
           Make no delay.
Summon all the dust to rise,
Till it stir and rub the eyes,
While this member jogs the other,   5
Each one whisp'ring, 'Live you, brother?'

              Come away,
           Make this the day.
Dust, alas, no music feels
But Thy trumpet; then it kneels,   10
As peculiar notes and strains
Cure tarantulae's raging pains.

              Come away,
           O make no stay!
Let the graves make their confession,   15
Lest at length they plead possession:
Flesh's stubbornness may have
Read that lesson to the grave.

              Come away,
           Thy flock doth stray.   20
Some to winds their body lend,
And in them may drown a friend:
Some in noisome vapours grow
To a plague and public woe.

              Come away,   25
           Help our decay.
Man is out of order hurled,
Parcelled out to all the world.
Lord, Thy broken consort raise,
And the music shall be praise.   30

Love [3]

Love bade me welcome; yet my soul drew back,
    Guilty of dust and sin.
But quick-eyed Love, observing me grow slack
    From my first entrance in,
Drew nearer to me, sweetly questioning   5
    If I lacked anything.

'A guest,' I answered, 'worthy to be here.'
    Love said, 'You shall be he.'
'I, the unkind, ungrateful? Ah my dear,
    I cannot look on Thee.'   10
Love took my hand, and smiling, did reply,
    'Who made the eyes but I?'

'Truth, Lord, but I have marred them; let my shame
    Go where it doth deserve.'
'And know you not,' says Love, 'who bore the blame?'   15
    'My dear, then I will serve.'
'You must sit down,' says Love, 'and taste my meat.'
    So I did sit and eat.

Finis

Glory be to God *on high,*
    And on earth peace,
    Good will towards men.
                    (*The Temple*, 1633)

THOMAS CAREW
(1594/5–1640)

Although it is conventional to regard Carew as a gifted minor poet who comes near to greatness in a few poems, to read through the whole corpus of his poetry is to discover a remarkable evenness of high achievement, and to recognize just how disciplined and intelligent an artist he was. His life outside of his art, notable for its lack of discipline, somewhat obscures this view of him: described by his own father as 'vagrant and debauched', an elegant but syphilitic courtier, he is reported to have been refused the sacrament and absolution on his deathbed. In the punning wit of his best poetry, and in the abandoned eroticism of 'A Rapture', one can see the points of creative contact between the witty courtier and the serious artist; but in the great epitaph on Maria Wentworth, the elegy on Donne, or the poem to Sandys, Carew's elegant, ironic urbanity fuses with a profundity of vision and a depth of feeling beyond the resources of a courtly minor poet.

Carew's poems circulated widely in manuscript during his lifetime, and, published within months of his death, went through five editions by 1671. The standard modern edition by R. Dunlap (Oxford, 1949) includes the masque, *Coelum Britannicum*, and a biography. There is critical discussion by F. R. Leavis in *Revaluation* (London, 1936) and E. I. Selig, *The Flourishing Wreath* (New Haven, 1957).

Song: To My Inconstant Mistress

When thou, poor excommunicate
  From all the joys of love, shalt see
The full reward, and glorious fate,
    Which my strong faith shall purchase me,
    Then curse thine own inconstancy.   5

A fairer hand than thine shalt cure
   That heart which thy false oaths did wound;
And to my soul, a soul more pure
   Than thine shall by Love's hand be bound,
   And both with equal glory crowned.   10

Then shalt thou weep, entreat, complain
   To Love, as I did once to thee;
When all thy tears shall be as vain
   As mine were then, for thou shalt be
   Damned for thy false apostasy.   15

To Saxham

Though frost and snow locked from mine eyes
That beauty which without door lies,
Thy gardens, orchards, walks, that so
I might not all thy pleasures know,
Yet, Saxham, thou within thy gate   5
Art of thyself so delicate,
So full of native sweets that bless
Thy roof with inward happiness,
As neither from nor to thy store
Winter takes aught, or spring adds more.   10
The cold and frozen air had starved
Much poor, if not by thee preserved,
Whose prayers have made thy table blest
With plenty, far above the rest.
The season hardly did afford   15
Coarse cates unto thy neighbours' board,
Yet thou hadst dainties as the sky
Had only been thy volary;
Or else the birds, fearing the snow
Might to another Deluge grow,   20
The pheasant, partridge, and the lark
Flew to thy house as to the Ark.
The willing ox of himself came
Home to the slaughter, with the lamb,
And every beast did thither bring   25
Himself to be an offering.

The scaly herd more pleasure took,
Bathed in thy dish, than in the brook.
Water, earth, air, did all conspire
To pay their tributes to thy fire,   30
Whose cherishing flames themselves divide
Through every room, where they deride
The night and cold abroad; whilst they,
Like suns within, keep endless day.
Those cheerful beams send forth their light   35
To all that wander in the night,
And seem to beckon from aloof
The weary pilgrim to thy roof;
Where if, refreshed, he will away,
He's fairly welcome, or if stay   40
Far more, which he shall hearty find,
Both from the master and the hind.
The stranger's welcome each man there
Stamped on his cheerful brow doth wear;
Nor doth this welcome or his cheer   45
Grow less 'cause he stays longer here:
There's none observes (much less repines)
How often this man sups or dines.
Thou hast no porter at the door
T' examine, or keep back the poor;   50
Nor locks nor bolts: thy gates have been
Made only to let strangers in;
Untaught to shut, they do not fear
To stand wide open all the year;
Careless who enters, for they know   55
Thou never didst deserve a foe;
And as for thieves, thy bounty's such,
They cannot steal, thou giv'st so much.

A Rapture

I will enjoy thee now, my Celia, come
And fly with me to Love's Elysium:
The giant, Honour, that keeps cowards out,
Is but a masquer, and the servile rout
Of baser subjects only bend in vain   5
To the vast idol, whilst the nobler train

Of valiant soldiers daily sail between
The huge Colossus' legs, and pass unseen
Unto the blissful shore. Be bold and wise,
And we shall enter: the grim Swiss denies   10
Only tame fools a passage, that not know
He is but form, and only frights in show
The duller eyes that look from far; draw near,
And thou shalt scorn what we were wont to fear.
We shall see how the stalking pageant goes   15
With borrowed legs, a heavy load to those
That made and bear him; not as we once thought
The seed of gods, but a weak model wrought
By greedy men that seek t' enclose the common
And within private arms impale free woman.   20
    Come, then, and mounted on the wings of Love
We'll cut the flitting air, and soar above
The monster's head, and in the noblest seats
Of those blest shades quench and renew our heats.
There shall the Queen of Love, and Innocence,   25
Beauty, and Nature, banish all offence
From our close ivy-twines; there I'll behold
Thy bared snow and thy unbraided gold;
There my enfranchised hand on every side
Shall o'er thy naked polished ivory slide.   30
No curtain there, though of transparent lawn,
Shall be before thy virgin-treasure drawn;
But the rich mine, to the enquiring eye
Exposed, shall ready still for mintage lie,
And we will coin young Cupids. There a bed   35
Of roses and fresh myrtles shall be spread
Under the cooler shade of cypress groves,
Our pillows of the down of Venus' doves,
Whereon our panting limbs we'll gently lay
In the faint respites of our active play,   40
That so our slumbers may in dreams have leisure
To tell the nimble fancy our past pleasure;
And so our souls, that cannot be embraced,
Shall the embraces of our bodies taste.
Meanwhile the bubbling stream shall court the shore;   45
Th' enamoured chirping wood-choir shall adore
In varied tunes the deity of Love;
The gentle blasts of western winds shall move

The trembling leaves, and through their close boughs breathe
Still music, whilst we rest ourselves beneath   50
Their dancing shade; till a soft murmur, sent
From souls entranced in am'rous languishment,
Rouse us, and shoot into our veins fresh fire,
Till we in their sweet ecstasy expire.
   Then, as the empty bee, that lately bore   55
Into the common treasure all her store,
Flies 'bout the painted field with nimble wing,
Deflow'ring the fresh virgins of the spring,
So will I rifle all the sweets that dwell
In my delicious paradise, and swell   60
My bag with honey, drawn forth by the power
Of fervent kisses, from each spicy flower.
I'll seize the rosebuds in their perfumed bed,
The violet knots, like curious mazes spread
O'er all the garden, taste the ripened cherry,   65
The warm firm apple, tipped with coral berry;
Then will I visit, with a wandering kiss,
The vale of lilies and the bower of bliss;
And, where the beauteous region doth divide
Into two milky ways, my lips shall slide   70
Down those smooth alleys, wearing as I go
A tract for lovers on the printed snow;
Thence climbing o'er the swelling Apennine
Retire into thy grove of eglantine,
Where I will all those ravished sweets distil   75
Through love's alembic, and with chemic skill
From the mixed mass one sovereign balm derive,
Then bring that great elixir to thy hive.
   Now in more subtle wreaths I will entwine
My sin'wy thighs, my legs and arms, with thine;   80
Thou like a sea of milk shalt lie displayed,
Whilst I the smooth, calm ocean invade
With such a tempest as when Jove of old
Fell down on Danae in a storm of gold:
Yet my tall pine shall in the Cyprian strait   85
Ride safe at anchor, and unlade her freight;
My rudder with thy bold hand, like a tried
And skilful pilot, thou shalt steer, and guide
My bark into love's channel, where it shall
Dance, as the bounding waves do rise or fall.   90

Then shall thy circling arms embrace and clip
My willing body, and thy balmy lip
Bathe me in juice of kisses, whose perfume
Like a religious incense shall consume,
And send up holy vapours to those powers   95
That bless our loves and crown our sportful hours,
That with such halcyon calmness fix our souls
In steadfast peace as no affright controls.
There no rude sounds shake us with sudden starts;
No jealous ears, when we unrip our hearts,   100
Suck our discourse in; no observing spies
This blush, that glance, traduce; no envious eyes
Watch our close meetings; nor are we betrayed
To rivals by the bribed chambermaid.
No wedlock bonds unwreathe our twisted loves;   105
We seek no midnight arbour, no dark groves,
To hide our kisses; there the hated name
Of husband, wife, lust, modest, chaste, or shame,
Are vain and empty words, whose very sound
Was never heard in the Elysian ground.   110
All things are lawful there that may delight
Nature or unrestrained appetite;
Like and enjoy, to will and act, is one:
We only sin when Love's rites are not done.
    The Roman Lucrece there reads the divine   115
Lectures of love's great master, Aretine,
And knows as well as Lais how to move
Her pliant body in the act of love.
To quench the burning ravisher, she hurls
Her limbs into a thousand winding curls,   120
And studies artful postures, such as be
Carved on the bark of every neighb'ring tree
By learned hands that so adorned the rind
Of those fair plants, which as they lay entwined
Have fanned their glowing fires. The Grecian Dame,   125
That in her endless web toiled for a name
As fruitless as her work, doth there display
Herself before the Youth of Ithaca,
And th' amorous sport of gamesome nights prefer
Before dull dreams of the lost Traveller.   130
Daphne hath broke her bark, and that swift foot
Which th' angry gods had fastened with a root

To the fixed earth doth now unfettered run
To meet th' embraces of the youthful Sun:
She hangs upon him like his Delphic lyre; 135
Her kisses blow the old and breathe new fire;
Full of her god, she sings inspired lays,
Sweet odes of love, such as deserve the bays,
Which she herself was. Next her, Laura lies
In Petrarch's learned arms, drying those eyes 140
That did in such sweet smooth-paced numbers flow
As made the world enamoured of his woe.
These, and ten thousand beauties more, that died
Slave to the tyrant, now enlarged deride
His cancelled laws, and for their time misspent 145
Pay into Love's exchequer double rent.
   Come then, my Celia, we'll no more forbear
To taste our joys, struck with a Panic fear,
But will depose from his imperious sway
This proud usurper and walk free as they, 150
With necks unyoked; nor is it just that he
Should fetter your soft sex with chastity,
Which Nature made unapt for abstinence;
When yet this false impostor can dispense
With human justice, and with sacred right, 155
And maugre both their laws command me fight
With rivals, or with em'lous loves, that dare
Equal with thine their mistress' eyes or hair:
If thou complain of wrong, and call my sword
To carve out thy revenge, upon that word 160
He bids me fight and kill, or else he brands
With marks of infamy my coward hands;
And yet Religion bids from bloodshed fly,
And damns me for that act. Then tell me why
   This goblin Honour, which the world adores, 165
   Should make men atheists, and not women whores.

Maria Wentworth

Thomae Comitis Cleveland Filia Praemortua
Prima Virgineam Animam Exhalavit:
Anno Domini 1632. Aetatis Suae 18

And here the precious dust is laid,
Whose purely tempered clay was made
So fine that it the guest betrayed.

Else the soul grew so fast within
It broke the outward shell of sin,　　　　　5
And so was hatched a cherubin.

In heighth it soared to God above;
In depth it did to knowledge move,
And spread in breadth to general love.

Before a pious duty shined　　　　　　　10
To parents; courtesy behind;
On either side, an equal mind.

Good to the poor, to kindred dear,
To servants kind, to friendship clear,
To nothing but herself severe.　　　　　15

So, though a virgin, yet a bride
To every grace, she justified
A chaste polygamy, and died.

Learn from hence, Reader, what small trust
We owe this world, where virtue must,　　20
Frail as our flesh, crumble to dust.

An Elegy upon the Death of the Dean of Paul's,
Doctor John Donne

Can we not force from widowed poetry,
Now thou art dead, great Donne, one elegy
To crown thy hearse? Why yet dare we not trust,
Though with unkneaded dough-baked prose, thy dust,

Such as th' unscissored churchman, from the flower   5
Of fading rhetoric, short-lived as his hour,
Dry as the sand that measures it, should lay
Upon thy ashes on the funeral day?
Have we no voice, no tune? Didst thou dispense
Through all our language both the words and sense?   10
'Tis a sad truth. The pulpit may her plain
And sober Christian precepts still retain;
Doctrines it may, and wholesome uses, frame,
Grave homilies and lectures; but the flame
Of thy brave soul – that shot such heat and light   15
As burnt our earth, and made our darkness bright,
Committed holy rapes upon our will,
Did through the eye the melting heart distil,
And the deep knowledge of dark truths so teach,
As sense might judge what fancy could not reach –   20
Must be desired for ever. So the fire
That fills with spirit and heat the Delphic choir,
Which, kindled first by thy Promethean breath,
Glowed here awhile, lies quenched now in thy death.
The Muses' garden, with pedantic weeds   25
O'erspread, was purged by thee; the lazy seeds
Of servile imitation thrown away,
And fresh invention planted; thou didst pay
The debts of our penurious bankrupt age;
Licentious thefts, that make poetic rage   30
A mimic fury, when our souls must be
Possessed, or with Anacreon's ecstasy
Or Pindar's, not their own; the subtle cheat
Of sly exchanges, and the juggling feat
Of two-edged words, or whatsoever wrong   35
By ours was done the Greek or Latin tongue,
Thou hast redeemed, and opened us a mine
Of rich and pregnant fancy; drawn a line
Of masculine expression, which had good
Old Orpheus seen, or all the ancient brood   40
Our superstitious fools admire, and hold
Their lead more precious than thy burnished gold,
Thou hadst been their exchequer, and no more
They each in other's dust had raked for ore.
Thou shalt yield no precedence, but of time   45
And the blind fate of language whose tuned chime

More charms the outward sense; yet thou may'st claim
From so great disadvantage greater fame,
Since to the awe of thy imperious wit
Our stubborn language bends, made only fit   50
With her tough thick-ribbed hoops to gird about
Thy giant fancy, which had proved too stout
For their soft melting phrases. As in time
They had the start, so did they cull the prime
Buds of invention many a hundred year,   55
And left the rifled fields, besides the fear
To touch their harvest; yet from those bare lands
Of what is purely thine thy only hands
(And that thy smallest work) have gleaned more
Than all those times and tongues could reap before.   60
    But thou art gone, and thy strict laws will be
Too hard for libertines in poetry.
They will repeal the goodly exiled train
Of gods and goddesses, which in thy just reign
Were banished nobler poems; now with these   65
The silenced tales o' th' *Metamorphoses*
Shall stuff their lines and swell the windy page,
Till verse, refined by thee, in this last age
Turn ballad-rhyme, or those old idols be
Adored again with new apostasy.   70
    O pardon me, that break with untuned verse
The reverend silence that attends thy hearse,
Whose awful solemn murmurs were to thee
More than these faint lines a loud elegy,
That did proclaim in a dumb eloquence   75
The death of all the arts, whose influence,
Grown feeble, in these panting numbers lies
Gasping short-winded accents, and so dies:
So doth the swiftly turning wheel not stand
In th' instant we withdraw the moving hand,   80
But some small time maintain a faint weak course
By virtue of the first impulsive force;
And so, whilst I cast on thy funeral pile
Thy crown of bays, oh, let it crack awhile,
And spit disdain, till the devouring flashes   85
Suck all the moisture up, then turn to ashes.
    I will not draw thee envy to engross
All thy perfections, or weep all our loss:

Those are too num'rous for an elegy,
And this too great to be expressed by me.   90
Though every pen should share a distinct part,
Yet art thou theme enough to tire all art;
Let others carve the rest; it shall suffice
I on thy tomb this epitaph incise:

> *Here lies a king, that ruled as he thought fit*   95
> *The universal monarchy of wit;*
> *Here lie two flamens, and both those the best:*
> *Apollo's first, at last the true God's priest.*

To My Worthy Friend Master George Sandys, On His Translation of the Psalms

I press not to the quire, nor dare I greet
The holy place with my unhallowed feet;
My unwashed Muse pollutes not things divine,
Nor mingles her profaner notes with thine;
Here humbly at the porch she listening stays,   5
And with glad ears sucks in thy sacred lays.
So devout penitents of old were wont,
Some without door and some beneath the font,
To stand and hear the Church's liturgies,
Yet not assist the solemn exercise: 10
Sufficeth her that she a lay-place gain,
To trim thy vestments or but bear thy train;
Though nor in tune nor wing she reach thy lark,
Her lyric feet may dance before the Ark.
Who knows but that her wandering eyes, that run   15
Now hunting glow-worms, may adore the sun?
A pure flame may, shot by Almighty Power
Into her breast, the earthy flame devour.
My eyes in penitential dew may steep
That brine which they for sensual love did weep.   20
So (though 'gainst Nature's course) fire may be quenched
With fire, and water be with water drenched.
Perhaps my restless soul – tired with pursuit
Of mortal beauty, seeking without fruit
Contentment there, which hath not, when enjoyed,   25
Quenched all her thirst, nor satisfied, though cloyed –

Weary of her vain search below, above
In the first Fair may find th' immortal Love.
Prompted by thy example then, no more
In moulds of clay will I my God adore,   30
But tear those idols from my heart, and write
What His blest Sp'rit, not fond love, shall indite;
Then I no more shall court the verdant bay,
But the dry leaveless trunk on Golgotha;   .
And rather strive to gain from thence one thorn,   35
Than all the flour'shing wreaths by laureates worn.

(*Poems*, 1640)

JOHN MILTON
(1608–74)

Milton's poetry came under attack in the 1920s and 1930s by Eliot,
Leavis and others who believed that his undeniable genius was
perversely dissipated through the cultivation of a style that grew
increasingly remote from the idiomatic strengths and energies of the
English language. In the poems included here it can be seen that
Milton's attitude to poetic language is indeed different from his
contemporaries, but that, paradoxically, it anticipates not just the
weak diffusions of eighteenth- and nineteenth-century 'Miltonic'
verse, but the richer symbolist techniques of those modernists who
reacted against him. Like the modern symbolist, Milton exploits to
the full the connotative functions of language, orchestrating
rhythm and imagery in such a way as to convey an emotion through
what Eliot would have called its 'objective correlatives'. No
structure of rational argument will be found in L'Allegro' or 'Il
Penseroso', and the resolution of 'Lycidas' is prepared by image and
rhythm more than by theological justification. If Milton is in this
sense radical, he is also deeply traditional, his allegiances, like those
of Jonson (whose erudition he more than matched and whose view
of the dignity of the poet he shared), being to the classical tradition;
unlike Jonson, he also turns to the more recent European tradition of
Dante, Tasso and Spenser. The poems reprinted here are thus deeply
original and in the best sense conventional. By the date of the two
sonnets Milton has, however, moved beyond the masterly use of a
conventional voice to one which is radically and unmistakably
original. Between 'Lycidas' (1637) and the sonnets of the 1650s lie
his prolific years as a prose pamphleteer in defence of religious
liberty, in favour of divorce and against censorship (the great
Areopagitica), and in defence of the Puritan revolution and the Re-
public itself. After the sonnets, and beyond the limits of this book
(both in length and in date) comes the great epic to which his life and
studies before the Civil Wars had been dedicated. *Paradise Lost*

appeared in 1667, followed in 1671 by the lesser epic *Paradise Regained* and the tragic poem *Samson Agonistes*.

Amongst a huge bibliography, there are recent editions of the poems by J. Carey and A. Fowler (London, 1968) and Douglas Bush (London, 1965); the chief biographies are the massive *Life* by David Masson (6 volumes, Cambridge, 1859–80) and W. R. Parker's *Milton: a Biography* (2 volumes, Oxford, 1968). Samuel Johnson's life of Milton in his *Lives of the Poets* (1779) and F. R. Leavis's essay in *Revaluation* (London, 1936) are important, while J. H. Hanford's *Milton Handbook* (5th edn, New York, 1970) is a very useful compendium. A good short introduction is that given by Bush in his *English Literature in the Earlier 17th Century* (2nd edn, Oxford, 1962), while the earlier poetry is well discussed by Cleanth Brooks and J. E. Hardy in *Poems of Mr. John Milton* (New York, 1951), by F. T. Prince in *The Italian Element in Milton's Verse* (Oxford, 1954) and by Rosamond Tuve in *Images and Themes in Five Poems by Milton* (Cambridge, Mass., 1957).

From *At a Vacation Exercise in the College*

The Latin Speeches ended, the English thus began

Hail native language, that by sinews weak
Didst move my first endeavouring tongue to speak,
And mad'st imperfect words with childish trips,
Half unpronounced, slide through my infant lips,
Driving dumb silence from the portal door,   5
Where he had mutely sat two years before:
Here I salute thee and thy pardon ask,
That now I use thee in my latter task:
Small loss it is that thence can come unto thee,
I know my tongue but little grace can do thee.   10
Thou need'st not be ambitious to be first,
Believe me I have thither packed the worst:
And, if it happen as I did forecast,
The daintiest dishes shall be served up last.
I pray thee then deny me not thy aid   15
For this same small neglect that I have made;
But haste thee straight to do me once a pleasure,
And from thy wardrobe bring thy chiefest treasure;

Not those new-fangled toys, and trimming slight
Which takes our late fantastics with delight,   20
But cull those richest robes, and gayest attire
Which deepest spirits, and choicest wits desire:
I have some naked thoughts that rove about
And loudly knock to have their passage out;
And weary of their place do only stay   25
Till thou hast decked them in thy best array;
That so they may without suspect or fears
Fly swiftly to this fair assembly's ears;
Yet I had rather, if I were to choose,
Thy service in some graver subject use,   30
Such as may make thee search thy coffers round,
Before thou clothe my fancy in fit sound:
Such where the deep transported mind may soar
Above the wheeling poles, and at heaven's door
Look in, and see each blissful deity   35
How he before the thunderous throne doth lie,
Listening to what unshorn Apollo sings
To the touch of golden wires, while Hebe brings
Immortal nectar to her kingly sire:
Then passing through the spheres of watchful fire,   40
And misty regions of wide air next under,
And hills of snow and lofts of piled thunder,
May tell at length how green-eyed Neptune raves,
In heaven's defiance mustering all his waves;
Then sing of secret things that came to pass   45
When beldam Nature in her cradle was;
And last of kings and queens and heroes old,
Such as the wise Demodocus once told
In solemn songs at king Alcinous' feast,
While sad Ulysses' soul and all the rest   50
Are held with his melodious harmony
In willing chains and sweet captivity.
But fie my wandering Muse how thou dost stray!
Expectance calls thee now another way,
Thou knowest it must be now thy only bent   55
To keep in compass of thy predicament:
Then quick about thy purposed business come,
That to the next I may resign my room.

                              (*Poems*, 1673)

L'Allegro

Hence loathed Melancholy
   Of Cerberus, and blackest Midnight born,
In Stygian cave forlorn
   'Mongst horrid shapes, and shrieks, and sights unholy,
Find out some uncouth cell,   5
   Where brooding Darkness spreads his jealous wings,
And the night-raven sings;
   There under ebon shades, and low-browed rocks,
As ragged as thy locks,
   In dark Cimmerian desert ever dwell.   10
But come thou goddess fair and free,
In heaven yclept Euphrosyne,
And by men, heart-easing Mirth,
Whom lovely Venus at a birth
With two sister Graces more   15
To ivy-crowned Bacchus bore;
Or whether (as some sager sing)
The frolic wind that breathes the spring,
Zephyr with Aurora playing,
As he met her once a-Maying,   20
There on beds of violets blue,
And fresh-blown roses washed in dew,
Filled her with thee a daughter fair,
So buxom, blithe, and debonair.
Haste thee nymph, and bring with thee   25
Jest and youthful Jollity,
Quips and cranks, and wanton wiles,
Nods, and becks, and wreathed smiles,
Such as hang on Hebe's cheek,
And love to live in dimple sleek;   30
Sport that wrinkled Care derides,
And Laughter holding both his sides.
Come, and trip it as you go
On the light fantastic toe,
And in thy right hand lead with thee,   35
The mountain nymph, sweet Liberty;
And if I give thee honour due,
Mirth, admit me of thy crew
To live with her, and live with thee,
In unreproved pleasures free;   40

To hear the lark begin his flight,
And singing startle the dull night,
From his watch-tower in the skies,
Till the dappled dawn doth rise;
Then to come in spite of sorrow,   45
And at my window bid good morrow,
Through the sweet-briar, or the vine,
Or the twisted eglantine.
While the cock with lively din,
Scatters the rear of darkness thin,   50
And to the stack, or the barn door,
Stoutly struts his dames before,
Oft list'ning how the hounds and horn
Cheerly rouse the slumb'ring morn,
From the side of some hoar hill,   55
Through the high wood echoing shrill.
Sometime walking not unseen
By hedgerow elms, on hillocks green,
Right against the eastern gate,
Where the great sun begins his state,   60
Robed in flames, and amber light,
The clouds in thousand liveries dight,
While the ploughman near at hand,
Whistles o'er the furrowed land,
And the milkmaid singeth blithe,   65
And the mower whets his scythe,
And every shepherd tells his tale
Under the hawthorn in the dale.
Straight mine eye hath caught new pleasures
Whilst the landscape round it measures,   70
Russet lawns, and fallows grey,
Where the nibbling flocks do stray,
Mountains on whose barren breast
The labouring clouds do often rest:
Meadows trim with daisies pied,   75
Shallow brooks, and rivers wide.
Towers, and battlements it sees
Bosomed high in tufted trees,
Where perhaps some beauty lies,
The cynosure of neighbouring eyes.   80
Hard by, a cottage chimney smokes,
From betwixt two aged oaks,

Where Corydon and Thyrsis met,
Are at their savoury dinner set
Of herbs, and other country messes,   85
Which the neat-handed Phillis dresses;
And then in haste her bower she leaves,
With Thestylis to bind the sheaves;
Or if the earlier season lead
To the tanned haycock in the mead,   90
Sometimes with secure delight
The upland hamlets will invite,
When the merry bells ring round,
And the jocund rebecks sound
To many a youth, and many a maid,   95
Dancing in the chequered shade;
And young and old come forth to play
On a sunshine holiday, ·
Till the livelong daylight fail;
Then to the spicy nut-brown ale,   100
With stories told of many a feat,
How Faery Mab the junkets eat,
She was pinched, and pulled she said,
And by the friar's lantern led;
Tells how the drudging goblin sweat,   105
To earn his cream-bowl duly set,
When in one night, ere glimpse of morn,
His shadowy flail hath threshed the corn,
That ten day-labourers could not end;
Then lies him down the lubber fiend,   110
And stretched out all the chimney's length,
Basks at the fire his hairy strength;
And crop-full out of doors he flings,
Ere the first cock his matin rings.
Thus done the tales, to bed they creep,   115
By whispering winds soon lulled asleep.
Towered cities please us then,
And the busy hum of men,
Where throngs of knights and barons bold,
In weeds of peace high triumphs hold,   120
With store of ladies, whose bright eyes
Rain influence, and judge the prize,
Of wit, or arms, while both contend
To win her grace, whom all commend.

There let Hymen oft appear   125
In saffron robe, with taper clear,
And pomp, and feast, and revelry,
With masks, and antique pageantry,
Such sights as youthful poets dream
On summer eves by haunted stream.   130
Then to the well-trod stage anon,
If Jonson's learned sock be on,
Or sweetest Shakespeare fancy's child,
Warble his native wood-notes wild,
And ever against eating cares,   135
Lap me in soft Lydian airs,
Married to immortal verse
Such as the meeting soul may pierce
In notes, with many a winding bout
Of linked sweetness long drawn out   140
With wanton heed, and giddy cunning,
The melting voice through mazes running;
Untwisting all the chains that tie
The hidden soul of harmony.
That Orpheus' self may heave his head   145
From golden slumber on a bed
Of heaped Elysian flowers, and hear
Such strains as would have won the ear
Of Pluto, to have quite set free
His half-regained Eurydice.   150
These delights, if thou canst give,
Mirth with thee, I mean to live.

Il Penseroso

Hence vain deluding Joys,
    The brood of Folly without father bred,
How little you bestead,
    Or fill the fixed mind with all your toys;
Dwell in some idle brain,   5
    And fancies fond with gaudy shapes possess,
As thick and numberless
    As the gay motes that people the sunbeams,
Or likest hovering dreams
    The fickle pensioners of Morpheus' train.   10

But hail thou goddess, sage and holy,
Hail divinest Melancholy,
Whose saintly visage is too bright
To hit the sense of human sight;
And therefore to our weaker view,   15
O'erlaid with black, staid wisdom's hue.
Black, but such as in esteem,
Prince Memnon's sister might beseem,
Or that starred Ethiop queen that strove
To set her beauty's praise above   20
The sea-nymphs, and their powers offended,
Yet thou art higher far descended,
Thee bright-haired Vesta long of yore,
To solitary Saturn bore;
His daughter she (in Saturn's reign,   25
Such mixture was not held a stain)
Oft in glimmering bowers, and glades
He met her, and in secret shades
Of woody Ida's inmost grove,
Whilst yet there was no fear of Jove.   30
Come pensive nun, devout and pure,
Sober, steadfast, and demure,
All in a robe of darkest grain,
Flowing with majestic train,
And sable stole of cypress lawn,   35
Over thy decent shoulders drawn.
Come, but keep thy wonted state,
With even step, and musing gait,
And looks commercing with the skies,
Thy rapt soul sitting in thine eyes: 40
There held in holy passion still,
Forget thyself to marble, till
With a sad leaden downward cast,
Thou fix them on the earth as fast.
And join with thee calm Peace, and Quiet,   45
Spare Fast, that oft with gods doth diet,
And hears the Muses in a ring,
Ay round about Jove's altar sing.
And add to these retired Leisure,
That in trim gardens takes his pleasure;   50
But first, and chiefest, with thee bring,
Him that yon soars on golden wing,

Guiding the fiery-wheeled throne,
The cherub Contemplation,
And the mute Silence hist along,   55
'Less Philomel will deign a song,
In her sweetest, saddest plight,
Smoothing the rugged brow of night,
While Cynthia checks her dragon yoke,
Gently o'er the accustomed oak;   60
Sweet bird that shunn'st the noise of folly,
Most musical, most melancholy!
Thee chauntress oft the woods among,
I woo to hear thy even-song;
And missing thee, I walk unseen   65
On the dry smooth-shaven green,
To behold the wandering moon,
Riding near her highest noon,
Like one that had been led astray
Through the heaven's wide pathless way;   70
And oft, as if her head she bowed,
Stooping through a fleecy cloud.
Oft on a plat of rising ground,
I hear the far-off curfew sound,
Over some wide-watered shore,   75
Swinging slow with sullen roar;
Or if the air will not permit,
Some still removed place will fit,
Where glowing embers through the room
Teach light to counterfeit a gloom,   80
Far from all resort of mirth,
Save the cricket on the hearth,
Or the bellman's drowsy charm,
To bless the doors from nightly harm:
Or let my lamp at midnight hour,   85
Be seen in some high lonely tower,
Where I may oft outwatch the Bear,
With thrice great Hermes, or unsphere
The spirit of Plato to unfold
What worlds, or what vast regions hold   90
The immortal mind that hath forsook
Her mansion in this fleshly nook:
And of those demons that are found
In fire, air, flood, or under ground,

Whose power hath a true consent   95
With planet, or with element.
Sometime let gorgeous Tragedy
In sceptred pall come sweeping by,
Presenting Thebes, or Pelops' line,
Or the tale of Troy divine.   100
Or what (though rare) of later age,
Ennobled hath the buskined stage.
But, O sad virgin, that thy power
Might raise Musaeus from his bower,
Or bid the soul of Orpheus sing   105
Such notes as warbled to the string,
Drew iron tears down Pluto's cheek,
And made hell grant what love did seek.
Or call up him that left half-told
The story of Cambuscan bold,   110
Of Camball, and of Algarsife,
And who had Canace to wife,
That owned the virtuous ring and glass,
And of the wondrous horse of brass,
On which the Tartar king did ride;   115
And if aught else, great bards beside,
In sage and solemn tunes have sung,
Of tourneys and of trophies hung;
Of forests, and enchantments drear,
Where more is meant than meets the ear.   120
Thus Night oft see me in thy pale career,
Till civil-suited Morn appear,
Not tricked and frounced as she was wont,
With the Attic boy to hunt,
But kerchieft in a comely cloud,   125
While rocking winds are piping loud,
Or ushered with a shower still,
When the gust hath blown his fill,
Ending on the rustling leaves,
With minute drops from off the eaves.   130
And when the sun begins to fling
His flaring beams, me goddess bring
To arched walks of twilight groves,
And shadows brown that Sylvan loves
Of pine, or monumental oak,   135
Where the rude axe with heaved stroke,

Was never heard the nymphs to daunt,
Or fright them from their hallowed haunt.
There in close covert by some brook,
Where no profaner eye may look, 140
Hide me from day's garish eye,
While the bee with honied thigh,
That at her flowery work doth sing,
And the waters murmuring
With such consort as they keep, 145
Entice the dewy-feathered Sleep;
And let some strange mysterious dream,
Wave at his wings in airy stream,
Of lively portraiture displayed,
Softly on my eyelids laid. 150
And as I wake, sweet music breathe
Above, about, or underneath,
Sent by some spirit to mortals good,
Or the unseen genius of the wood.
But let my due feet never fail, 155
To walk the studious cloister's pale,
And love the high embowed roof,
With antique pillars' massy proof,
And storied windows richly dight,
Casting a dim religious light. 160
There let the pealing organ blow,
To the full-voiced choir below,
In service high, and anthems clear,
As may with sweetness, through mine ear,
Dissolve me into ecstasies, 165
And bring all heaven before mine eyes.
And may at last my weary age
Find out the peaceful hermitage,
The hairy gown and mossy cell,
Where I may sit and rightly spell 170
Of every star that heaven doth shew,
And every herb that sips the dew;
Till old experience do attain
To something like prophetic strain.
These pleasures Melancholy give, 175
And I with thee will choose to live.

Lycidas

In this monody the author bewails a learned friend, unfortunately drowned in his passage from Chester on the Irish Seas, 1637. And by occasion foretells the ruin of our corrupted clergy then in their height.

Yet once more, O ye laurels, and once more
Ye myrtles brown, with ivy never sere,
I come to pluck your berries harsh and crude,
And with forced fingers rude,
Shatter your leaves before the mellowing year.   5
Bitter constraint, and sad occasion dear,
Compels me to disturb your season due:
For Lycidas is dead, dead ere his prime,
Young Lycidas, and hath not left his peer:
Who would not sing for Lycidas? he knew   10
Himself to sing, and build the lofty rhyme.
He must not float upon his watery bier
Unwept, and welter to the parching wind,
Without the meed of some melodious tear.
    Begin then, sisters of the sacred well,   15
That from beneath the seat of Jove doth spring,
Begin, and somewhat loudly sweep the string.
Hence with denial vain, and coy excuse;
So may some gentle muse
With lucky words favour my destined urn,   20
And as he passes turn,
And bid fair peace be to my sable shroud.
For we were nursed upon the self-same hill,
Fed the same flock; by fountain, shade, and rill.
    Together both, ere the high lawns appeared   25
Under the opening eyelids of the morn,
We drove a-field, and both together heard
What time the grey-fly winds her sultry horn,
Battening our flocks with the fresh dews of night,
Oft till the star that rose, at evening, bright,   30
Toward heaven's descent had sloped his westering wheel.
Meanwhile the rural ditties were not mute,
Tempered to the oaten flute,
Rough satyrs danced, and fauns with cloven heel,
From the glad sound would not be absent long,   35
And old Damaetas loved to hear our song.
    But O the heavy change, now thou art gone,

Now thou art gone, and never must return!
Thee shepherd, thee the woods, and desert caves,
With wild thyme and the gadding vine o'ergrown,   40
And all their echoes mourn.
The willows, and the hazel copses green,
Shall now no more be seen,
Fanning their joyous leaves to thy soft lays.
As killing as the canker to the rose,   45
Or taint-worm to the weanling herds that graze,
Or frost to flowers, that their gay wardrobe wear,
When first the whitethorn blows;
Such, Lycidas, thy loss to shepherd's ear.
    Where were ye nymphs when the remorseless deep   50
Closed o'er the head of your loved Lycidas?
For neither were ye playing on the steep,
Where your old bards, the famous Druids, lie,
Nor on the shaggy top of Mona high,
Nor yet where Deva spreads her wizard stream: 55
Ay me, I fondly dream!
Had ye been there: for what could that have done?
What could the muse herself that Orpheus bore,
The muse herself for her enchanting son
Whom universal nature did lament,   60
When by the rout that made the hideous roar,
His gory visage down the stream was sent,
Down the swift Hebrus to the Lesbian shore.
    Alas! What boots it with uncessant care
To tend the homely slighted shepherd's trade,   65
And strictly meditate the thankless muse,
Were it not better done as others use,
To sport with Amaryllis in the shade,
Or with the tangles of Neaera's hair?
Fame is the spur that the clear spirit doth raise   70
(That last infirmity of noble mind)
To scorn delights, and live laborious days;
But the fair guerdon when we hope to find,
And think to burst out into sudden blaze,
Comes the blind Fury with th' abhorred shears,   75
And slits the thin-spun life. But not the praise,
Phoebus replied, and touched my trembling ears;
Fame is no plant that grows on mortal soil,
Nor in the glistering foil

Set off to the world, nor in broad rumour lies,   80
But lives and spreads aloft by those pure eyes,
And perfect witness of all-judging Jove;
As he pronounces lastly on each deed,
Of so much fame in heaven expect thy meed.
    O fountain Arethuse, and thou honoured flood,   85
Smooth-sliding Mincius, crowned with vocal reeds,
That strain I heard was of a higher mood:
But now my oat proceeds,
And listens to the herald of the sea
That came in Neptune's plea,   90
He asked the waves, and asked the felon winds,
What hard mishap hath doomed this gentle swain?
And questioned every gust of rugged wings
That blows from off each beaked promontory;
They knew not of his story,   95
And sage Hippotades their answer brings,
That not a blast was from his dungeon strayed,
The air was calm, and on the level brine,
Sleek Panope with all her sisters played.
It was that fatal and perfidious bark,   100
Built in the eclipse, and rigged with curses dark,
That sunk so low that sacred head of thine.
    Next Camus, reverend sire, went footing slow,
His mantle hairy, and his bonnet sedge,
Inwrought with figures dim, and on the edge   105
Like to that sanguine flower inscribed with woe.
Ah; who hath reft (quoth he) my dearest pledge?
Last came, and last did go,
The pilot of the Galilean lake,
Two massy keys he bore of metals twain,   110
(The golden opes, the iron shuts amain)
He shook his mitred locks, and stern bespake,
How well could I have spared for thee, young swain,
Enow of such as for their bellies' sake,
Creep and intrude, and climb into the fold?   115
Of other care they little reckoning make,
Than how to scramble at the shearers' feast,
And shove away the worthy bidden guest;
Blind mouths! that scarce themselves know how to hold
A sheep-hook, or have learned aught else the least   120
That to the faithful herdman's art belongs!

What recks it them? What need they? They are sped;
And when they list, their lean and flashy songs
Grate on their scrannel pipes of wretched straw,
The hungry sheep look up, and are not fed,   125
But swoll'n with wind, and the rank mist they draw,
Rot inwardly, and foul contagion spread:
Besides what the grim wolf with privy paw
Daily devours apace, and nothing said,
But that two-handed engine at the door,   130
Stands ready to smite once, and smite no more.
    Return Alpheus, the dread voice is past,
That shrunk thy streams; return Sicilian muse,
And call the vales, and bid them hither cast
Their bells, and flowrets of a thousand hues.   135
Ye valleys low where the mild whispers use,
Of shades and wanton winds, and gushing brooks,
On whose fresh lap the swart star sparely looks,
Throw hither all your quaint enamelled eyes,
That on the green turf suck the honied showers,   140
And purple all the ground with vernal flowers.
Bring the rathe primrose that forsaken dies,
The tufted crow-toe, and pale jessamine,
The white pink, and the pansy freaked with jet,
The glowing violet   145
The musk-rose, and the well-attired woodbine,
With cowslips wan that hang the pensive head,
And every flower that sad embroidery wears:
Bid amaranthus all his beauty shed,
And daffadillies fill their cups with tears,   150
To strew the laureate hearse where Lycid lies.
For so to interpose a little ease,
Let our frail thoughts dally with false surmise.
Ay me! Whilst thee the shores, and sounding seas
Wash far away, where'er thy bones are hurled,   155
Whether beyond the stormy Hebrides
Where thou perhaps under the whelming tide
Visit'st the bottom of the monstrous world;
Or whether thou to our moist vows denied,
Sleep'st by the fable of Bellerus old,   160
Where the great vision of the guarded mount
Looks toward Namancos and Bayona's hold;
Look homeward angel now, and melt with ruth.

And, O ye dolphins, waft the hapless youth.
  Weep no more, woeful shepherds weep no more,   165
For Lycidas your sorrow is not dead,
Sunk though he be beneath the watery floor,
So sinks the day-star in the ocean bed,
And yet anon repairs his drooping head,
And tricks his beams, and with new spangled ore,   170
Flames in the forehead of the morning sky:
So Lycidas sunk low, but mounted high,
Through the dear might of Him that walked the waves;
Where other groves, and other streams along,
With nectar pure his oozy locks he laves,   175
And hears the unexpressive nuptial song,
In the blest kingdoms meek of joy and love.
There entertain him all the saints above,
In solemn troops, and sweet societies
That sing, and singing in their glory move,   180
And wipe the tears for ever from his eyes.
Now Lycidas the shepherds weep no more;
Henceforth thou art the genius of the shore,
In thy large recompense, and shalt be good
To all that wander in that perilous flood.   185
  Thus sang the uncouth swain to the oaks and rills,
While the still morn went out with sandals grey,
He touched the tender stops of various quills,
With eager thought warbling his Doric lay:
And now the sun had stretched out all the hills,   190
And now was dropped into the western bay;
At last he rose, and twitched his mantle blue:
Tomorrow to fresh woods, and pastures new.

                            (*Poems*, 1645)

Sonnet 15: On the Late Massacre in Piedmont

Avenge O Lord Thy slaughtered saints, whose bones
  Lie scattered on the Alpine mountains cold,
  Even them who kept Thy truth so pure of old
    When all our fathers worshipped stocks and stones,
Forget not: in Thy book record their groans   5

Who were Thy sheep and in their ancient fold
Slain by the bloody Piedmontese that rolled
Mother with infant down the rocks. Their moans
The vales redoubled to the hills, and they
    To heaven. Their martyred blood and ashes sow   10
    O'er all the Italian fields where still doth sway
The triple Tyrant: that from these may grow
    A hundredfold, who having learnt Thy way
    Early may fly the Babylonian woe.

Sonnet 16

When I consider how my light is spent,
    Ere half my days, in this dark world and wide,
    And that one talent which is death to hide,
    Lodged with me useless, though my soul more bent
To serve therewith my maker, and present   5
    My true account, lest He returning chide,
    Doth God exact day-labour, light denied,
    I fondly ask; but Patience to prevent
That murmur, soon replies, God doth not need
    Either man's work or His own gifts, who best   10
    Bear His mild yoke, they serve Him best, His state
Is kingly. Thousands at His bidding speed
    And post o'er land and ocean without rest:
    They also serve who only stand and wait.

(Poems, 1673)

RICHARD CRASHAW
(1612–49)

While Crashaw may seem like Donne in his use of the conceit and
his application of erotic imagery to religious experience, and while
the title of *Steps to the Temple* (1646) implies an allegiance to Herbert,
the resemblances to both are superficial, the differences funda-
mental. Amongst English poets of the period, Crashaw is the only
one to whom the term 'baroque' can be meaningfully applied. The
anonymous friend who introduced *Steps to the Temple* perfectly
described the aims of baroque art when he said 'they shall lift thee,
reader, some yards above the ground.' Baroque art is the art of the
Catholic Counter-Reformation, and Crashaw, a Roman Catholic
first by temperament, then by conversion, is very much an artist of
the Counter-Reformation, a poet who seeks by his use of rapturous
experience, of poignantly mixed emotions, of ingenuity and
dramatic surprise, of sensuous description, or by simple en-
thusiasm, to lift his readers towards heaven on the wings of
emotional response in the same way that the great baroque architects
and sculptors sought to lift those who came to their churches.
Inevitably Crashaw is a poet of excess, sometimes triumphant, but
sometimes, when the appeal to the senses is too blatant or the conceit
too bizarre, merely lurid or ludicrous.

Crashaw revised his poems considerably, so that those which
appeared in the posthumous collection *Carmen Deo Nostro* (Paris,
1652) often differ markedly, not always for the better, from their
counterparts in *Steps to the Temple*. The best modern editions are by
L. C. Martin (*Poetical Works*, 2nd edn, Oxford, 1957) and G. W.
Williams (*Complete Poetry*, New York, 1970); there are books by
Williams (*Image and Symbol in the Sacred Poetry of Richard Crashaw*,
Columbia, 1963), Ruth Wallerstein (*Richard Crashaw*, Madison,
1935), Austin Warren (*Richard Crashaw: A Study in Baroque
Sensibility*, Ann Arbor, 1939) and Mario Praz (*The Flaming Heart*,
Garden City, 1958).

Luke 11: 'Blessed be the paps which
Thou hast sucked'

Suppose He had been tabled at thy teats,
　　Thy hunger feels not what He eats.
He'll have His teat ere long (a bloody one);
　　The mother then must suck the Son.

New Year's Day

Rise thou best and brightest morning,
　　Rosy with a double red,
With thine own blush thy cheeks adorning
　　And the dear drops this day were shed.

All the purple pride that laces   5
　　The crimson curtains of thy bed
Gilds thee not with so sweet graces
　　Nor sets thee in so rich a red.

Of all the fair-cheeked flowers that fill thee,
　　None so fair thy bosom strows   10
As the modest maiden lily
　　Our sins have shamed into a rose.

Bid thy golden god, the sun,
　　Burnished in his best beams rise,
Put all his red-eyed rubies on;   15
　　These rubies shall put out their eyes.

Let him make poor the purple east,
　　Search what the world's close cabinets keep,
Rob the rich births of each bright nest
　　That flaming in their fair beds sleep.   20

Let him embrace his own bright tresses
　　With a new mourning made of gems,
And wear, in those his morning dresses,
　　Another day of diadems.

When he hath done all he may   25
   To make himself rich in his rise,
All will be darkness to the day
   That breaks from one of these bright eyes.

And soon this sweet truth shall appear
   Dear babe, ere many days be done,·
The morn shall come to meet Thee here   30
   And leave her own neglected sun.

Here are beauties shall bereave him
   Of all his eastern paramours;
His Persian lovers all shall leave him   35
   And swear faith to Thy sweeter powers.

Charitas Nimia, or The Dear Bargain

Lord, what is man? Why should he cost Thee
So dear? What had this ruin lost Thee?
Lord, what is man, that Thou hast overbought
   So much a thing of naught?

   Love is too kind, I see, and can   5
Make but a simple merchant man.
'Twas for such sorry merchandise
Bold painters have put out his eyes.

   Alas, sweet lord, what wer't to Thee
If there were no such worms as we?   10
Heaven ne'er the less still heaven would be,
   Should mankind dwell
   In the deep hell.
What have his woes to do with Thee?

     Let him go weep   15
    O'er his own wounds;
    Seraphims will not sleep
Nor spheres let fall their faithful rounds.

   Still would the youthful spirits sing,
And still Thy spacious palace ring;   20
Still would those beauteous ministers of light
   Burn all as bright,

And bow their flaming heads before Thee;
Still thrones and dominations would adore Thee;
Still would those ever-wakeful sons of fire   25
          Keep warm Thy praise
          Both nights and days,
And teach Thy loved name to their noble lyre.

     Let froward dust then do its kind,
And give itself for sport to the proud wind.   30
Why should a piece of peevish clay plead shares
In the eternity of Thy old cares?
Why shouldst Thou bow Thy awful breast to see
What mine own madnesses have done with me?

     Should not the king still keep his throne   35
Because some desperate fool's undone?
Or will the world's illustrious eyes
Weep for every worm that dies?

          Will the gallant sun
          E'er the less glorious run?   40
Will he hang down his golden head
Or e'er the sooner seek his western bed,
          Because some foolish fly
          Grows wanton and will die?

     If I were lost in misery   45
What was it to Thy heaven and thee?
What was it to Thy precious blood
If my foul heart called for a flood?

What if my faithless soul and I
          Would needs fall in   50
          With guilt and sin,
What did the lamb that He should die?
What did the lamb that He should need,
When the wolf sins, Himself to bleed?

          If my base lust   55
Bargained with death and well-beseeming dust,
          Why should the white
          Lamb's bosom write
          The purple name
          Of my sin's shame?   60

Why should His unstained breast make good
My blushes with His own heart-blood?
   O my saviour make me see
How dearly Thou hast paid for me,
     That, lost again, my life may prove   65
As then in death, so now in love.

                      (*Steps to the Temple*, 1646)

A Hymn to the Name and Honour of
the Admirable St Teresa

Foundress of the reformation of the Discalced Carmelites, both men
and women. A woman for angelical height of speculation, for
masculine courage of performance, more than a woman, who yet a
child outran maturity, and durst plot a martyrdom.

Love, thou art absolute sole lord
Of life and death. To prove the word,
We'll now appeal to none of all
Those thy old soldiers, great and tall,
Ripe men of martyrdom, that could reach down   5
With strong arms their triumphant crown,
Such as could with lusty breath
Speak loud into the face of death
Their great Lord's glorious name; to none
Of those whose spacious bosoms spread a throne   10
For love at large to fill; spare blood and sweat,
And see him take a private seat,
Making his mansion in the mild
And milky soul of a soft child.
   Scarce has she learned to lisp the name   15
Of martyr, yet she thinks it shame
Life should so long play with that breath
Which spent can buy so brave a death.
She never undertook to know
What death with love should have to do;   20
Nor has she e'er yet understood
Why to show love she should shed blood;
Yet though she cannot tell you why,
She can love and she can die.
   Scarce has she blood enough to make   25
A guilty sword blush for her sake;

Yet has she a heart dares hope to prove
How much less strong is death than love.
   Be love but there, let poor six years
Be posed with the maturest fears 30
Man trembles at, you straight shall find
Love knows nò nonage, nor the mind.
'Tis love, not years or limbs that can
Make the martyr or the man.
   Love touched her heart, and lo it beats 35
High, and burns with such brave heats,
Such thirsts to die, as dares drink up
A thousand cold deaths in one cup.
Good reason, for she breathes all fire;
Her weak breast heaves with strong desire 40
Of what she may with fruitless wishes
Seek for amongst her mother's kisses.
   Since 'tis not to be had at home,
She'll travel to a martyrdom.
No home for hers confesses she 45
But where she may a martyr be.
   She'll to the Moors, and trade with them
For this unvalued diadem.
She'll offer them her dearest breath,
With Christ's name in 't, in change for death. 50
She'll bargain with them, and will give
Them God, teach them how to live
In Him; or if they this deny,
For Him she'll teach them how to die.
So shall she leave amongst them sown 55
Her Lord's blood, or at least her own.
   Farewell then, all the world, adieu!
Teresa is no more for you.
Farewell, all pleasures, sports, and joys,
Never till now esteemed toys, 60
Farewell, whatever dear may be,
Mother's arms or father's knee;
Farewell house and farewell home,
She's for the Moors and martyrdom!
   Sweet, not so fast! lo, thy fair spouse 65
Whom thou seek'st with so swift vows
Calls thee back, and bids thee come
T' embrace a milder martyrdom.

Blest powers forbid thy tender life
Should bleed upon a barbarous knife;   70
Or some base hand have power to race
Thy breast's chaste cabinet and uncase
A soul kept there so sweet; oh no,
Wise heav'n will never have it so:
Thou art love's victim, and must die   75
A death more mystical and high;
Into love's arms thou shalt let fall
A still surviving funeral.
His is the dart must make the death
Whose stroke shall taste thy hallowed breath;   80
A dart thrice dipped in that rich flame
Which writes thy spouse's radiant name
Upon the roof of heav'n, where aye
It shines, and with a sovereign ray
Beats bright upon the burning faces   85
Of souls, which in that name's sweet graces
Find everlasting smiles. So rare,
So spiritual, pure, and fair
Must be th' immortal instrument
Upon whose choice point shall be sent   90
A life so loved; and that there be
Fit executioners for thee,
The fair'st and first-born sons of fire,
Blest seraphim, shall leave their choir
And turn love's soldiers, upon thee   95
To exercise their archery.
    Oh, how oft shalt thou complain
Of a sweet and subtle pain,
Of intolerable joys,
Of a death in which who dies   100
Loves his death, and dies again,
And would forever so be slain,
And lives and dies, and knows not why
To live, but that he thus may never leave to die.
    How kindly will thy gentle heart   105
Kiss the sweetly killing dart!
And close in his embraces keep
Those delicious wounds, that weep
Balsam to heal themselves with. Thus
When these thy deaths, so numerous,   110

Shall all at last die into one,
And melt thy soul's sweet mansion
Like a soft lump of incense, hasted
By too hot a fire, and wasted
Into perfuming clouds, so fast   115
Shalt thou exhale to heav'n at last
In a resolving sigh; and then,
Oh, what! Ask not the tongues of men;
Angels cannot tell; suffice,
Thyself shall feel thine own full joys   120
And hold them fast forever. There
So soon as thou shalt first appear,
The moon of maiden stars, thy white
Mistress, attended by such bright
Souls as thy shining self, shall come   125
And in her first ranks make thee room;
Where 'mongst her snowy family
Immortal welcomes wait for thee.
     Oh, what delight when revealed life shall stand
And teach thy lips heav'n with His hand,   130
On which thou now mayst to thy wishes
Heap up thy consecrated kisses.
What joys shall seize thy soul when she,
Bending her blessed eyes on thee,
Those second smiles of heaven, shall dart   135
Her mild rays through thy melting heart!
     Angels, thy old friends, there shall greet thee,
Glad at their own home now to meet thee.
     All thy good works which went before
And waited for thee at the door   140
Shall own thee there, and all in one
Weave a constellation
Of crowns, with which the King, thy spouse,
Shall build up thy triumphant brows.
     All thy old woes shall now smile on thee,   145
And thy pains sit bright upon thee;
All thy sorrow here shall shine,
All thy sufferings be divine;
Tears shall take comfort and turn gems,
And wrongs repent to diadems.   150
Even thy deaths shall live, and new
Dress the soul that erst they slew;

Thy wounds shall blush to such bright scars
As keep account of the Lamb's wars.
  Those rare works where thou shalt leave writ   155
Love's noble history, with wit
Taught thee by none but Him, while here
They feed our souls, shall clothe thine there.
Each heav'nly word by whose hid flame
Our hard hearts shall strike fire, the same   160
Shall flourish on thy brows, and be
Both fire to us and flame to thee,
Whose light shall live bright in thy face
By glory, in our hearts by grace.
  Thou shalt look round about and see   165
Thousands of crowned souls throng to be
Themselves thy crown; sons of thy vows,
The virgin-births with which thy sovereign spouse
Made fruitful thy fair soul, go now
And with them all about thee, bow   170
To Him. Put on, He'll say, put on,
My rosy love, that thy rich zone
Sparkling with the sacred flames
Of thousand souls whose happy names
Heav'n keeps upon thy score. Thy bright   175
Life brought them first to kiss the light
That kindled them to stars. And so
Thou with the Lamb, thy Lord, shalt go,
And wheresoe'er He sets his white
Steps, walk with Him those ways of light,   180
Which who in death would live to see
Must learn in life to die like thee.

*An Apology for the Foregoing Hymn, as having
been writ when the Author was yet among
the Protestants*

Thus have I back again to thy bright name
(Fair flood of holy fires!) transfused the flame
I took from reading thee; 'tis to thy wrong,
I know, that in my weak and worthless song

Thou here art set to shine where thy full day   5
Scarce dawns. O pardon if I dare to say
Thine own dear books are guilty, for from thence
I learned to know that love is eloquence.
That hopeful maxim gave me heart to try
If, what to other tongues is tuned so high,   10
Thy praise might not speak English too; forbid,
By all thy mysteries that here lie hid,
Forbid it, mighty love! let no fond hate
Of names and words so far prejudicate.
Souls are not Spaniards too; one friendly flood   15
Of baptism blends them all into a blood.
Christ's faith makes but one body of all souls,
And love's that body's soul; no law controls
Our free traffic for heav'n; we may maintain
Peace, sure, with piety, though it come from Spain.   20
What soul soe'er, in any language, can
Speak heav'n like hers is my soul's countryman.
Oh, 'tis not Spanish, but 'tis heav'n she speaks!
'Tis heaven that lies in ambush there, and breaks
From thence into the wond'ring reader's breast,   25
Who feels his warm heart hatched into a nest
Of little eagles and young loves, whose high
Flights scorn the lazy dust and things that die.
    There are enow whose draughts, as deep as hell,
Drink up all Spain in sack. Let my soul swell   30
With thee, strong wine of love! Let others swim
In puddles; we will pledge this seraphim
Bowls full of richer blood than blush of grape
Was ever guilty of; change we too our shape,
My soul: some drink from men to beasts – oh, then   35
Drink we till we prove more, not less, than men,
And turn not beasts but angels. Let the King
Me ever into these His cellars bring,
Where flows such wine as we can have of none
But Him who trod the winepress all alone,   40
Wine of youth, life, and the sweet deaths of love;
Wine of immortal mixture, which can prove
Its tincture from the rosy nectar; wine
That can exalt weak earth, and so refine
Our dust that at one draught mortality   45
May drink itself up, and forget to die.

To the Noblest and Best of Ladies, the Countess of Denbigh

(Persuading her to resolution in religion and to render
herself without further delay into the communion of the
Catholic church)

What heaven-entreated heart is this
Stands trembling at the gate of bliss;
Holds fast the door, yet dares not venture
Fairly to open it and enter?
Whose definition is a doubt   5
'Twixt life and death, 'twixt in and out?
Say, ling'ring fair, why comes the birth
Of your brave soul so slowly forth?
Plead your pretences, O you strong
In weakness, why you choose so long   10
In labour of yourself to lie,
Nor daring quite to live nor die.
Ah linger not, loved soul, a slow
And late consent was a long no:
Who grants at last, long time tried   15
And did his best to have denied.
What magic bolts, what mystic bars
Maintain the will in these strange wars!
What fatal yet fantastic bands
Keep the free heart from its own hands!   20
So when the year takes cold we see
Poor waters their own prisoners be:
Fettered and locked up fast they lie
In a sad self-captivity.
Th'astonished nymphs their flood's strange fate deplore   25
To see themselves their own securer shore.
Thou that alone canst thaw this cold
And fetch the heart from its stronghold:
Almighty love! End this long war
And of a meteor make a star.   30
O fix this fair indefinite;
And 'mongst thy shafts of sovereign light
Choose out that sure, decisive dart
Which has the key of this close heart,
Knows all the corners of't and can control   35
The self-shut cabinet of an unsearched soul.

O let it be at last love's hour;
Raise this tall trophy of thy power;
Come once the conquering way; not to confute
But kill this rebel word 'Irresolute',   40
That so, in spite of all this peevish strength
Of weakness, she may write 'Resolved' at length.
Unfold at last, unfold fair flower,
And use the season of love's shower,
Meet his well-meaning wounds, wise heart,   45
And haste to drink the wholesome dart:
That healing shaft which heav'n till now
Hath in love's quiver hid for you.
O dart of love, arrow of light!
O happy you if it hit right.   50
It must not fall in vain, it must
Not mark the dry, regardless dust.
Fair one it is your fate, and brings
Eternal worlds upon its wings.
Meet it with widespread arms and see   55
Its seat your soul's just centre be.
Disband dull fears, give faith the day.
To save your life kill your delay:
It is love's siege, and sure to be
Your triumph, though his victory.   60
'Tis cowardice that keeps this field,
And want of courage not to yield.
Yield then, O yield, that love may win
The fort at last and let life in.
Yield quickly: lest perhaps you prove   65
Death's prey before the prize of love.
This fort of your fair self, if't be not won
He is repulsed indeed – but you are undone.

                              (*Carmen Deo Nostro*, 1652)

ANDREW MARVELL
(1621–78)

Best known during the eighteenth and early nineteenth centuries as the MP and pamphleteer who defended during the Restoration the liberties fought for in the Civil Wars, Marvell is the only example in English literature of a major poet whose greatness remained largely unrecognized for over two hundred years. He was, according to Aubrey, an intensely private man, although a busy politician (and perhaps a spy). His poetry, like his life, is built on a series of creative antitheses: in his lyric poetry detached irony and passionate commitment coexist in elegant harmony, and consummate Augustan poise and urbanity go together with extravagant Metaphysical ingenuity. 'Balanced' is thus rightly one of the most common adjectives applied to Marvell's lyric poetry (his post-Restoration satires are anything but balanced), and yet it suggests a lukewarm detachment that is never evident in his poetry or his life. The balance of the great 'Horatian Ode', for example, is a quality of mature human and political judgement too complex to be summarized, but this finest of English political poems involves no fence-sitting. In his later poems, Marvell moved towards less qualified admiration for Cromwell, turning at the Restoration (with an integrity not exhibited by Dryden or Waller) to satires on the government of Charles II. It is, however, on his lyric poetry, most of it probably dating from the 1640s and 1650s, that his reputation rests. At Appleton House in the early 1650s he found, like the Lord General Fairfax in whose service he was, a retreat from the turmoils of the new-born Republic. It was perhaps here that Marvell began to see the world of nature, in a way that anticipates the Romantics, not only as the Book of God, but as a source of more immediate spiritual refreshment, of mystical, intuitive wisdom. As well as being the inheritor of ancient European traditions, he is also, like Vaughan, a precursor of Wordsworth.

Marvell's *Miscellaneous Poems* were published in 1681 by a woman who claimed to be, but almost certainly was not, his widow. The

Complete Works, including prose, were edited by Alexander Grosart (4 volumes, Blackburn, 1872–5). The best modern editions of the poems are N. M. Margoliouth's *Poems and Letters* (2 volumes, 3rd edn, Oxford, 1971) and E. S. Donno's *Complete Poems* (Harmondsworth, 1972). The slightly contentious biography is best covered by Pierre Legouis in *Andrew Marvell: Poet, Puritan, Patriot* (2nd edn, Oxford, 1968); while there are good critical studies by R. L. Colie (*My Echoing Song*, Princeton, 1969) and A. M. Patterson (*Marvell and The Civic Crown*, Princeton, 1979), and useful collections of essays edited by John Carey (*Andrew Marvell*, Harmondsworth, 1968), C. A. Patrides (*Approaches to Marvell*, London, 1978) and R. L. Brett (*Andrew Marvell*, Oxford, 1978).

The Definition of Love

My love is of a birth as rare
As 'tis for object strange and high:
It was begotten by Despair
Upon Impossibility.

Magnanimous Despair alone   5
Could show me so divine a thing,
Where feeble Hope could ne'er have flown
But vainly flapped its tinsel wing.

And yet I quickly might arrive
Where my extended soul is fixed,   10
But Fate does iron wedges drive,
And always crowds itself betwixt.

For Fate with jealous eye does see
Two perfect loves, nor lets them close:
Their union would her ruin be,   15
And her tyrannic power depose.

And therefore her decrees of steel
Us as the distant Poles have placed,
(Though Love's whole world on us doth wheel)
Not by themselves to be embraced,   20

Unless the giddy heaven fall,
And earth some new convulsion tear;
And, us to join, the world should all
Be cramped into a planisphere.

As lines (so loves) oblique may well   25
Themselves in every angle greet:
But ours so truly parallel,
Though infinite, can never meet.

Therefore the love which us doth bind,
But Fate so enviously debars,   30
Is the conjunction of the mind,
And opposition of the stars.

To His Coy Mistress

Had we but world enough, and time,
This coyness, Lady, were no crime.
We would sit down, and think which way
To walk, and pass our long love's day.
Thou by the Indian Ganges' side   5
Shouldst rubies find: I by the tide
Of Humber would complain. I would
Love you ten years before the flood:
And you should, if you please, refuse
Till the conversion of the Jews.   10
My vegetable love should grow
Vaster than empires, and more slow.
An hundred years should go to praise
Thine eyes, and on thy forehead gaze.
Two hundred to adore each breast: 15
But thirty thousand to the rest.
An age at least to every part,
And the last age should show your heart:
For, Lady, you deserve this state;
Nor would I love at lower rate.   20
   But at my back I always hear
Time's winged chariot hurrying near:
And yonder all before us lie
Deserts of vast eternity.

Thy beauty shall no more be found;   25
Nor, in thy marble vault, shall sound
My echoing song: then worms shall try
That long-preserved virginity:
And your quaint honour turn to dust;
And into ashes all my lust.   30
The grave's a fine and private place,
But none, I think, do there embrace.
   Now, therefore, while the youthful hue
Sits on thy skin like morning dew,
And while thy willing soul transpires   35
At every pore with instant fires,
Now let us sport us while we may;
And now, like amorous birds of prey,
Rather at once our time devour,
Than languish in his slow-chapped power.   40
Let us roll all our strength, and all
Our sweetness, up into one ball:
And tear our pleasures with rough strife,
Thorough the iron grates of life.
Thus, though we cannot make our sun   45
Stand still, yet we will make him run.

An Horatian Ode upon
Cromwell's Return from Ireland

The forward youth that would appear
Must now forsake his muses dear,
   Nor in the shadows sing
   His numbers languishing.
'Tis time to leave the books in dust,   5
And oil the unused armour's rust:
   Removing from the wall
   The corslet of the hall.
So restless Cromwell could not cease
In the inglorious arts of peace,   10
   But through adventurous war
   Urged his active star.
And, like the three-forked lightning, first
Breaking the clouds where it was nursed

Did thorough his own side   15
His fiery way divide.
(For 'tis all one to courage high
The emulous or enemy:
    And with such to inclose
    Is more than to oppose.)   20
Then burning through the air he went,
And palaces and temples rent:
    And Caesar's head at last
    Did through his laurels blast.
'Tis madness to resist or blame   25
The force of angry heaven's flame:
    And, if we would speak true,
    Much to the man is due,
Who, from his private gardens, where
He lived reserved and austere,   30
    As if his highest plot
    To plant the bergamot,
Could by industrious valour climb
To ruin the great work of time,
    And cast the kingdoms old   35
    Into another mould.
Though justice against fate complain,
And plead the ancient rights in vain:
    But those do hold or break
    As men are strong or weak.   40
Nature, that hateth emptiness,
Allows of penetration less:
    And therefore must make room
    Where greater spirits come.
What field of all the Civil Wars,   45
Where his were not the deepest scars?
    And Hampton shows what part
    He had of wiser art,
Where, twining subtle fears with hope,
He wove a net of such a scope,   50
    That Charles himself might chase
    To Carisbrooke's narrow case:
That thence the royal actor born
The tragic scaffold might adorn:
    While round the armed bands   55
    Did clap their bloody hands.

He nothing common did or mean
Upon that memorable scene:
 But with his keener eye
 The axe's edge did try: 60
Nor called the gods with vulgar spite
To vindicate his helpless right,
 But bowed his comely head,
 Down, as upon a bed.
This was that memorable hour   65
Which first assured the forced power.
 So when they did design
 The Capitol's first line,
A bleeding head where they begun,
Did fright the architects to run;   70
 And yet in that the State
 Foresaw its happy fate.
And now the Irish are ashamed
To see themselves in one year tamed:
 So much one man can do,   75
 That does both act and know.
They can affirm his praises best,
And have, though overcome, confessed
 How good he is, how just,
 And fit for highest trust: 80
Nor yet grown stiffer with command,
But still in the Republic's hand:
 How fit he is to sway
 That can so well obey.
He to the Commons' feet presents 85
A kingdom, for his first year's rents:
 And, what he may, forbears
 His fame, to make it theirs:
And has his sword and spoils ungirt,
To lay them at the public's skirt.   90
 So when the falcon high
 Falls heavy from the sky,
She, having killed, no more does search
But on the next green bough to perch,
 Where, when he first does lure, 95
 The falc'ner has her sure.
What may not then our isle presume
While Victory his crest does plume?

What may not others fear
If thus he crowns each year?   100
A Caesar, he, ere long to Gaul,
To Italy an Hannibal,
    And to all states not free
    Shall climacteric be.
The Pict no shelter now shall find   105
Within his parti-coloured mind,
    But from this valour sad
    Shrink underneath the plaid:
Happy, if in the tufted brake
The English hunter him mistake,   110
    Nor lay his hounds in near
    The Caledonian deer.
But thou, the Wars' and Fortune's son,
March indefatigably on,
    And for the last effect   115
    Still keep thy sword erect:
Besides the force it has to fright
The spirits of the shady night,
    The same arts that did gain
    A power, must it maintain.   120

The Picture of Little T.C.
in a Prospect of Flowers

See with what simplicity
This nymph begins her golden days!
In the green grass she loves to lie,
And there with her fair aspect tames
The wilder flowers, and gives them names: 5
But only with the roses plays;
         And them does tell
What colour best becomes them, and what smell.

Who can foretell for what high cause
This Darling of the Gods was born!   10
Yet this is she whose chaster laws
The wanton Love shall one day fear,
And, under her command severe,
See his bow broke and ensigns torn.
         Happy, who can   15
Appease this virtuous enemy of man!

O, then let me in time compound,
And parley with those conquering eyes;
Ere they have tried their force to wound,
Ere, with their glancing wheels, they drive   20
In triumph over hearts that strive,
And them that yield but more despise.
            Let me be laid,
Where I may see thy glories from some shade.

Meantime, whilst every verdant thing   25
Itself does at thy beauty charm,
Reform the errors of the spring;
Make that the tulips may have share
Of sweetness, seeing they are fair;
And roses of their thorns disarm: 30
            But most procure
That violets may a longer age endure.

But, O young beauty of the woods,
Whom Nature courts with fruits and flowers,
Gather the flowers, but spare the buds;   35
Lest Flora angry at thy crime,
To kill her infants in their prime,
Do quickly make the example yours;
            And, ere we see,
Nip in the blossom all our hopes and thee.

From *Upon Appleton House,*
to my Lord Fairfax

36

From that blest bed the hero came,
Whom France and Poland yet does fame:
Who, when retired here to peace,
His warlike studies could not cease;
But laid these gardens out in sport   285
In the just figure of a fort;
And with five bastions it did fence,
As aiming one for every sense.

37

When in the east the morning ray
Hangs out the colours of the day,   290
The bee through these known alleys hums,
Beating the *dian* with its drums.
Then flowers their drowsy eyelids raise,
Their silken ensigns each displays,
And dries its pan yet dank with dew,   295
And fills its flask with odours new.

38

These, as their Governor goes by,
In fragrant volleys they let fly;
And to salute their Governess
Again as great a charge they press: 300
None for the virgin Nymph; for she
Seems with the flowers a flower to be.
And think so still! though not compare
With breath so sweet, or cheek so fair.

39

Well shot, ye firemen! Oh how sweet,   305
And round your equal fires do meet
Whose shrill report no ear can tell,
But echoes to the eye and smell.
See how the flowers, as at parade,
Under their colours stand displayed: 310
Each regiment in order grows,
That of the tulip, pink, and rose.

40

But when the vigilant patrol
Of stars walks round about the Pole,   315
Their leaves, that to the stalks are curled,
Seem to their staves the ensigns furled.
Then in some flower's beloved hut
Each bee as sentinel is shut,
And sleeps so too: but, if once stirred,
She runs you through, nor asks the word.   320

41

Oh thou, that dear and happy isle
The garden of the world ere while,
Thou paradise of four seas,
Which heaven planted us to please,
But, to exclude the world, did guard   325
With watery if not flaming sword;
What luckless apple did we taste,
To make us mortal, and thee waste?

42

Unhappy! shall we never more
That sweet militia restore,   330
When gardens only had their towers,
And all the garrisons were flowers,
When roses only arms might bear,
And men did rosy garlands wear?
Tulips, in several colours barred,   335
Were then the Switzers of our Guard.

43

The gardener had the soldier's place,
And his more gentle forts did trace.
The nursery of all things green
Was then the only magazine.   340
The winter quarters were the stoves,
Where he the tender plants removes.
But war all this doth overgrow;
We ordnance plant and powder sow.

44

And yet there walks one on the sod   345
Who, had it pleased him and God,
Might once have made our gardens spring
Fresh as his own and flourishing.
But he preferred to the Cinque Ports
These five imaginary forts,   350
And, in those half-dry trenches, spanned
Power which the ocean might command.

45

For he did, with his utmost skill,
Ambition weed, but conscience till:
Conscience, that heaven-nursed plant,   355
Which most our earthy gardens want.
A prickling leaf it bears, and such
As that which shrinks at every touch;
But flowers eternal, and divine,
That in the crowns of saints do shine.   360

[. . .]

63

When first the eye this forest sees
It seems indeed as wood not trees:
As if their neighbourhood so old
To one great trunk them all did mould.   500
There the huge bulk takes place, as meant
To thrust up a fifth element,
And stretches still so closely wedged
As if the night within were hedged.

64

Dark all without it knits; within   505
It opens passable and thin;
And in as loose an order grows,
As the Corinthean porticoes.
The arching boughs unite between
The columns of the temple green;   510
And underneath the winged choirs
Echo about their tuned fires.

65

The nightingale does here make choice
To sing the trials of her voice.
Low shrubs she sits in, and adorns   515
With music high the squatted thorns.
But highest oaks stoop down to hear,
And listening elders prick the ear.
The thorn, lest it should hurt her, draws
Within the skin its shrunken claws.   520

66

But I have for my music found
A sadder, yet more pleasing sound:
The stock-doves, whose fair necks are graced
With nuptial rings, their ensigns chaste;
Yet always, for some cause unknown,   525
Sad pair unto the elms they moan.
O why should such a couple mourn,
That in so equal flames do burn!

67

Then as I careless on the bed
Of gelid strawberries do tread,   530
And through the hazels thick espy
The hatching throstles shining eye,
The heron from the ash's top,
The eldest of its young lets drop,
As if it stork-like did pretend   535
That tribute to its Lord to send.

68

But most the hewel's wonders are,
Who here has the holtfelster's care.
He walks still upright from the root,
Measuring the timber with his foot,   540
And all the way, to keep it clean,
Doth from the bark the woodmoths glean.
He, with his beak, examines well
Which fit to stand and which to fell.

69

The good he numbers up, and hacks,   545
As if he marked them with the axe.
But where he, tinkling with his beak,
Does find the hollow oak to speak,
That for his building he designs,
And through the tainted side he mines.   550
Who could have thought the tallest oak
Should fall by such a feeble stroke!

70

Nor would it, had the tree not fed
A traitor-worm, within it bred,
(As first our flesh corrupt within   555
Tempts impotent and bashful sin).
And yet that worm triumphs not long,
But serves to feed the hewel's young,
While the oak seems to fall content,
Viewing the treason's punishment.   560

71

Thus I, easy philosopher,
Among the birds and trees confer.
And little now to make me wants
Or of the fowls, or of the plants:
Give me but wings as they, and I   565
Straight floating on the air shall fly:
Or turn me but, and you shall see
I was but an inverted tree.

72

Already I begin to call
In their most learn'd original: 570
And where I language want, my signs
The bird upon the bough divines;
And more attentive there doth sit
Than if she were with lime-twigs knit.
No leaf does tremble in the wind   575
Which I, returning, cannot find.

73

Out of these scattered sibyl's leaves
Strange prophecies my fancy weaves:
And in one history consumes,
Like Mexique paintings, all the plumes.   580
What Rome, Greece, Palestine, ere said
I in this light mosaic read.
Thrice happy he who, not mistook,
Hath read in Nature's mystic book.

74

And see how chance's better wit   585
Could with a mask my studies hit!
The oak leaves me embroider all,
Between which caterpillars crawl:
And ivy, with familiar trails,
Me licks, and clasps, and curls, and hales.   590
Under this antic cope I move
Like some great prelate of the grove.

75

Then, languishing with ease, I toss
On pallets swollen of velvet moss,
While the wind, cooling through the boughs,   595
Flatters with air my panting brows.
Thanks for my rest, ye mossy banks;
And unto you, cool zephyrs, thanks,
Who, as my hair, my thoughts too shed,
And winnow from the chaff my head.   600

76

How safe, methinks, and strong, behind
These trees have I encamped my mind;
Where beauty, aiming at the heart,
Bends in some tree its useless dart;
And where the world no certain shot   605
Can make, or me it toucheth not.
But I on it securely play,
And gall its horsemen all the day.

The Garden

How vainly men themselves amaze
To win the palm, the oak, or bays,
And their uncessant labours see
Crowned from some single herb or tree,
Whose short and narrow verged shade   5
Does prudently their toils upbraid,
While all flowers and all trees do close
To weave the garlands of repose.

Fair Quiet, have I found thee here,
And Innocence, thy sister dear!   10
Mistaken long, I sought you then
In busy companies of men.
Your sacred plants, if here below,
Only among the plants will grow.
Society is all but rude,   15
To this delicious solitude.

No white nor red was ever seen
So am'rous as this lovely green.
Fond lovers, cruel as their flame,
Cut in these trees their mistress' name.   20
Little, alas, they know, or heed,
How far these beauties hers exceed!
Fair trees! wheres'e'er your barks I wound,
No name shall but your own be found.

When we have run our passion's heat,   25
Love hither makes his best retreat.
The gods, that mortal beauty chase,
Still in a tree did end their race.
Apollo hunted Daphne so,
Only that she might laurel grow.   30
And Pan did after Syrinx speed,
Not as a nymph, but for a reed.

What wondrous life in this I lead!
Ripe apples drop about my head;
The luscious clusters of the vine   35
Upon my mouth do crush their wine;
The nectarene, and curious peach,
Into my hands themselves do reach;
Stumbling on melons, as I pass,
Ensnared with flowers, I fall on grass.   40

Meanwhile the mind, from pleasure less,
Withdraws into its happiness:
The mind, that ocean where each kind
Does straight its own resemblance find;
Yet it creates, transcending these,   45
Far other worlds, and other seas,

Annihilating all that's made
To a green thought in a green shade.

Here at the fountain's sliding foot,
Or at some fruit-tree's mossy root,   50
Casting the body's vest aside,
My soul into the boughs does glide:
There like a bird it sits, and sings,
Then whets, and combs its silver wings;
And, till prepared for longer flight,   55
Waves in its plumes the various light.

Such was that happy garden-state,
While man there walked without a mate:
After a place so pure, and sweet,
What other help could yet be meet!   60
But 'twas beyond a mortal's share
To wander solitary there:
Two paradises 'twere in one
To live in paradise alone.

How well the skilful gardener drew   65
Of flowers and herbs this dial new,
Where from above the milder sun
Does through a fragrant zodiac run;
And, as it works, the industrious bee
Computes its time as well as we.   70
How could such sweet and wholesome hours
Be reckoned but with herbs and flowers!

On a Drop of Dew

See how the orient dew,
Shed from the bosom of the morn
    Into the blowing roses,
Yet careless of its mansion new,
For the clear region where 'twas born   5
    Round in itself incloses:
    And in its little globe's extent,
Frames as it can its native element.

How it the purple flower does slight,
  Scarce touching where it lies,   10
But gazing back upon the skies,
  Shines with a mournful light,
    Like its own tear,
Because so long divided from the sphere.
  Restless it rolls and unsecure,   15
    Trembling lest it grow impure,
  Till the warm sun pity its pain,
And to the skies exhale it back again.
    So the soul, that drop, that ray
Of the clear fountain of eternal day,   20
Could it within the human flower be seen,
    Remembering still its former height,
    Shuns the sweet leaves and blossoms green,
    And, recollecting its own light,
Does, in its pure and circling thoughts, express   25
The greater heaven in an heaven less.
    In how coy a figure wound,
    Every way it turns away:
  So the world excluding round,
    Yet receiving in the day,   30
    Dark beneath, but bright above,
    Here disdaining, there in love.
  How loose and easy hence to go,
  How girt and ready to ascend,
    Moving but on a point below,   35
  It all about does upwards bend.
Such did the manna's sacred dew distil,
White and entire, though congealed and chill,
Congealed on earth: but does, dissolving, run
Into the glories of th' almighty sun.   40

A Dialogue between the Soul and Body

SOUL

Oh, who shall from this dungeon raise
A soul, enslaved so many ways,
With bolts of bones, that fettered stands
In feet, and manacled in hands.

Here blinded with an eye; and there   5
Deaf with the drumming of an ear,
A soul hung up, as 'twere, in chains
Of nerves, and arteries, and veins,
Tortured, besides each other part,
In a vain head, and double heart?   10

BODY

Oh, who shall me deliver whole,
From bonds of this tyrannic soul,
Which, stretched upright, impales me so,
That mine own precipice I go;
And warms and moves this needless frame   15
(A fever could but do the same),
And, wanting where its spite to try,
Has made me live to let me die,
A body that could never rest,
Since this ill spirit it possessed?   20

SOUL

What magic could me thus confine
Within another's grief to pine,
Where, whatsoever it complain,
I feel, that cannot feel, the pain,
And all my care itself employs,   25
That to preserve, which me destroys:
Constrained not only to endure
Diseases, but, what's worse, the cure:
And ready oft the port to gain,
Am shipwrecked into health again?   30

BODY

But physic yet could never reach
The maladies thou me dost teach:
Whom first the cramp of hope does tear,
And then the palsy shakes of fear;
The pestilence of love does heat,   35
Or hatred's hidden ulcer eat;

Joy's cheerful madness does perplex,
Or sorrow's other madness vex;
Which knowledge forces me to know,
And memory will not forgo.   40
What but a soul could have the wit
To build me up for sin so fit?
So architects do square and hew,
Green trees that in the forest grew.

Damon the Mower

Hark how the Mower Damon sung,
With love of Juliana stung!
While everything did seem to paint
The scene more fit for his complaint.
Like her fair eyes the day was fair,   5
But scorching like his am'rous care.
Sharp like his scythe his sorrow was,
And withered like his hopes the grass.

'Oh what unusual heats are here,
Which thus our sunburned meadows sear!   10
The grasshopper its pipe gives o'er;
And hamstringed frogs can dance no more.
But in the brook the green frog wades;
And grasshoppers seek out the shades.
Only the snake, that kept within,   15
Now glitters in its second skin.

'This heat the sun could never raise,
Nor Dog Star so inflame the days.
It from an higher beauty grow'th,
Which burns the fields and mower both: 20
Which mads the dog, and makes the sun
Hotter than his own Phaëton.
Not July causeth these extremes,
But Juliana's scorching beams.

'Tell me where I may pass the fires   25
Of the hot day, or hot desires.
To what cool cave shall I descend,
Or to what gelid fountain bend?

Alas! I look for ease in vain,
When remedies themselves complain. 30
No moisture but my tears do rest,
Nor cold but in her icy breast.

'How long wilt thou, fair shepherdess,
Esteem me, and my presents less?
To thee the harmless snake I bring, 35
Disarmed of its teeth and sting;
To thee chameleons, changing hue,
And oak leaves tipped with honey dew.
Yet thou, ungrateful, hast not sought
Nor what they are, nor who them brought. 40

'I am the Mower Damon, known
Through all the meadows I have mown.
On me the morn her dew distils
Before her darling daffodils.
And, if at noon my toil me heat, 45
The sun himself licks off my sweat.
While, going home, the evening sweet
In cowslip-water bathes my feet.

'What, though the piping shepherd stock
The plains with an unnumbered flock, 50
This scythe of mine discovers wide
More ground than all his sheep do hide.
With this the golden fleece I shear
Of all these closes every year.
And though in wool more poor than they, 55
Yet am I richer far in hay.

'Nor am I so deformed to sight,
If in my scythe I looked right;
In which I see my picture done,
As in a crescent moon the sun. 60
The deathless fairies take me oft
To lead them in their dances soft:
And, when I tune myself to sing,
About me they contract their ring.

'How happy might I still have mowed,   65
Had not Love here his thistles sowed!
But now I all the day complain,
Joining my labour to my pain;
And with my scythe cut down the grass,
Yet still my grief is where it was: 70
But, when the iron blunter grows,
Sighing, I whet my scythe and woes.'

While thus he threw his elbow round,
Depopulating all the ground,
And, with his whistling scythe, does cut   75
Each stroke between the earth and root,
The edged steel by careless chance
Did into his own ankle glance;
And there among the grass fell down,
By his own scythe, the Mower mown.   80

'Alas!' said he, 'these hurts are slight
To those that die by love's despite.
With shepherd's-purse, and clown's-all-heal,
The blood I staunch, and wound I seal.
Only for him no cure is found,   85
Whom Juliana's eyes do wound.
'Tis death alone that this must do:
For Death thou art a Mower too.'

Bermudas

Where the remote Bermudas ride
In the ocean's bosom unespied,
From a small boat, that rowed along:
The listening winds received this song.
    'What should we do but sing his praise   5
That led us through the watery maze,
Unto an isle so long unknown,
And yet far kinder than our own?
Where he the huge sea-monsters wracks,
That lift the deep upon their backs,   10
He lands us on a grassy stage,
Safe from the storms, and prelate's rage.

He gave us this eternal spring,
Which here enamels everything,
And sends the fowl to us in care,   15
On daily visits through the air.
He hangs in shades the orange bright,
Like golden lamps in a green night,
And does in the pom'granates close
Jewels more rich than Ormus shows.   20
He makes the figs our mouths to meet,
And throws the melons at our feet,
But apples plants of such a price,
No tree could ever bear them twice.
With cedars, chosen by his hand,   25
From Lebanon, he stores the land,
And makes the hollow seas, that roar,
Proclaim the ambergris on shore.
He cast (of which we rather boast)
The gospel's pearl upon our coast,   30
And in these rocks for us did frame
A temple, where to sound his name.
Oh let our voice his praise exalt,
Till it arrive at heaven's vault:
Which thence (perhaps) rebounding, may   35
Echo beyond the Mexique Bay.'
   Thus sung they, in the English boat,
An holy and a cheerful note,
And all the way, to guide their chime,
With falling oars they kept the time.   40

From *Upon the Death of*
His Late Highness the Lord Protector

I saw him dead. A leaden slumber lies
And mortal sleep over those wakeful eyes:
Those gentle rays under the lids were fled,
Which through his looks that piercing sweetness shed;   250
That port which so majestic was and strong,
Loose and deprived of vigour, stretched along:
All withered, all discoloured, pale and wan –
How much another thing, nor more that man?

Oh human glory vain, oh death, oh wings,   255
Oh worthless world, oh transitory things!
   Yet dwelt that greatness in his shape decayed,
That still though dead, greater than death he laid;
And in his altered face you something feign
That threatens death he yet will live again.   260
   Not much unlike the sacred'oak which shoots
To heaven its branches and through earth its roots,
Whose spacious boughs are hung with trophies round,
And honoured wreaths have oft the victor crowned.
When angry Jove darts lightning through the air,   265
At mortals' sins, nor his own plant will spare,
(It groans, and bruises all below, that stood
So many years the shelter of the wood.)
The tree erewhile foreshortened to our view,
When fall'n shows taller yet than as it grew: 270
   So shall his praise to after times increase,
When truth shall be allowed, and faction cease,
And his own shadows with him fall. The eye
Detracts from objects than itself more high:
But when death takes them from that envied seat,   275
Seeing how little, we confess how great.
   Thee, many ages hence in martial verse
Shall the English soldier, ere he charge, rehearse,
Singing of thee, inflame themselves to fight,
And with the name of *Cromwell*, armies fright.   280
As long as rivers to the seas shall run,
As long as Cynthia shall relieve the sun,
While stags shall fly unto the forests thick,
While sheep delight the grassy downs to pick,
As long as future times succeed the past,   285
Always thy honour, praise, and name shall last.

On Mr Milton's 'Paradise Lost'

When I beheld the poet blind, yet bold,
In slender book his vast design unfold,
Messiah crowned, God's reconciled decree,
Rebelling Angels, the Forbidden Tree,
Heaven, Hell, Earth, Chaos, all; the argument   5
Held me a while, misdoubting his intent

That he would ruin (for I saw him strong)
The sacred truths to fable and old song,
(So Sampson groped the temple's posts in spite)
The world o'erwhelming to revenge his sight.   10
    Yet as I read, soon growing less severe,
I liked his project, the success did fear;
Through that wide field how he his way should find
O'er which lame faith leads understanding blind;
Lest he perplexed the things he would explain,   15
And what was easy he should render vain.
    Or if a work so infinite he spanned,
Jealous I was that some less skilful hand
(Such as disquiet always what is well,
And by ill imitating would excel)   20
Might hence presume the whole Creation's day
To change in scenes, and show it in a play.
    Pardon me, Mighty Poet, nor despise
My causeless, yet not impious, surmise.
But I am now convinced that none will dare   25
Within thy labours to pretend a share.
Thou hast not missed one thought that could be fit,
And all that was improper dost omit:
So that no room is here for writers left,
But to detect their ignorance or theft.   30
That majesty which through thy work doth reign
Draws the devout, deterring the profane.
And things divine thou treat'st of in such state
As them preserves, and thee, inviolate.
At once delight and horror on us seize,   35
Thou sing'st with so much gravity and ease;
And above human flight dost soar aloft,
With plume so strong, so equal, and so soft.
The bird named from that paradise you sing
So never flags, but always keeps on wing.   40
    Where couldst thou words of such a compass find?
Whence furnish such a vast expense of mind?
Just heaven thee, like Tiresias, to requite,
Rewards with prophecy thy loss of sight.
    Well mightst thou scorn thy readers to allure   45
With tinkling rhyme, of thine own sense secure;
While the *Town-Bayes* writes all the while and spells,
And like a pack-horse tires without his bells.

Their fancies like our bushy points appear,
The poets tag them; we for fashion wear.   50
I too, transported by the mode, offend,
And while I meant to *praise* thee must *commend*.
Thy verse created like thy theme sublime,
In number, weight, and measure, needs not rhyme.

(*Miscellaneous Poems*, 1681)

HENRY VAUGHAN
(1621/2–95)

Vaughan began his career as a poet with the mediocre and decidedly secular *Poems* of 1646; in 1650 he published *Silex Scintillans* ('sparkling flint') a collection of such different character and quality that one inevitably looks to the intervening years to find what could have transformed an irredeemably minor Caroline lyrist into one of the most strikingly profound and individual religious poets of the century. Several things seem to have contributed: the events of the Civil Wars, the more private grief of the death of his younger brother William, a close reading of the Bible, and, most important of all to the form his poetry took, a reading of George Herbert. To speak of Herbert strongly influencing Vaughan would be to under-state the case: Vaughan is saturated with Herbert. He set out (as did several others, like Ralph Knevet or Christopher Harvey) to imitate him closely, taking or echoing titles, phrases, images, whole lines, from *The Temple*. Instead of stifling his poetic voice, Herbert apparently opened for Vaughan ways in which to express his own distinctive religious experience. That experience differs most obviously from Herbert in its emphasis on the cherished moment of insight into the eternal, usually expressed in terms of radiant light and contrasted with the bleak darkness of man's fallen, earthly state. Vaughan is in this a Christian neo-Platonist, much influenced also by the mystic theories of his twin brother Thomas, one of the last of the serious alchemists. Vaughan is a mystical neo-Platonist, too, in his emphasis on God's immanence in the world around him. As in the case of Marvell, one sees in his treatment of nature, and of child-hood in a poem like 'The Retreat', the beginnings of attitudes which, nipped in the bud by the cool rational consensus of the later seventeenth century, were to re-emerge in the work of the Romantic poets more than a century later.

There are good modern editions of Vaughan by L. C. Martin (*Works*, 2nd edn, Oxford, 1957) and by F. Fogle (*Complete Poetry*,

New York, 1964). There is a critical biography, now somewhat dated, by F. E. Hutchinson (*Henry Vaughan: A Life and Interpretation*, Oxford, 1947), and studies by R. Garner (*Henry Vaughan: Experience and the Tradition*, Chicago, 1959), E. C. Pettet (*Of Paradise and Light*, Cambridge, 1960), R. A. Durr (*On the Mystical Poetry of Henry Vaughan*, Cambridge, Mass., 1962) and J. D. Simmonds (*Masques of God*, Pittsburgh, 1972).

Regeneration

A ward and still in bonds, one day
  I stole abroad:
It was high spring, and all the way
  Primrosed and hung with shade;
   Yet was it frost within,
    And surly winds   5
Blasted my infant buds, and sin
  Like clouds eclipsed my mind.

Stormed thus I straight perceived my spring
  Mere stage and show,   10
My walk a monstrous, mountained thing
  Rough-cast with rocks and snow;
   And as a pilgrim's eye
    Far from relief
Measures the melancholy sky   15
  Then drops and rains for grief,

So sighed I upwards still: at last,
  'Twixt steps and falls,
I reached the pinnacle, where placed
  I found a pair of scales.   20
   I took them up and laid
    In the one late pains;
The other smoke and pleasures weighed
  But proved the heavier grains.

With that some cried 'Away': straight I 25
  Obeyed, and led
Full east, a fair, fresh field could spy;
  Some called it Jacob's bed,

A virgin soil which no
   Rude feet e'er trod,   30
Where, since He stepped there, only go
   Prophets and friends of God.

Here I reposed; but, scarce well set,
   A grove descried
Of stately height, whose branches met   35
   And mixed on every side.
   I entered, and once in
     (Amazed to see't)
Found all was changed, and a new spring
   Did all my senses greet.   40

The unthrift sun shot vital gold
   A thousand pieces,
And heaven its azure did unfold
   Chequered with snowy fleeces:
   The air was all in spice   45
     And every bush
A garland wore. Thus fed my eyes
   But all the ear lay hush.

Only a little fountain lent
   Some use for ears,   50
And on the dumb shades language spent
   The music of her tears.
   I drew her near and found
     The cistern full
Of diverse stones, some bright and round,   55
   Others ill-shaped and dull.

The first – pray mark – as quick as light
   Danced through the flood,
But the last, more heavy than the night,
   Nailed to the centre stood.   60
   I wondered much, but tired
     At last with thought,
My restless eye that still desired
   As strange an object brought.

It was a bank of flowers, where I descried   65
    (Though 'twas midday)
Some fast asleep, others broad-eyed
    And taking in the ray.
    Here musing long I heard
      A rushing wind   70
Which still increased, but whence it stirred
    Nowhere I could not find.

I turned me round and to each shade
    Dispatched an eye,
To see if any leaf had made   75
    Least motion or reply:
    But while I listening sought
      My mind to ease
By knowing where 'twas or where not,
    It whispered 'Where I please'.   80

    'Lord,' then said I, 'On me one breath,
    And let me die before my death.'

Cant. Cap. 5. ver. 17
Arise, O north, and come thou south wind, and blow upon my garden, that the
spices thereof may flow out.

The Retreat

Happy those early days when I
Shined in my angel-infancy;
Before I understood this place
Appointed for my second race,
Or taught my soul to fancy aught   5
But a white, celestial thought;
When yet I had not walked above
A mile or two from my first love,
And looking back, at that short space,
Could see a glimpse of His bright face;   10
When on some gilded cloud or flower
My gazing soul would dwell an hour,
And in those weaker glories spy
Some shadows of eternity;
Before I taught my tongue to wound   15
My conscience with a sinful sound,

Or had the black art to dispense
A several sin to every sense,
But felt through all this fleshy dress
Bright shoots of everlastingness.   20
    O how I long to travel back
And tread again that ancient track,
That I might once more reach that plain
Where first I left my glorious train,
From whence the enlightened spirit sees   25
That shady city of palm trees;
But (ah!) my soul with too much stay
Is drunk and staggers in the way.
Some men a forward motion love
But I by backward steps would move,   30
And when this dust falls to the urn
In that state I came return.

¶

Silence and stealth of days! 'Tis now
    Since thou art gone
Twelve hundred hours, and not a brow
    But clouds hang on.
As he that in some cave's thick damp   5
    Locked from the light,
Fixeth a solitary lamp
    To brave the night,
And, walking from his sun, when past
    That glimmering ray   10
Cuts through the heavy mists in haste
    Back to his day,
So o'er fled minutes I retreat
    Unto that hour
Which showed thee last but did defeat   15
    Thy light and power.
I search and rack my soul to see
    Those beams again,
But nothing but the snuff to me
    Appeareth plain;   20
That, dark and dead, sleeps in its known
    And common urn,
But those fled to their Maker's throne
    There shine and burn;

O could I track them! But souls must   25
   Track one the other,
And now the spirit, not the dust
   Must be thy brother.
Yet I have one pearl by whose light
   All things I see,   30
And in the heart of earth and night
   Find Heaven and thee.

Corruption

Sure it was so: man in those early days
   Was not all stone and earth;
He shined a little, and by those weak rays
   Had some glimpse of his birth.
He saw Heaven o'er his head, and knew from whence   5
   He came, condemned, hither,
And, as first love draws strongest, so from hence
   His mind sure progressed thither.
Things here were strange unto him: sweat and till,
   All was a thorn or weed.   10
Nor did those last but, like himself, died still
   As soon as they did seed:
They seemed to quarrel with him, for that act
   That fell him, foiled them all,
He drew the curse upon the world and cracked   15
   The whole frame with his fall.
This made him long for home, as loth to stay
   With murmurers and foes:
He sighed for Eden and would often say
   'Ah what bright lights were those?'   20
Nor was Heaven cold unto him, for each day
   The valley or the mountain
Afforded visits, and still Paradise lay
   In some green shade or fountain.
Angels lay lieger here: each bush and cell,   25
   Each oak and highway knew them.
Walk but the fields or sit down at some well,
   And he was sure to view them.

Almighty love! Where art thou now? Mad man
   Sits down and freezeth on: 30
He raves and swears to stir nor fire nor fan
   But bids the thread be spun.
I see thy curtains are close-drawn; thy bow
   Looks dim too in the cloud;
Sin triumphs still and man is sunk below   35
   The centre and his shroud:
All's in deep sleep and night; thick darkness lies
   And hatcheth o'er thy people:
But hark! What trumpet's that? What angel cries
   'Arise! Thrust in thy sickle'?   40

The World

I saw eternity the other night
   Like a great ring of pure and endless light,
     All calm as it was bright;
And round beneath it Time in hours, days, years,
     Driven by the spheres   5
Like a vast shadow moved, in which the world
   And all her train were hurled:
The doting lover in his quaintest strain
     Did there complain;
Near him his lute, his fancy and his flights,   10
     Wit's sour delights,
With gloves and knots, the silly snares of pleasure.
     Yet his dear treasure
All scattered lay, while he his eyes did pour
     Upon a flower.   15

The darksome statesman, hung with weights and woe,
Like a thick midnight fog moved there so slow
   He did nor stay nor go:
Condemning thoughts, like sad eclipses, scowl
     Upon his soul,   20
And clouds of crying witnesses without
   Pursued him with one shout.
Yet digged the mole and lest his ways be found
     Worked underground,

Where he did clutch his prey, but one did see   25
   That policy;
Churches and altars fed him; perjuries
    Were gnats and flies;
It rained about him blood and tears but he
   Drank them as free.   30

The fearful miser on a heap of rust
Sat pining all his life there, did scarce trust
   His own hands with the dust,
Yet would not place one piece above, but lives
   In fear of thieves.   35
Thousands there were as frantic as himself
   And hugged each one his pelf.
The downright epicure placed heaven in sense
   And scorned pretence,
While others, slipped into a wide excess,   40
   Said little less.
The weaker sort slight, trivial wares enslave
   Who think them brave,
And poor, despised truth sat counting by
   Their victory.   45

Yet some, who all this while did weep and sing,
And sing and weep, soared up into the ring,
   But most would use no wing.
'O fools,' said I, 'thus to prefer dark night
   Before true light;   50
To live in grots and caves and hate the day
   Because it shows the way;
The way which from this dead and dark abode
   Leads up to God;
A way where you might tread the sun and be   55
   More bright than he.'
But as I did their madness so discuss,
   One whispered thus:
'This ring the bridegroom did for none provide
   But for his bride.'

John Cap. 2. Ver. 16, 17
All that is in the world, the lust of the flesh, the lust of the eyes, and the pride
of life, is not of the father, but is of the world.
And the world passeth away, and the lusts thereof, but he that doth the will
of God abideth for ever.

¶

I walked the other day (to spend my hour)
    Into a field
Where I sometimes had seen the soil to yield
    A gallant flower,
But winter now had ruffled all the bower   5
    And curious store
  I knew there heretofore.

Yet I whose search loved not to peep and peer
    I' the face of things
Thought with myself there might be other springs   10
    Besides this here
Which, like cold friends, sees us but once a year,
    And so the flower
  Might have some other bower.

Then taking up what I could nearest spy   15
    I digged about
That place where I had seen him to grow out,
    And by and by
I saw the warm recluse alone to lie
    Where, fresh and green,   20
  He lived of us unseen.

Many a question intricate and rare
    Did I there strow,
But all I could extort was that he now
    Did there repair   25
Such losses as befell him in this air,
    And would ere long
  Come forth most fair and young.

This past, I threw the clothes quite o'er his head,
    And stung with fear   30
Of my own frailty, dropped down many a tear
    Upon his bed;
Then sighing whispered 'Happy are the dead!
    What peace doth now
  Rock him asleep below?'   35

And yet how few believe such doctrine springs
    From a poor root,
Which all the winter sleeps here under foot
    And hath no wings
To raise it to the truth and light of things,   40
    But is still trod
  By every wandering clod.

O Thou, whose spirit did at first inflame
    And warm the dead,
And by a sacred incubation fed   45
    With life this frame,
Which once had neither being, form, nor name,
    Grant I may so
  Thy steps track here below

That in these masques and shadows I may see   50
    Thy sacred way,
And by those hid ascents climb to that day
    Which breaks from thee
Who art in all things, though invisibly;
    Show me Thy peace,   55
  Thy mercy, love and ease,

And from this care, where dreams and sorrows reign,
    Lead me above
Where light, joy, leisure, and true comforts move
    Without all pain: 60
There, hid in thee, show me his life again
    At whose dumb urn
  Thus all the year I mourn.
              (*Silex Scintillans*, 1650)

¶

They are all gone into the world of light!
    And I alone sit lingering here:
Their very memory is fair and bright,
    And my sad thoughts doth clear.

It glows and glitters in my cloudy breast   5
   Like stars upon some gloomy grove,
Or those faint beams in which this hill is dressed
   After the sun's remove.

I see them walking in an air of glory,
   Whose light doth trample on my days;   10
My days which are at best but dull and hoary,
   Mere glimmering and decays.

O holy hope and high humility,
   High as the heavens above!
These are your walks, and you have showed them me   15
   To kindle my cold love.

Dear, beauteous death! The jewel of the just,
   Shining nowhere but in the dark:
What mysteries do lie beyond thy dust,
   Could man outlook that mark!   20

He that hath found some fledged bird's nest may know
   At first sight if the bird be flown;
But what fair well or grove he sings in now,
   That is to him unknown.

And yet, as angels in some brighter dreams   25
   Call to the soul when man doth sleep,
So some strange thoughts transcend our wonted themes
   And into glory peep.

If a star were confined into a tomb
   Her captive flames must needs burn there,   30
But when the hand that locked her up gives room
   She'll shine through all the sphere.

O father of eternal life, and all
   Created glories under thee,
Resume thy spirit from this world of thrall   35
   Into true liberty.

Either disperse these mists, which blot and fill
   My perspective, still, as they pass,
Or else remove me hence unto that hill
   Where I shall need no glass.   40

The Book

Eternal God, maker of all
That have lived here since the man's fall;
The rock of ages, in whose shade
They live unseen when here they fade!

Thou knew'st this paper when it was   5
Mere seed, and after that but grass;
Before 'twas dressed or spun, and when
Made linen who did wear it then;
What were their lives, their thoughts and deeds,
Whether good corn or fruitless weeds.   10

Thou knew'st this tree when a green shade
Covered it, since a cover made,
And where it flourished, grew and spread
As if it never should be dead.

Thou knew'st this harmless beast, when he   15
Did live and feed by thy decree
On each green thing, then slept (well fed)
Clothed with this skin, which now lies spread
A covering o'er this aged book,
Which makes me wisely weep and look   20
On my own dust – mere dust it is,
But not so dry and clean as this.
Thou knew'st and saw'st them all, and though
Now scattered thus, dost know them so.

O knowing, glorious spirit! When   25
Thou shalt restore trees, beasts and men;
When Thou shalt make all new again,
Destroying only death and pain,
Give him amongst Thy works a place
Who in them loved and sought Thy face!   30

(Silex Scintillans, 1655)

PART TWO
MISCELLANY

FULKE GREVILLE,
FIRST BARON BROOKE
(1554–1628)

From CAELICA

Sonnet 38

Caelica, I overnight was finely used,
Lodged in the midst of paradise, your heart:
Kind thoughts had charge I might not be refused,
Of every fruit and flower I had part.
But curious knowledge, blown with busy flame,   5
The sweetest fruits had down in shadows hidden,
And for it found mine eyes had seen the same,
I from my paradise was straight forbidden.
Where that cur, Rumour, runs in every place,
Barking with Care, begotten out of Fear;   10
And glassy Honour, tender of Disgrace,
Stands Seraphin to see I come not there;
   While that fine soil, which all these joys did yield,
   By broken fence is proved a common field.

Sonnet 40

The nurse-life wheat within his green husk growing,
Flatters our hope and tickles our desire,
Nature's true riches in sweet beauties showing,
Which set all hearts, with labour's love, on fire.
No less fair is the wheat when golden ear   5
Shows unto hope the joys of near enjoying:
Fair and sweet is the bud, more sweet and fair
The rose, which proves that time is not destroying.
Caelica, your youth, the morning of delight,
Enamelled o'er with beauties white and red,   10
All sense and thoughts did to belief invite,
That love and glory there are brought to bed;
   And your ripe year's love-noon (he goes no higher)
   Turns all the spirits of man into desire.

Sonnet 85

Love is the peace, whereto all thoughts do strive,
Done and begun with all our powers in one:
The first and last in us that is alive,
End of the good, and therewith pleased alone.
Perfection's spirit, goddess of the mind,   5
Passed through hope, desire, grief and fear,
A simple goodness in the flesh refined,
Which of the joys to come doth witness bear.
Constant, because it sees no cause to vary,
A quintessence of passions overthrown,   10
Raised above all that change of objects carry,
A nature by no other nature known:
    For glory's of eternity a frame,
    That by all bodies else obscures her name.

Sonnet 86

The earth with thunder torn, with fire blasted,
With waters drowned, with windy palsy shaken
Cannot for this with heavens be distasted,
Since thunder, rain and winds from earth are taken:
Man torn with love, with inward furies blasted,   5
Drowned with despair, with fleshly lustings shaken,
Cannot for this with heaven be distasted,
Love, fury, lustings out of man are taken.
Then man, endure thyself, those clouds will vanish;
Life is a top which whipping Sorrow driveth;   10
Wisdom must bear what our flesh cannot banish,
The humble lead, the stubborn bootless striveth:
    Or man, forsake thyself, to heaven turn thee,
    Her flames enlighten nature, never burn thee.

Sonnet 88

Man, dream no more of curious mysteries,
As what was here before the world was made,
The first man's life, the state of Paradise,
Where Heaven is, or Hell's eternal shade,

For God's works are like him, all infinite;   5
And curious search, but crafty sin's delight.

The flood that did, and dreadful fire that shall,
Drown, and burn up the malice of the earth,
The divers tongues, and Babylon's downfall,
Are nothing to the man's renewed birth;   10
   First, let the Law plough up thy wicked heart,
   That Christ may come, and all these types depart.

When thou hast swept the house that all is clear,
When thou the dust hast shaken from thy feet,
When God's all-might doth in thy flesh appear,   15
Then seas with streams above thy sky do meet;
   For goodness only doth God comprehend,
   Knows what was first, and what shall be the end.

CHORUSES *from* MUSTAPHA

[Eternity's Speech against Time]

What means this new-born child of planets' motion?
This finite elf of man's vain acts, and errors?   80
Whose changing wheels in all thoughts stir commotion?
And in her own face, only, bears the mirror.
   A mirror in which, since Time took her fall,
   Mankind sees ill increase; no good at all.

Because in your vast mouth you hold your tail,   85
As coupling ages past with times to come:
Do you presume your trophies shall not fail,
As both creation's cradle, and her tomb?
   Or for beyond yourself you cannot see,
   By days, and hours, would you eternal be?   90

Time is the weakest work of my creation,
And, if not still repaired, must straight decay:
The mortal take not my true constellation,
And so are dazzled, by her nimble sway,
   To think her course long; which if measured right, 95
   Is but a minute of my infinite.

A minute which doth her subsistence tie;
Subsistences which, in not being, be:
Shall is to come; and *Was* is passed by;
Time present cements this duplicity: 100
   And if one must, of force, be like the other,
   Of Nothing is not Nothing made the mother?

Why strives Time then to parallel with me?
What be her types of longest lasting glory?
Arts, mitres, laws, moments, supremacy,   105
Of Nature's erring alchemy the story:
   From Nothing sprang this point, and must, by course,
   To that confusion turn again, or worse.

For she, and all her mortal offsprings, built
Upon the moving base of self-conceit;   110
Which constant form can neither take, nor yield;
But still change shapes, to multiply deceit;
   Like playing atomi, in vain contending,
   Though they beginning had, to have no ending.

I, that at once see Time's distinct progression;   115
I, in whose bosom *Was*, and *Shall*, still be;
I, that in causes work th' effect's succession,
Giving both good, and ill, their destiny;
   Thought I bind all, yet can receive no bound;
   But see the finite still itself confound.   120

Time! therefore know thy limits, and strive not
To make thyself, or thy works infinite,
Whose essence only is to write, and blot:
Thy changes prove thou hast no 'stablished right.
   Govern thy mortal sphere, deal not with mine: 125
   Time but the servant is of Power Divine.

Chorus Sacerdotum

Oh wearisome condition of humanity!
Born under one law, to another bound:
Vainly begot, and yet forbidden vanity,
Created sick, commanded to be sound:

What meaneth Nature by these diverse laws?   5
Passion and reason, self-division cause:
Is it the mark, or majesty of power
To make offences that it may forgive?
Nature herself, doth her own self deflower,
To hate those errors she herself doth give.   10
For how should man think that, he may not do
If Nature did not fail, and punish too?
Tyrant to others, to herself unjust,
Only commands things difficult and hard;
Forbids us all things, which it knows we lust,   15
Makes easy pains, unpossible reward.
If Nature did not take delight in blood,
She would have made more easy ways to good.
We that are bound by vows, and by promotion,
With pomp of holy sacrifice and rites,   20
To teach belief in good and still devotion,
To preach of Heaven's wonders, and delights:
Yet when each of us, in his own heart looks,
He finds the God there, far unlike his books.
                    (*Certain Learned and Elegant Works*, 1633)

GEORGE CHAPMAN
(*c.* 1559–1634)

[*The Poet questions Peace*]

                    As we went
I felt a scruple, which I durst not vent,
No not to Peace herself, whom it concerned
For fear to wrong her; so well I have learned,
To shun injustice, even to doves, or flies;   170
But, to the Devil or the Destinies,
Where I am just, and know I honour Truth,
I'll speak my thoughts, in scorn of what ensu'th.
Yet (not resolved in th'other) there did shine
A beam of Homer's freer soul in mine,   175
That made me see I might propose my doubt,
Which was, if this were true Peace I found out,

That felt such passion? I proved her sad part,
And prayed her call her voice out of her heart
(There kept a wrongful prisoner to her woe)   180
To answer, why she was afflicted so,
Or how in her such contraries could fall,
That taught all joy, and was the life of all?
She answered: 'Homer told me that there are
Passions in which corruption hath no share;   185
There is a joy of soul: and why not then
A grief of soul, that is no scathe to men?
For both are passions, though not such as reign
In blood and humour, that engender pain.
Free sufferance for the truth makes sorrow sing,   190
And mourning far more sweet than banqueting.
Good, that deserveth joy (receiving ill)
Doth merit justly as much sorrow still.
And is it a corruption to do right?
Grief, that dischargeth conscience, is delight: 195
One sets the other off. To stand at gaze
In one position is a stupid maze,
Fit for a statue.' This resolved me well,
That grief, in peace, and peace in grief might dwell.
        And now fell all things from their natural birth: 200
Passion in Heaven; stupidity in earth,
Inverted all; the Muses, Virtues, Graces,
Now suffered rude and miserable chases
From men's societies, to that desert heath;
And after them, Religion (chased by Death)   205
Came weeping, bleeding to the funeral;
Sought her dear mother, Peace, and down did fall
Before her fainting on her horned knees –
Turned horn, with praying for the miseries
She left the world in, desperate in their sin;   210
Marble her knees pierced, but Heaven could not win
To stay the weighty ruin of his glory
In her sad exile. All the memory
Of Heaven and heavenly things razed of all hands:
Heaven moves so far off, that men say it stands,   215
And Earth is turned the true and moving Heaven.
And so 'tis left, and so is all truth driven
From her false bosom; all is left alone,
Till all be ordered with confusion.
                (*Euthymiae Raptus, or The Tears of Peace,* 1609)

[Ulysses leaves the Nymph Calypso]

The great-in-counsels made her this reply:
'Renowned, and to be rev'renced, Deity!
Let it not move thee, that so much I vow
My comforts to my wife; though well I know   285
All cause myself why wise Penelope
In wit is far inferior to thee,
In feature, stature, all the parts of show,
She being a mortal, an immortal thou,
Old ever growing, and yet never old.   290
Yet her desire shall all my days see told,
Adding the sight of my returning day,
And natural home. If any God shall lay
His hand upon me as I pass the seas,
I'll bear the worst of what his hand shall please, 295
As having given me such a mind as shall
The more still rise the more his hand lets fall.
In wars and waves my suff'rings were not small.
I now have suff'red much, as much before,
Hereafter let as much result, and more.'   300
    This said, the sun set, and earth shadows gave;
When these two (in an in-room of the cave,
Left to themselves) left love no rites undone.
The early Morn up, up he rose, put on
His in and out weed. She herself enchases   305
Amidst a white robe, full of all the Graces,
Ample, and pleated thick like fishy scales;
A golden girdle then her waist impales
Her head a veil decks; and abroad they come.
And now began Ulysses to go home.   310
    A great axe first she gave, that two ways cut,
In which a fair well-polished helm was put,
That from an olive bough received his frame.
A planer then. Then led she, till they came
To lofty woods that did the isle confine.   315
The fir-tree, poplar, and heaven-scaling pine,
Had there their offspring. Of which, those that were
Of driest matter, and grew longest there,
He choosed for light sail. This place thus shown,
The Nymph turned home. He fell to felling down,   320
And twenty trees he stooped in little space,
Planed, used his plumb, did all with artful grace.

In meantime did Calypso wimbles bring;
He bored, closed, nailed, and ordered every thing,
And look how much a shipwright will allow   325
A ship of burden (one that best doth know
What fits his art) so large a keel he cast,
Wrought up her decks, and hatches, sideboards, mast,
With willow watlings armed her to resist
The billows' outrage, added all she missed,   330
Sail-yards, and stern for guide. The Nymph then brought
Linen for sails, which with dispatch he wrought,
Gables, and halsters, tacklings. All the frame
In four days' space to full perfection came
The fifth day, they dismissed him from the shore,   335
Weeds neat, and odorous, gave him, victuals store,
Wine, and strong waters, and a prosp'rous wind,
To which, Ulysses (fit-to-be-divined)
His sails exposed, and hoisted. Off he gat;
And cheerful was he. At the stern he sat,   340
And steered right artfully. Nor sleep could seize
His eyelids. He beheld the Pleiades;
The Bear, surnamed the Wain, that round doth move
About Orion, and keeps still above
The billowy ocean; the slow-setting star   345
Boötes called, by some the Wagoner.

(*Homer's Odysseys*, Book V, 1614)

SIR HENRY WOTTON
(1568–1639)

On His Mistress, the Queen of Bohemia

You meaner beauties of the night,
    That poorly satisfy our eyes
More by your number than your light,
    You common people of the skies
        What are you when the sun shall rise?   5

You curious chanters of the wood
   That warble forth Dame Nature's lays,
Thinking your voices understood
    By your weak accents, what's your praise
    When Philomel her voice shall raise?   10

You violets that first appear,
   By your pure purple mantles known
Like the proud virgins of the year,
    As if the spring were all your own
    What are you when the rose is blown?   15

So, when my mistress shall be seen
   In form and beauty of her mind,
By virtue first, then choice, a queen,
    Tell me if she were not designed
    Th' eclipse and glory of her kind?   20

Upon the Sudden Restraint of the Earl of Somerset,
then Falling from Favour

Dazzled thus with height of place,
   Whilst our hopes our wits beguile,
No man marks the narrow space
   'Twixt a prison and a smile.

Then, since Fortune's favours fade,   5
   You, that in her arms do sleep,
Learn to swim and not to wade,
   For the hearts of kings are deep.

But if greatness be so blind
   As to trust in towers of air,   10
Let it be with goodness lined,
   That at least the fall be fair.

Then, though dark'ned, you shall say,
   When friends fail and princes frown,
Virtue is the roughest way   15
   But proves at night a bed of down.
                   (*Reliquiae Wottonianae*, 1651)

GEORGE SANDYS
(1578–1644)

[The death of Eurydice and Orpheus' journey to Hell]

Th' event worse than the omen; as his bride
Troops with the Naiades by Hebrus' side
A serpent bit her by the heel, which forced
Life from her hold and nuptial ties divorced.
Whom when the Thracian poet had above   5
Enough bewailed, that his complaints might move
The under shades, by Tenarus descends
To Stygian floods; and his bold steps extends,
By airy shapes and fleeting souls that boast
Of sepulture, through that unpleasant coast   10
To Pluto's court; when, having tuned his strings,
Thus to his harp the godlike poet sings:
　　'You pow'rs that sway the world beneath the earth,
The last abode of all our human birth,
If we the truth without offence may tell,   15
I come not hither to discover hell,
Nor bind that scowling cur who barking shakes
About his triple brows Medusa's snakes.
My wife this journey urged, who by the tooth
Of trod-on viper perished in her youth.   20
I would, and strove t' have borne her loss, but Love
Won in that strife – a god well-known above,
Nor here perhaps unknown. If truly fame
Report old rapes, you also felt his flame.
By these obscure abodes so full of dread,   25
By this huge chaos and deep silence spread
Through your vast empire, by these prayers of mine,
Eurydice's too-hasty fate untwine.
We all are yours, and after a short stay,
Early or late we all must run one way.   30
Hither we throng for our last home assigned,
Th' eternal habitation of mankind.

She, when her time by nature shall expire,
Again is yours; I but the use desire.
If Fate deny me this, my second choice   35
Is here t' abide: in both our deaths rejoice.'
   While thus he sung and struck the quavering strings,
The bloodless shadows wept; nor flattering springs
Tempt Tantalus, Ixion's wheel stood still,
Their urn the Belides no longer fill,   40
The vultures feed not, Tityus left to groan,
And Sisyphus sat list'ning on his stone.
The Furies, vanquished by his verse, were seen
To weep, that never wept before. Hell's Queen,
The King of Darkness yield t' his pow'rful plea.   45
Among the late-come souls Eurydice
They call; she came, yet halting of her wound;
Given Orpheus with this law: 'Till thou the bound
Of pale Avernus pass, if back thou cast
Thy careful eyes thou losest what thou hast.'   50
A steep ascent, dark, thick with fogs, they climb
Through everlasting silence; by this time
Approach the confines of illustrious light.
Fearing to lose and longing for a sight,
His eyes th' impatient lover backward threw,   55
When she, back-sliding, presently withdrew.
He catches at her, in his wits distraught,
And yielding air for her (unhappy!) caught.
Nor did she, dying twice, her spouse reprove,
For what could she complain of but his love?   60
                    (*Ovid's Metamorphoses English'd*, 1632)

Psalm 23

   The Lord my shepherd, me His sheep
   Will from consuming famine keep.
   He fosters me in fragrant meads,
   By softly sliding waters leads,
   My soul refreshed with pleasant juice,   5
   And lest they should His name traduce,
   Then when I wander in the maze
   Of tempting sin, informs my ways.

No terror can my courage quail,
Though shaded in death's gloomy veil;   10
By Thy protection fortified,
Thy staff my stay, Thy rod my guide.
My table Thou hast furnished,
Poured precious odours on my head;
My mazer flows with pleasant wine,   15
While all my foes with envy pine.
Thy mercy and beneficence
Shall ever join in my defence;
Who in Thy house will sacrifice,
Till aged Time close up mine eyes.   20
                (*A Paraphrase upon the Psalms of David*, 1636)

EDWARD,
LORD HERBERT OF CHERBURY
(1582–1648)

To His Watch, When He Could Not Sleep

Uncessant minutes, whilst you move you tell
    The time that tells our life, which though it run
Never so fast or far, your new begun
    Short steps shall overtake; for though life well
May 'scape his own account, it shall not yours: 5
    You are Death's auditors, that both divide
And sum whate'er that life inspired endures
    Past a beginning; and through you we bide
The doom of Fate, whose unrecalled decree
    You date, bring, execute, making what's new   10
Ill and good old; for as we die in you,
    You die in Time, Time in Eternity.

To Her Eyes

Black eyes, if you seem dark,
It is because your beams are deep,
And with your soul united keep.

Who could discern
Enough into them, there might learn   5
    Whence they derive that mark,
    And how their power is such
That all the wonders which proceed from thence,
    Affecting more the mind than sense,
        Are not so much   10
    The works of light as influence.

    As you then joined are
Unto the soul, so it again
By its connection doth pertain
    To that First Cause,   15
Who, giving all their proper laws,
    By you doth best declare
    How He at first b'ing hid
Within the veil of an eternal night,
    Did frame for us a second light,   20
        And after bid
    It serve for ordinary sight.

    His image then you are.
If there be any yet who doubt
What power it is that doth look out   25
    Through that your black,
He will not an example lack,
    If he suppose that there
    Were gray or hazel glass,
And that through them though sight or soul might shine, 30
    He must yet at the last define
        That beams which pass
    Through black cannot but be divine.

Sonnet Made upon the Groves near Merlou Castle

You well-compacted groves, whose light and shade,
    Mixed equally, produce nor heat nor cold,
    Either to burn the young or freeze the old,
But to one even temper being made,
Upon a green embroidering through each glade   5

An airy silver and a sunny gold,
So clothe the poorest that they do behold
Themselves in riches which can never fade;
While the wind whistles, and the birds do sing,
While your twigs clip, and while the leaves do friss,   10
While the fruit ripens which those trunks do bring,
Senseless to all but love, do you not spring
Pleasure of such a kind as truly is
A self-renewing vegetable bliss?

An Ode upon a Question Moved,
Whether Love Should Continue Forever

Having interred her infant-birth,
    The watery ground that late did mourn
    Was strewed with flowers for the return
Of the wished bridegroom of the earth.

The well-accorded birds did sing   5
    Their hymns unto the pleasant time,
    And in a sweet consorted chime
Did welcome in the cheerful spring.

To which, soft whistles of the wind,
    And warbling murmurs of a brook,   10
    And varied notes of leaves that shook,
An harmony of parts did bind.

While doubling joy unto each other,
    All in so rare consent was shown,
    No happiness that came alone,   15
Nor pleasure that was not another.

When with a love none can express,
    That mutually happy pair,
    Melander and Celinda fair,
The season with their loves did bless.   20

Walking towards a pleasant grove,
    Which did, it seemed, in new delight
    The pleasures of the time unite,
To give a triumph to their love,

They stayed at last, and on the grass   25
    Reposed so, as o'er his breast
    She bowed her gracious head to rest,
Such a weight as no burden was.

While over either's compassed waist
    Their folded arms were so composed,   30
    As if in straitest bonds enclosed,
They suffered for joys they did taste.

Long their fixed eyes to heaven bent,
    Unchanged, they did never move,
    As if so great and pure a love   35
No glass but it could represent.

When with a sweet though troubled look,
    She first brake silence, saying, 'Dear friend,
    O, that our love might take no end,
Or never had beginning took!   40

I speak not this with a false heart,'
    (Wherewith his hand she gently strained)
    'Or that would change a love maintained
With so much faith on either part.

Nay, I protest, though death with his   45
    Worst counsel should divide us here,
    His terrors could not make me fear
To come where your loved presence is.

Only if love's fire with the breath
    Of life be kindled, I doubt   50
    With our last air 'twill be breathed out,
And quenched with the cold of death.

That if affection be a line,
    Which is closed up in our last hour;
    O how 'twould grieve me, any power   55
Could force so dear a love as mine!'

She scarce had done, when his shut eyes
   An inward joy did represent,
   To hear Celinda thus intent
To a love he so much did prize.   60

Then with a look, it seemed, denied
   All earthly power but hers, yet so,
   As if to her breath he did owe
This borrowed life, he thus replied:

'O you, wherein they say souls rest,   65
   Till they descend pure heavenly fires,
   Shall lustful and corrupt desires
With your immortal seed be blessed?

And shall our love, so far beyond
   That low and dying appetite,   70
   And which so chaste desires unite,
Not hold in an eternal bond?

Is it because we should decline
   And wholly from our thoughts exclude
   Objects that may the sense delude,   75
And study only the divine?

No sure, for if none can ascend
   Even to the visible degree
   Of things created, how should we
The invisible comprehend?   80

Or rather, since that Power expressed
   His greatness in his works alone,
   Being here best in his creatures known,
Why is he not loved in them best?

But it's not true, which you pretend,   85
   That since our love and knowledge here
   Only as parts of life appear,
So they with it should take their end.

O no, beloved, I am most sure,
   Those virtuous habits we acquire,   90
   As being with the soul entire,
Must with it evermore endure.

For if, where sins and vice reside,
   We find so foul a guilt remain,
   As never dying in his stain,   95
Still punished in the soul doth bide,

Much more that true and real joy,
   Which in a virtuous love is found,
   Must be more solid in its ground,
Than fate or death can e'er destroy.   100

Else should our souls in vain elect,
   And vainer yet were heaven's laws,
   When to an everlasting cause
They gave a perishing effect.

Nor here on earth then, nor above,   105
   Our good affection can impair,
   For where God doth admit the fair,
Think you that he excludeth love?

These eyes again, then, eyes shall see,
   And hands again these hands enfold,   110
   And all chaste pleasures can be told
Shall with us everlasting be.

For if no use of sense remain
   When bodies once this life forsake,
   Or they could no delight partake,   115
Why should they ever rise again?

And if every imperfect mind
   Make love the end of knowledge here,
   How perfect will our love be, where
All imperfection is refined!   120

Let then no doubt, Celinda, touch,
　　Much less your fairest mind invade,
　　Were not our souls immortal made,
Our equal loves can make them such.

So when one wing can make no way,　　　　125
　　Two joined can themselves dilate,
　　So can two persons propagate,
When singly either would decay.

So when from hence we shall be gone,
　　And be no more, nor you, nor I,　　　　130
　　As one another's mystery,
Each shall be both, yet both but one.'

This said, in her uplifted face,
　　Her eyes which did that beauty crown,
　　Were like two stars, that having fallen down,　　135
Look up again to find their place:

While such a moveless silent peace
　　Did seize on their becalmed sense,
　　One would have thought some influence
Their ravished spirits did possess.　　　　140

(Occasional Verses, 1655)

PHINEAS FLETCHER
(1582–1650)

[The all-seeing Intellect]

The Island's Prince, of frame more than celestial,　　190
Is rightly called the all-seeing Intellect:
All glorious bright, such nothing is terrestrial,
Whose sun-like face and most divine aspect
　　No human sight may ever hope descry,
　　For when himself on's self reflects his eye　　195
Dull and amazed he stands at so bright majesty.

Look as the sun, whose ray and searching light
Here, there, and everywhere itself displays,
No nook or corner flies his piercing sight;
Yet on himself when he reflects his rays   200
   Soon back he flings the too bold venturing gleam,
   Down to the earth the flames all broken stream:
Such is this famous Prince, such his unpierced beam.

His strangest body is not bodily,
But matter without matter; never filled,   205
Nor filling; though within his compass high
All heaven and earth, and all in both, are held,
   Yet thousand thousand heavens he could contain,
   And still as empty as at first remain,
And when he takes in most, readiest to take again.   210

Though travelling all places, changing none:
Bid him soar up to heaven, and thence down throwing
The centre search, and Dis dark realm: he's gone,
Returns, arrives, before thou saw'st him going;
   And while his weary kingdom safely sleeps,   215
   All restless night he watch and warding keeps,
Never his careful head on resting pillow steeps.

In every quarter of this blessed Isle
Himself both present is, and President;
Nor once retires (ah happy realm the while,   220
That by no officer's lewd ravishment
   With greedy lust and wrong consumed art!).
   He all in all, and all in every part,
Does share to each his due, and equal dole impart.

He knows nor death, nor years, nor feeble age,   225
But as his time, his strength and vigour grows:
And when his kingdom by intestine rage
Lies broke and wasted, open to his foes,
   And battered sconce now flat and even lies,
   Sooner than thought to that great Judge he flies,   230
Who weighs him just reward of good or injuries.

For he the Judge's viceroy here is placed,
Where if he live as knowing he may die,
He never dies, but with fresh pleasures graced
Bathes his crowned head in soft eternity,   235
   Where thousand joys, and pleasures ever new,
   And blessings thicker than the morning dew,
With endless sweets rain down on that immortal crew.

There golden stars set in the crystal snow;
There dainty joys laugh at white-headed caring;   240
There day no night, delight no end shall know;
Sweets without surfeit, fullness without sparing,
   And by its spending, growing happiness.
   There God Himself in glories lavishness
Diffused in all, to all, is all full blessedness.   245

But if he here neglect his master's law,
And with those traitors 'gainst his Lord rebels,
Down to the deeps ten thousand fiends him draw:
Deeps where night, death, despair and horror dwells,
   And in worst ills, still worse expecting fears;   250
   Where fell despite for spite his bowels tears,
And still increasing grief, and torment never wears.

Prayers there are idle, death is wooed in vain;
In midst of death, poor wretches long to die;
Night without day or rest, still doubling pain,   255
Woes spending still, yet still their end less nigh;
   The soul there restless, helpless, hopeless lies,
   The body frying roars, and roaring fries:
There's life that never lives, and death that never dies.

Hence while unsettled here, he fighting reigns,   260
Shut in a tower where thousand enemies
Assault the fort; with wary care and pains
He guards all entrance, and by divers spies
   Searches into his foes' and friends' designs,
   For most he fears his subjects' wavering minds: 265
This tower then only falls when treason undermines.
                  (Canto VI, verses 28–38)

    (*The Purple Island, or The Isle of Man*, 1633)

AURELIAN TOWNSHEND
(*c*. 1583–*c*. 1651)

¶

Let not thy beauty make thee proud,
    Though princes do adore thee,
Since time and sickness were allowed
    To mow such flowers before thee.

Nor be not shy to that degree   5
    Thy friends may hardly know thee,
Nor yet so coming or so free
    That every fly may blow thee.

A state in every princely brow
    As decent is required,   10
Much more in thine, to whom they bow
    By Beauty's lightnings fired,

And yet a state so sweetly mixt
    With an attractive mildness
It may like Virtue sit betwixt   15
    The extremes of pride and vileness.

Then every eye that sees thy face
    Will in thy beauty glory,
And every tongue that wags will grace
    Thy virtue with a story.   20

¶

Though regions far divided
    And tedious tracts of time,
By my misfortune guided
    Make absence thought a crime;

Though we were set asunder   5
  As far as East from West,
Love still would work this wonder,
  Thou shouldst be in my breast.

How slow alas are paces
  Compared to thoughts that fly   10
In moment back to places
  Whole ages scarce descry.
The body must have pauses,
  The mind requires no rest.
Love needs no second causes   15
  To guide thee to my breast.

Accept in that poor dwelling
  But welcome, nothing great,
With pride no turrets swelling,
  But lowly as the seat;   20
Where, though not much delighted,
  In peace thou mayst be blest,
Unfeasted yet unfrighted
  By rivals, in my breast.

But this is not the diet   25
  That doth for glory strive;
Poor beauties seek in quiet
  To keep one heart alive.
The price of this ambition,
  That looks for such a guest,   30
Is, hopeless of fruition,
  To beat an empty breast.

See then my last lamenting:
  Upon a cliff I'll sit,
Rock Constancy presenting   35
  Till I grow part of it;
My tears a quicksand feeding,
  Whereon no foot can rest,
My sighs a tempest breeding
  About my stony breast.   40

Those arms wherein wide open
   Love's fleet was wont to put,
Shall laid across betoken
   That haven's mouth is shut.
Mine eyes no light shall cherish   45
   For ships at sea distrest,
But darkling let them perish,
   Or split against my breast.

Yet if I can discover
   When thine before it rides,   50
To show I was thy lover
   I'll smooth my ragged sides,
And so much better measure
   Afford thee than the rest,
Thou shalt have no displeasure   55
   By knocking at my breast.

                 (*Poems and Masks*, 1912)

SIR JOHN BEAUMONT
(*c.* 1583–1627)

To His Late Majesty Concerning the
True Form of English Poetry

Great king, the sovereign ruler of this land,
By whose grave care our hopes securely stand,
Since you, descending from that spacious reach,
Vouchsafe to be our master, and to teach
Your English poets to direct their lines,   5
To mix their colours, and express their signs;
Forgive my boldness that I here present
The life of Muses yielding true consent
In pondered numbers, which with ease I tried
When your judicious rules have been my guide.   10
   He makes sweet music who, in serious lines,
Light dancing tunes and heavy prose declines;

When verses like a milky torrent flow,
They equal temper in the poet show.
He paints true forms who with a modest heart   15
Gives lustre to his work, yet covers art.
Uneven swelling is no way to fame,
But solid joining of the perfect frame,
So that no curious finger there can find
The former chinks, or nails that fastly bind;   20
Yet most would have the knots of stitches seen,
And holes where men may thrust their hands between.
On halting feet the ragged poem goes
With accents neither fitting verse nor prose;
The style mine ear with more contentment fills   25
In lawyers' pleadings or physicians' bills,
For though in terms of art their skill they close,
And joy in darksome words as well as those,
They yet have perfect sense more pure and clear
Than envious Muses which sad garlands wear   30
Of dusky clouds, their strange conceits to hide
From human eyes; and, lest they should be spied
By some sharp Oedipus, the English tongue
For this their poor ambition suffers wrong.
In every language now in Europe spoke   35
By nations which the Roman Empire broke,
The relish of the Muse consists in rhyme;
One verse must meet another like a chime.
Our Saxon shortness hath peculiar grace
In choice of words fit for the ending place,   40
Which leave impression in the mind as well
As closing sounds of some delightful bell.
These must not be with disproportion lame,
Nor should an echo still repeat the same.
In many changes these may be expressed   45
But those that join most simply run the best;
Their form, surpassing far the fettered staves,
Vain care and needless repetition saves.
These outward ashes keep those inward fires
Whose heat the Greek and Roman works inspires;   50
Pure phrase, fit epithets, a sober care
Of metaphors, descriptions clear yet rare,
Similitudes contracted smooth and round,
Not vexed by learning, but with nature crowned;

Strong figures drawn from deep invention's springs,   55
Consisting less in words and more in things;
A language not affecting ancient times,
Nor Latin shreds, by which the pedant climbs;
A noble subject which the mind may lift
To easy use of that peculiar gift   60
Which poets in their raptures hold most dear,
When actions by the lively sound appear:
Give me such helps, I never will despair
But that our heads which suck the freezing air,
As well as hotter brains, may verse adorn,   65
And be their wonder, as we were their scorn.

An Epitaph upon My Dear Brother, Francis Beaumont

On Death, thy murd'rer, this revenge I take:
I slight his terror, and just question make
Which of us two the best precedence have,
Mine to this wretched world, thine to the grave.
Thou shouldst have followed me; but death, to blame,   5
Miscounted years and measured age by fame:
So dearly hast thou bought thy precious lines;
Their praise grew swiftly: so thy life declines.
Thy Muse, the hearer's queen, the reader's love,
All ears, all hearts but Death's could please and move. 10

Of My Dear Son, Gervase Beaumont

Can I, who have for others oft compiled
The songs of death, forget my sweetest child,
Which like a flower crushed with a blast is dead,
And ere full time hangs down his smiling head,
Expecting with clear hope to live anew   5
Among the angels fed with heavenly dew?
We have this sign of joy: that many days
While on the earth his struggling spirit stays,
The name of Jesus in his mouth contains
His only food, his sleep, his ease from pains.   10
O may that sound be rooted in my mind,
Of which in him such strong effect I find.

Dear Lord, receive my son, whose winning love
To me was like a friendship far above
The course of nature or his tender age,   15
Whose looks could all my bitter griefs assuage;
Let his pure soul, ordained seven years to be
In that frail body which was part of me,
Remain my pledge in heaven, as sent to show
How to this port at every step I go.   20

From BOSWORTH FIELD

[Richard III's speech]

He rides about the ranks, and strives t'inspire
Each breast with part of his unwearied fire.
To those who had his brother's servants been,
And had the wonders of his valour seen,   200
He saith: 'My fellow-soldiers, though your swords
Are sharp, and need not whetting by my words,
Yet call to mind those many glorious days
In which we treasured up immortal praise.
If when I served I ever fled from foe,   205
Fly ye from mine, let me be punished so:
But if my father, when at first he tried
How all his sons could shining blades abide,
Found me an eagle, whose undazzled eyes
Affront the beams which from the steel arise,   210
And if I now in action teach the same,
Know then ye have but changed your gen'ral's name.
Be still yourselves: ye fight against the dross
Of those that oft have run from you with loss.
How many Somersets, dissention's brands,   215
Have felt the force of our revengeful hands!
From whom this youth, as from a princely flood,
Derives his best, yet not untainted blood.
Have our assaults made Lancaster to droop?
And shall this Welshman with his ragged troop   220
Subdue the Norman and the Saxon line,
That only Merlin may be thought divine?
See what a guide these fugitives have chose!
Who, bred among the French, our ancient foes,

Forgets the English language, and the ground,   225
And knows not what our drums and trumpets sound.'
To other's minds, their willing oaths he draws,
He tells his just decrees, and healthful laws,
And makes large proffers of his future grace.
Thus having ended, with as cheerful face   230
As Nature, which his stepdame still was thought,
Could lend to one without proportion wrought,
Some with loud shouting make the valleys ring,
But most with murmur sigh 'God save the King'.

(*Bosworth Field, with a Taste of the Variety of
Other Poems*, 1629)

WILLIAM DRUMMOND OF HAWTHORNDEN
(1585–1649)

From POEMS: THE FIRST PART

Sonnet 2

I know that all beneath the moon decays,
And what by mortals in this world is brought
In time's great periods shall return to nought,
That fairest states have fatal nights and days.
I know how all the Muses' heavenly lays,   5
With toil of sprite which are so dearly bought,
As idle sounds of few or none are sought,
And that nought lighter is than airy praise.
I know frail beauty like the purple flower
To which one morn oft birth and death affords;   10
That love a jarring is of minds' accords,
Where sense and will invassal reason's power;
    Know what I list, this all can not me move,
    But that, oh me, I both must write and love!

Sonnet 11

Lamp of heaven's crystal hall that brings the hours,
Eye-dazzler, who makes the ugly night
At thine approach fly to her slumb'ry bow'rs,
And fills the world with wonder and delight;
Life of all lives, death-giver by thy flight   5
To southern pole from these six signs of ours,
Goldsmith of all the stars, with silver bright
Who moon enamels, Apelles of the flowers;
Ah! from those watery plains thy golden head
Raise up, and bring the so long lingering morn;   10
A grave, nay, hell, I find become this bed,
This bed so grievously where I am torn;
    But, woe is me! though thou now brought the day,
    Day shall but serve more sorrow to display.

From POEMS: THE SECOND PART

Sonnet 6

Sweet soul, which in the April of thy years
So to enrich the heaven mad'st poor this round,
And now with golden rays of glory crowned,
Most blest abid'st above the sphere of spheres;
If heavenly laws, alas! have not thee bound   5
From looking to this globe that all upbears,
If ruth and pity there above be found,
O deign to lend a look unto these tears.
Do not disdain, dear ghost, this sacrifice,
And though I raise not pillars to thy praise,   10
Mine offerings take; let this for me suffice,
My heart a living pyramid I raise;
    And whilst kings' tombs with laurels flourish green,
    Thine shall with myrtles and these flowers be seen.
                                        (*Poems*, 1616)

Sonnet 24: Content and Resolute

As when it happ'neth that some lovely town
Unto a barbarous besieger falls,
Who there by sword and flame himself installs,
And, cruel, it in tears and blood doth drown;
Her beauty spoiled, her citizens made thralls,   5
His spite yet so cannot her all throw down,
But that some statue, arch, fane or renown
Yet lurks unmaimed within her weeping walls:
So, after all the spoil, disgrace, and wrack,
That time, the world, and death could bring combined,   10
Amidst that mass of ruins they did make,
Safe and all scarless yet remains my mind:
   From this so high transcending rapture springs,
   That I, all else defaced, not envy kings.

Sonnet 25: Death's Last Will

More oft than once Death whispered in mine ear,
'Grave what thou hears in diamond and gold:
I am that monarch whom all monarchs fear,
Who hath in dust their far-stretched pride uprolled;
All, all is mine beneath moon's silver sphere,   5
And nought, save virtue, can my power withhold:
This, not believed, experience true thee told,
By danger late when I to thee came near.
As bugbear then my visage I did show,
That of my horrors thou right use might'st make,   10
And a more sacred path of living take:
Now still walk armed for my ruthless blow,
   Trust flattering life no more, redeem time past,
   And live each day as if it were thy last.'
                         (*Flowers of Sion*, 1630)

GILES FLETCHER
(1585/6–1623)

[Mercy pleads for Mankind]

'What hath man done that man shall not undo,
Since God to him is grown so near a kin?
Did his foe slay him? He shall slay his foe.
Hath he lost all? He all again shall win.
Is sin his master? He shall master sin.   605
    Too hardy soul with sin the field to try,
    The only way to conquer was to fly;
But thus long Death hath lived, and now Death's self shall die.

'He is a path, if any be misled;
He is a robe, if any naked be;   610
If any chance to hunger, He is bread;
If any be a bondman, He is free;
If any be but weak, how strong is He:
    To dead men life He is, to sick men health,
    To blind men sight, and to the needy wealth: 615
A pleasure without loss, a treasure without stealth.

'Who can forget, never to be forgot,
The time that all the world in slumber lies,
When, like the stars, the singing angels shot
To earth, and heaven awaked all his eyes   620
To see another Sun at midnight rise?
    On earth was never sight of pareil fame,
    For God before man like himself did frame,
But God Himself now like a mortal man became.

'A child He was and had not learned to speak   625
That with His Word the world before did make;
His mother's arms Him bore, He was so weak
That with one hand the vaults of heaven could shake.
See how small room my infant Lord doth take,
    Whom all the world is not enough to hold.   630
    Who of His years or of His age hath told?
Never such age so young, never a child so old.

'And yet bu newly He was infanted,
And yet already He was sought to die;
Yet scarcely born, already banished,   635
Not able yet to go, and forced to fly;
   But scarcely fled away when by and by
     The tyrant's sword with blood is all defiled,
    And Rachel, for her sons with fury wild,
Cries, "O thou cruel king" and "O my sweetest child."   640

'Egypt his nurse became, where Nilus springs,
Who straight to entertain the rising sun
The hasty harvest in his bosom brings;
But now for drieth the fields were all undone,
And now with waters all is overrun,   645
   So fast the Cynthian mountains poured their snow
    When once they felt the sun so near them glow
That Nilus Egypt lost, and to a sea did grow.

'The angels carolled loud their song of peace;
The cursed oracles were strucken dumb;   650
To see their Shepherd the poor shepherds press;
To see their King the kingly sophies come;
And them to guide unto his Master's home
   A star comes dancing up the orient,
    That springs for joy over the strawy tent,   655
Where gold, to make their Prince a crown, they all present.

'Young John, glad child, before he could be born
Leapt in the womb, his joy to prophesy;
Old Anna, though with age all spent and worn,
Proclaims her Saviour to posterity;   660
And Simeon fast his dying notes doth ply.
   O how the blessed souls about him trace:
    It is the fire of heaven thou dost embrace.
Sing, Simeon, sing! sing, Simeon, sing apace!'

With that the mighty thunder dropped away   665
From God's unwary arm, now milder grown
And melted into tears, as if to pray
For pardon and for pity it had known,
That should have been for sacred vengeance thrown.
   Thereto the armies angelic devowed   670
    Their former rage, and all to Mercy bowed;
Their broken weapons at her feet they gladly strowed.

Bring, bring, ye Graces, all your silver flaskets,
Painted with every choicest flower that grows,
That I may soon unflower your fragrant baskets   675
To strow the fields with odours where He goes;
Let whatsoe'er He treads on be a rose.
 So down she let her eyelids fall, to shine
 Upon the rivers of bright Palestine,
Whose woods drop honey, and her rivers skip with wine.   680
                    (Canto I, verses 76–85)

                (*Christ's Victory and Triumph*, 1610)

WILLIAM BROWNE OF TAVISTOCK
(*c.* 1590–*c.* 1645)

BOOK II: THE SECOND SONG

 The Muses' friend (grey-eyed Aurora) yet
Held all the meadows in a cooling sweat,
The milk-white gossamers not upwards snowed,
Nor was the sharp and useful-steering goad
Laid on the strong-necked ox; no gentle bud   5
The sun had dried; the cattle chewed the cud
Low levelled on the grass; no fly's quick sting
Enforced the stonehorse in a furious ring
To tear the passive earth, nor lash his tail
About his buttocks broad; the slimy snail   10
Might on the wainscot, by his many mazes,
Winding meanders and self-knitting traces,
Be followed where he stuck, his glittering slime
Not yet wiped off. It was so early time,
The careful smith had in his sooty forge   15
Kindled no coal; nor did his hammers urge
His neighbours' patience: owls abroad did fly,
And day as then might plead his infancy.
Yet of fair Albion all the western swains
Were long since up, attending on the plains   20
When Nereus' daughter with her mirthful host
Should summon them on their declining coast.

But since her stay was long, for fear the sun
Should find them idle, some of them begun
To leap and wrestle, others threw the bar;   25
Some from the company removed are
To meditate the songs they meant to play,
Or make a new round for next holiday.
Some tales of love their lovesick fellows told:
Others were seeking stakes to pitch their fold.   30
This, all alone was mending of his pipe:
That, for his lass sought fruits most sweet, most ripe.
Here from the rest a lovely shepherd's boy
Sits piping on a hill, as if his joy
Would still endure, or else that age's frost   35
Should never make him think what he had lost.
Yonder a shepherdess knits by the springs,
Her hands still keeping time to what she sings:
Or seeming, by her song, those fairest hands
Were comforted in working. Near the sands   40
Of some sweet river sits a musing lad,
That moans the loss of what he sometime had,
His love by death bereft: when fast by him
An aged swain takes place, as near the brim
Of 's grave as of the river, showing how   45
That as those floods, which pass along right now,
Are followed still by others from their spring,
And in the sea have all their burying:
Right so our times are known, our ages found,
(Nothing is permanent within this round,)   50
One age is now, another that succeeds,
Extirping all things which the former breeds:
Another follows that, doth new times raise,
New years, new months, new weeks, new hours, new days,
Mankind thus goes like rivers from their spring,   55
And in the earth have all their burying.
Thus sat the old man counselling the young;
Whilst, underneath a tree which overhung
The silver stream (as some delight it took
To trim his thick boughs in the crystal brook)   60
Were set a jocund crew of youthful swains,
Wooing their sweetings with delicious strains.
Sportive Oreades the hills descended,
The Hamadryades their hunting ended,

And in the high woods left the long-lived harts   65
To feed in peace, free from their winged darts;
Floods, mountains, valleys, woods, each vacant lies
Of nymphs that by them danced their haydigyes:
For all those powers were ready to embrace
The present means to give our shepherds grace.   70
                    (*Britannia's Pastorals*, 1613–16)

In Obitum M.S., X° Maii 1614

May, be thou never graced with birds that sing,
        Nor Flora's pride!
In thee all flowers and roses spring;
        Mine only died.

On the Countess Dowager of Pembroke

Underneath this sable hearse
Lies the subject of all verse:
Sidney's sister, Pembroke's mother.
Death, ere thou hast slain another
Fair and learned and good as she,   5
Time shall throw a dart at thee.

Marble piles let no man raise
To her name, for after days;
Some kind woman born as she,
Reading this, like Niobe   10
Shall turn marble, and become
Both her mourner and her tomb.
                    (*Lansdowne MS*)

HENRY KING
(1592–1669)

The Exequy

Accept, thou shrine of my dead saint,
Instead of dirges, this complaint;
And for sweet flowers to crown thy hearse,
Receive a strew of weeping verse
From thy grieved friend, whom thou might'st see   5
Quite melted into tears for thee.

Dear loss! since thy untimely fate
My task hath been to meditate
On thee, on thee; thou art the book,
The library whereon I look,   10
Though almost blind. For thee, loved clay,
I languish out, not live, the day,
Using no other exercise
But what I practise with mine eyes;
By which wet glasses I find out   15
How lazily time creeps about
To one that mourns; this, only this,
My exercise and business is.
So I compute the weary hours
With sighs dissolved into showers.   20

Nor wonder if my time go thus
Backward and most preposterous;
Thou hast benighted me; thy set
This eve of blackness did beget,
Who wast my day, though overcast   25
Before thou hadst thy noontide passed;
And I remember must in tears,
Thou scarce hadst seen so many years
As day tells hours. By thy clear sun
My love and fortune first did run;   30

But thou wilt never more appear
Folded within my hemisphere,
Since both thy light and motion
Like a fled star is fall'n and gone;
And 'twixt me and my soul's dear wish   35
An earth now interposed is,
Which such a strange eclipse doth make
As ne'er was read in almanac.

I could allow thee for a time
To darken me and my sad clime;   40
Were it a month, a year, or ten,
I would thy exile live till then,
And all that space my mirth adjourn,
So thou wouldst promise to return,
And putting off thy ashy shroud,   45
At length disperse this sorrow's cloud.

But woe is me! the longest date
Too narrow is to calculate
These empty hopes; never shall I
Be so much blest as to descry   50
A glimpse of thee, till that day come
Which shall the earth to cinders doom,
And a fierce fever must calcine
The body of this world like thine,
My little world. That fit of fire   55
Once off, our bodies shall aspire
To our souls' bliss; then we shall rise
And view ourselves with clearer eyes
In that calm region where no night
Can hide us from each other's sight.   60

Meantime, thou hast her, earth; much good
May my harm do thee. Since it stood
With Heaven's will I might not call
Her longer mine, I give thee all
My short-lived right and interest   65
In her whom living I loved best;
With a most free and bounteous grief,
I give thee what I could not keep.

Be kind to her, and prithee look
Thou write into thy doomsday book   70
Each parcel of this rarity
Which in thy casket shrined doth lie.
See that thou make thy reck'ning straight,
And yield her back again by weight;
For thou must audit on thy trust   75
Each grain and atom of this dust,
As thou wilt answer Him that lent,
Not gave thee, my dear monument.

So close the ground, and 'bout her shade
Black curtains draw; my bride is laid.   80

Sleep on, my love, in thy cold bed,
Never to be disquieted!
My last good-night! Thou wilt not wake
Till I thy fate shall overtake;
Till age, or grief, or sickness must   85
Marry my body to that dust
It so much loves, and fill the room
My heart keeps empty in thy tomb.
Stay for me there, I will not fail
To meet thee in that hollow vale.   90
And think not much of my delay;
I am already on the way,
And follow thee with all the speed
Desire can make, or sorrows breed.
Each minute is a short degree,   95
And ev'ry hour a step towards thee.
At night when I betake to rest,
Next morn I rise nearer my west
Of life, almost by eight hours' sail,
Than when sleep breathed his drowsy gale.   100

Thus from the sun my bottom steers,
And my day's compass downward bears;
Nor labour I to stem the tide
Through which to thee I swiftly glide.

'Tis true, with shame and grief I yield,   105
Thou like the van first took'st the field,

And gotten hath the victory
In thus adventuring to die
Before me, whose more years might crave
A just precedence in the grave.   110
But hark! my pulse like a soft drum
Beats my approach, tells thee I come;
And slow howe'er my marches be,
I shall at last sit down by thee.

The thought of this bids me go on,   115
And wait my dissolution
With hope and comfort. Dear, forgive
The crime, I am content to live
Divided, with but half a heart,
Till we shall meet and never part.   120

The Anniverse: An Elegy

So soon grown old! Hast thou been six years dead,
Poor earth, once by my love inhabited?
And must I live to calculate the time
To which thy blooming youth could never climb,
But fell in the ascent? Yet have not I   5
Studied enough thy loss's history?

How happy were mankind if Death's strict laws
Consumed our lamentations like the cause!
Or that our grief, turning to dust, might end
With the dissolved body of a friend!   10

But sacred heaven, O how just thou art
In stamping Death's impression on that heart
Which through thy favours would grow insolent
Were it not physicked by sharp discontent.
If, then, it stand resolved in thy decree   15
That still I must doomed to a desert be
Sprung out of my lone thoughts, which know no path
But what my own misfortune beaten hath;
If thou wilt bind me living to a corse
And I must slowly waste, I then of force   20
Stoop to thy great appointment, and obey
That will, which nought avails me to gainsay.

For whilst in sorrow's maze I wander on,
I do but follow life's vocation.
Sure we were made to grieve: at our first birth   25
With cries we took possession of the earth;
And though the lucky man reputed be
Fortune's adopted son, yet only he
Is Nature's true-born child who sums his years
(Like me) with no arithmetic, but tears.   30

The Surrender

My once dear love, hapless that I no more
Must call thee so, the rich affection's store
That fed our hopes lies now exhaust and spent,
Like sums of treasure unto bankrupts lent.

We that did nothing study but the way   5
To love each other, with which thoughts the day
Rose with delight to us, and with them set,
Must learn the hateful art how to forget.

We that did nothing wish that Heav'n could give
Beyond ourselves, nor did desire to live   10
Beyond that wish, all these now cancel must
As if not writ in faith, but words and dust.

Yet witness those clear vows which lovers make,
Witness the chaste desires that never brake
Into unruly heats; witness that breast   15
Which in thy bosom anchored his whole rest,
'Tis no default in us; I dare acquite
Thy maiden faith, thy purpose fair and white
As thy pure self. Cross planets did envy
Us to each other, and Heav'n did untie   20
Faster than vows could bind. Oh, that the stars,
When lovers meet, should stand opposed in wars!

Since, then, some higher destinies command,
Let us not strive, nor labour to withstand
What is past help. The longest date of grief   25
Can never yield a hope of our relief;

And though we waste ourselves in moist laments,
Tears may drown us, but not our discontents.

Fold back our arms, take home our fruitless loves.
That must new fortunes try, like turtledoves   30
Dislodged from their haunts. We must in tears
Unwind a love knit up in many years.
In this last kiss I here surrender thee
Back to thyself, so thou again art free;
Thou in another, sad as that, resend   35
The truest heart that lover e'er did lend.

Now turn from each. So fare our severed hearts
As the divorced soul from her body parts.
        (*Poems, Elegies, Paradoxes and Sonnets*, 1657)

JAMES SHIRLEY
(1596–1666)

Io!

You virgins that did late despair
    To keep your wealth from cruel men,
Tie up in silk your careless hair,
    Soft peace is come again.

Now lovers' eyes may gently shoot   5
    A flame that will not kill:
The drum was angry, but the lute
    Shall whisper what you will.

Sing Io! Io! for his sake,
    Who hath restored your drooping heads,   10
With choice of sweetest flowers make
    A garden where he treads.

Whilst we whole groves of laurel bring,
   A petty triumph to his brow,
Who is the master of our spring,   15
   And all the bloom we owe.

(Poems, 1646)

¶

The glories of our blood and state
   Are shadows, not substantial things;
There is no armour against fate;
   Death lays his icy hand on kings.
      Sceptre and crown   5
      Must tumble down,
And in the dust be equal made
With the poor crooked scythe and spade.

Some men with swords may reap the field,
   And plant fresh laurels where they kill;   10
But their strong nerves at last must yield;
   They tame but one another still.
      Early or late,
      They stoop to fate,
And must give up their murmuring breath,   15
When they, pale captives, creep to death.

The garlands wither on your brow,
   Then boast no more your mighty deeds;
Upon death's purple altar now,
   See where the victor–victim bleeds.   20
      Your heads must come
      To the cold tomb;
Only the actions of the just
Smell sweet and blossom in their dust.

(Ajax and Ulysses, 1659)

RALPH KNEVET
(1601–72)

The Passion

Who can review, without a precious loss
Of tears, the bitter sorrows of Thy cross
    (Oh dearest Lord)
    Whose corpse was gored
In every member by remorseless steel,   5
That we (thy members) might not Tophet feel:
    Thy feet (Oh God)
    Which never trod
In sinful paths, with bloody nails were pierced,
Because we in ungodly ways were versed;   10
    Thy hands most pure
    Were forced t'endure
The self-same pains, because our hands have been
Vile instruments of wickedness and sin;
    Thy temples blest   15
    With thorns were prest,
Because we have, upon our pillows soft,
Mischievous stratagems imagined oft;
    Thy heart most just
    And free from lust,   20
Was wounded too, because our hearts most evil
Through pride and lust were censers for the devil.
    What I express
    Must needs be less
Than thy sharp pains, for the whole continent   25
Of thy chaste corpse was into one wound rent;
    Who can reflect
    With dry aspect
Upon thy torments? Oh, that I could weep
Till I did swim in my repentance deep,   30
    Since for my guilt
    Thy blood was spilt.

But I am whelmed in sorrows and in fears,
Because I cannot drown my sins in tears.
What shall I say?   35
I thus will pray:
As blood and water issued from thy wound,
So with thy blood, do Thou my tears compound.

(*Shorter Poems*, 1966)

WILLIAM STRODE
(1602–45)

On the Death of Mistress Mary Prideaux

Weep not because this child hath died so young,
But weep because yourselves have lived so long.
Age is not filled by growth of time, for then
What old man lives to see th'estate of men?
Who sees the age of grand Methusalem?   5
Ten years make us as old as hundreds him.
Ripeness is from ourselves, and then we die
When nature hath obtained maturity.
Summer and winter fruits there be, and all
Not at one time, but being ripe, must fall.   10
Death did not err; your mourners are beguiled:
She died more like a mother than a child.
Weigh the composure of her pretty parts:
Her gravity in childhood, all her arts
Of womanly behaviour; weigh her tongue,   15
So wisely measured, not too short nor long.
Add only to the growth some inches more,
She took up now what due was at threescore.
She lived seven years, our age's first degree:
Journeys at first step ended happy be.   20
Yet, take her stature with the age of man,
They well are fitted: both are but a span.

On Westwell Downs

When Westwell Downs I gan to tread,
Where cleanly winds the green do sweep,
Methought a landscape there was spread,
Here a bush and there a sheep;
    The pleated wrinkles on the face   5
    Of wave-swollen earth did lend such grace
    As shadows do in imagery,
    Which both deceive and please the eye.

The sheep sometimes do tread a maze
By often winding in and in,   10
And sometimes round about they trace
Which milkmaids call a fairy ring;
    Such semicircles they have run,
    Such lines across so lively spun,
    That shepherds learn whene'er they please   15
    A new geometry with ease.

The slender food upon the down
Is always even, always bare,
Which neither spring nor winter's frown
Can aught improve or aught impair;   20
    Such is the barren eunuch's chin,
    Which thus doth evermore begin
    With tender down to be o'ercast,
    Which never comes to hair at last.

Here and there two hilly crests   25
Amidst them hug a pleasant green,
And these are like two swelling breasts
That close a tender fall between.
    Here could I read, or sleep, or pray,
    From early morn till flight of day;   30
    But hark! a sheep's bell calls me up,
    Like Oxford college bells, to sup.

                                 (*Poetical Works*, 1907)

On Chloris Walking in the Snow

I saw fair Chloris walk alone
Where feathered rain came softly down,
Then Jove descended from his tower
To court her in a silver shower;
The wanton snow flew to her breast   5
Like little birds into their nest,
But overcome with whiteness there
For grief it thawed into a tear,
Then falling down her garment hem
To deck her, froze into a gem.   10

(*Parnassus Biceps*, 1656)

OWEN FELLTHAM
(*c*. 1604–1668)

¶

When, dearest, I but think on thee,
Methinks all things that lovely be
Are present, and my soul delighted:
    For beauties that from worth arise
    Are, like the grace of deities,   5
Still present with us, though unsighted.

Thus while I sit and sigh the day
With all his spreading lights away,
Till night's black wings do overtake me:
    Thinking on thee, thy beauties then,   10
    As sudden lights do sleeping men,
So they by their bright rays awake me.

Thus absence dies, and dying proves
No absence can consist with loves
That do partake of fair perfection: 15
    Since in the darkest night they may
    By their quick motion find a way
To see each other by reflection.

The waving sea can with such flood
Bathe some high palace that hath stood   20
Far from the main up in the river:
　O think not then but love can do
　As much, for that's an ocean too,
That flows not every day, but ever.

On the Duke of Buckingham, slain by Felton, the 23rd August, 1628

Sooner I may some fixed statue be
Than prove forgetful of thy death or thee!
Canst thou be gone so quickly? Can a knife
Let out so many titles and a life?
　Now I'll mourn thee! Oh that so huge a pile   5
Of state should pash thus in so small a while!
Let the rude Genius of the giddy train
Brag in a fury that they have stabbed Spain,
Austria and the skipping French, yea all
Those home-bred papists that would sell our fall;   10
Th'eclipse of two wise princes' judgements; more,
The waste whereby our land was still kept poor.
I'll pity yet at least thy fatal end,
Shot like a lightning from a violent hand,
Taking thee hence unsummed. Thou art to me   15
The great example of mortality,
And when the times to come shall want a name
To startle greatness, here is Buckingham
Fall'n like a meteor. And 'tis hard to say
Whether it was that went the stranger way,   20
Thou or the hand that slew thee: thy estate
Was high, and he was resolute above that.
Yet since I hold of none engaged to thee,
Death and that liberty shall make me free.
Thy mists I knew not: if thou hadst a fault,   25
My charity shall leave it in the vault,
There for thine own accounting; 'tis undue
To speak ill of the dead, though it be true.
And this even those that envied thee confess,
Thou hadst a mind, a flowing nobleness,   30

A fortune, friends, and such proportion
As call for sorrow to be thus undone.
  Yet should I speak the vulgar, I should boast
Thy bold assassinate and wish almost
He were no Christian, that I up might stand   35
To praise th'intent of his misguided hand.
And sure when all the patriots in the shade
Shall rank, and their full musters there be made,
He shall sit next to Brutus, and receive
Such bays as heath'nish ignorance can give.   40
But then the Christian, poising that, shall say
Though he did good, he did it the wrong way:
They oft decline into the worst of ill
That act the people's wish without law's will.

(Lusoria, 1661)

THOMAS RANDOLPH
(1605–35)

A Gratulatory to Mr Ben Jonson
for His Adopting of Him to be His Son

I was not born to Helicon, nor dare
Presume to think myself a Muse's heir.
I have no title to Parnassus hill,
Nor any acre of it by the will
Of a dead ancestor, nor could I be   5
Aught but a tenant unto poetry.
But thy adoption quits me of all fear,
And makes me challenge a child's portion there.
I am akin to heroes, being thine,
And part of my alliance is divine.   10
Orpheus, Musaeus, Homer too, beside
Thy brothers by the Roman mother's side,
As Ovid, Virgil, and the Latin lyre
That is so like thy Horace – the whole choir
Of poets are by thy adoption all   15
My uncles; thou hast given me power to call

Phoebus himself my grandsire; by this grant
Each sister of the Nine is made my aunt.
Go, you that reckon from a large descent
Your lineal honours, and are well content   20
To glory in the age of your great name,
Though on a herald's faith you build the same,
I do not envy you, nor think you blest
Though you may bear a gorgon on your crest
By direct line from Perseus; I will boast   25
No farther than my father; that's the most
I can, or should be proud of, and I were
Unworthy his adoption if that here
I should be dully modest; boast I must,
Being son of his adoption, not his lust.   30
And to say truth, that which is best in me
May call you father, 'twas begot by thee.
Have I a spark of that celestial flame
Within me, I confess I stole the same,
Prometheus-like, from thee; and may I feed   35
His vulture when I dare deny the deed.
Many more moons thou hast that shine by night,
All bankrupts, were 't not for a borrowed light,
Yet can forswear it; I the debt confess
And think my reputation ne'er the less.   40
For father, let me be resolved by you:
Is 't a disparagement from rich Peru
To ravish gold, or theft, for wealthy ore
To ransack Tagus', or Pactolus' shore?
Or does he wrong Alcinous, that for want   45
Doth take from him a sprig or two to plant
A lesser orchard? Sure it cannot be;
Nor is it theft to steal some flames from thee.
Grant this, and I'll cry, Guilty, as I am,
And pay a filial reverence to thy name.   50
For when my muse upon obedient knees
Asks not a father's blessing, let her leese
The fame of this adoption; 'tis a curse
I wish her, 'cause I cannot think a worse.
And here, as piety bids me, I entreat   55
Phoebus to lend thee some of his own heat
To cure thy palsy, else I will complain
He has no skill in herbs; poets in vain

Make him the god of physic. 'Twere his praise
To make thee as immortal as thy bays,   60
As his own Daphne; 'twere a shame to see
The god not love his priest more than his tree.
   But if heaven take thee, envying us thy lyre,
   'Tis to pen anthems for an angels' choir.

A Parley with His Empty Purse

Purse, who'll not know you have a poet's been,
When he shall look and find no gold herein?
What respect (think you) will there now be shown
To this foul nest when all the birds are flown?
Unnatural vacuum, can your emptiness   5
Answer to some slight questions, such as these?
How shall my debts be paid? or can my scores
Be cleared with verses to my creditors?
Hexameter's no sterling, and I fear
What the brain coins goes scarce for current there: 10
Can metre cancel bonds? Is here a time
Ever to hope to wipe out chalk with rhyme?
Or if I now were hurrying to the jail,
Are the nine Muses held sufficient bail?
Would they to any composition come,   15
If we should mortgage our Elysium,
Tempe, Parnassus, and the golden streams
Of Tagus and Pactolus: those rich dreams
Of active fancy? Can our Orpheus move
Those rocks and stones with his best strains of love? 20
Should I (like Homer) sing in lofty tones
To them Achilles and his myrmidons!
Hector and Ajax are but sergeant's names,
They relish basalt 'bove the epigrams
Of the most seasoned brain; nor will they be   25
Content with ode, or paid with elegy.
Muse, burn thy bays, and thy fond quill resign,
One cross of theirs is worth whole books of mine.
Of all the treasure which the poets hold
There's none at all they weigh, except our gold;   30

And mine's returned to th' Indies, and hath swore
Never to visit this cold climate more.
Then crack your strings, good purse, for you need none!
Gape on, as they do to be paid, gape on!

On a Maid of Honour Seen by a Scholar
in Somerset Garden

As once in black I disrespected walked,
Where glittering courtiers in their tissues stalked,
I cast by chance my melancholy eye
Upon a woman (as I thought) passed by.
But when I viewed her muff, and beaver reared   5
As if Priapus-like she would have feared
The ravenous Harpies from the clustered grape,
Then I began much to mistrust her shape;
When viewing curiously, away she slipped,
And in a fount her whited hand she dipped,   10
The angry water as if wronged thereby,
Ran murmuring thence a second touch to fly,
At which away she stalks, and as she goes
She views the situation of each rose;
And having higher raised her gown, she gazed   15
Upon her crimson stocking which, amazed,
Blushed at her open impudence, and sent
Reflection to her cheek, for punishment.
As thus I stood the gardener chanced to pass,
'My friend' (quoth I) 'what is this stately lass?'   20
'A maid of honour, Sir,' said he, and goes
Leaving a riddle, was enough to pose
The crafty Oedipus, for I could see
Nor maid, nor honour, sure no honesty.
(*Poems, with the Muses' Looking-glass and Amyntas*, 1638)

WILLIAM HABINGTON
(1605–54)

To the World: the Perfection of Love

You who are earth and cannot rise
   Above your sense,
Boasting the envied wealth which lies
Bright in your mistress' lips or eyes,
Betray a pitied eloquence.   5

That which doth join our souls, so light
   And quick doth move
That like the eagle in his flight
It doth transcend all human sight,
Lost in the element of love.   10

You poets reach not this who sing
   The praise of dust
But kneaded, when by theft you bring
The rose and lily from the spring
T' adorn the wrinkled face of lust.   15

When we speak love, nor art nor wit
   We gloss upon;
Our souls engender and beget
Ideas, which you counterfeit
In your dull propagation.   20

While Time seven ages shall disperse
   We'll talk of love,
And when our tongues hold no commerce
Our thoughts shall mutually converse,
And yet the blood no rebel prove.   25

And though we be of several kind
   Fit for offence,
Yet we are so by love refined,
From impure dross we are all mind;
Death could not more have conquered sense.   30

How suddenly those flames expire
    Which scorch our clay;
Prometheus-like, when we steal fire
From heaven, 'tis endless and entire;
It may know age, but not decay.   35

Against Them Who Lay Unchastity to the
Sex of Women

They meet but with unwholesome springs,
And summers which infectious are;
They hear but when the mermaid sings,
And only see the falling star,
        Who ever dare   5
Affirm no woman chaste and fair.

Go cure your fevers, and you'll say
The dog days scorch not all the year;
In copper mines no longer stay,
But travel to the West, and there   10
        The right ones see,
And grant all gold's not alchemy.

What madman, 'cause the glow-worm's flame
Is cold, swears there's no warmth in fire?
'Cause some make forfeit of their name,   15
And slave themselves to man's desire,
        Shall the sex free
From guilt, damned to the bondage be?

Nor grieve Castara, though 'twere frail,
Thy virtue then would brighter shine   20
When thy example should prevail,
And every woman's faith be thine:
        And were there none,
'Tis majesty to rule alone.

'Nox nocti indicat scientiam.' David

When I survey the bright
   Celestial sphere,
So rich with jewels hung that night
Doth like an Ethiop bride appear,

My soul her wings doth spread   5
   And heavenward flies,
Th' Almighty's mysteries to read
In the large volumes of the skies.

For the bright firmament
   Shoots forth no flame   10
So silent, but is eloquent
In speaking the Creator's name.

No unregarded star
   Contracts its light
Into so small a character,   15
Removed far from our human sight,

But if we steadfast look,
   We shall discern
In it, as in some holy book,
How man may heavenly knowledge learn.   20

It tells the conqueror
   That far-stretched power
Which his proud dangers traffic for,
Is but the triumph of an hour;

That from the farthest north   25
   Some nation may,
Yet undiscovered, issue forth
And o'er his new-got conquest sway.

Some nation yet shut in
   With hills of ice   30
May be let out to scourge his sin
Till they shall equal him in vice.

And then they likewise shall
　　Their ruin have;
For as yourselves, your empires fall,   35
And every kingdom hath a grave.

Thus those celestial fires,
　　Though seeming mute,
The fallacy of our desires
And all the pride of life confute.   40

For they have watched since first
　　The world had birth;
And found sin in itself accurst,
And nothing permanent on earth.

(*Castara*, 1640)

SIR WILLIAM D'AVENANT
(1606–68)

For the Lady Olivia Porter.
A Present upon a New Year's Day

Go! hunt the whiter ermine, and present
His wealthy skin as this day's tribute sent
To my Endymion's love; though she be far
More gently smooth, more soft, than ermines are!
Go! climb that rock, and when thou there hast found   5
A star, contracted in a diamond,
Give it Endymion's love, whose glorious eyes
Darken the starry jewels of the skies!
Go! dive into the Southern Sea, and when
Th'ast found, to trouble the nice sight of men,   10
A swelling pearl, and such whose single worth
Boasts all the wonders which the seas bring forth,
Give it Endymion's love, whose ev'ry tear
Would more enrich the skilful jeweller.
How I command! how slowly they obey!   15
The churlish Tartar will not hunt today;

Nor will that lazy sallow Indian strive
To climb the rock, nor that dull Negro dive.
Thus poets, like to kings by trust deceived,
Give oftener what is heard of than received.   20

(*Madagascar, with Other Poems*, 1638)

The Mistress

When Nature heard men thought her old,
    Her skill in beauteous forms decayed,
Her eyes grown dim, and fingers cold,
    Then to her poet thus she said:

'Catch as it falls the Scythian snow   5
    Bring blushing roses steeped in milk;
From early meadows scent and show,
    And from the Persian worm her silk.

Fetch from the East the morning's breath;
    And from the Phoenix gums and spice,   10
Such as she calls when at her death,
    The world does smell her sacrifice.'

Nature of these a mistress made;
    But would have formed a Lover too;
And such as might this nymph persuade,   15
    To all that love for love should do.

This second work she well began,
    With leisure, and by slow degrees;
But found it hard to make a man,
    That could so choice a beauty please.   20

She wrought, and wrought, and then gave o'er;
    Then did another model try;
But less contented than before,
    She laid the work for ever by.

I asked the cause, and straight she said: 25
    ''Tis very possible I find,
To match the body which I made,
    But I can never fit her mind.

For that still various seems and strange;
   And since all lovers various be,   30
And apt as mistresses to change,
   I cannot make my work agree.

Now sexes meet not by design
   When they the world's chief work advance;
But in the dark they sometimes join,   35
   As wandering atoms meet by chance.'

'Goddess,' I cried, 'pray pardon me!
   You little know our lovers hearts.
The Devil take 'em! they agree!
   And, nature failing, want no arts.'   40
          (*Poems on Several Occasions*, 1672)

¶

My lodging it is on the cold ground,
   And very hard is my fare,
But that which troubles me most, is
   The unkindness of my dear.
Yet still I cry, 'O turn love,'   5
   And I prithee love turn to me,
For thou art the man that I long for,
   And alack, what remedy.

I'll crown thee with a garland of straw then,
   And I'll marry thee with a rush ring,   10
My frozen hopes shall thaw then,
   And merrily we will sing,
O turn to me my dear love,
   And prithee love turn to me,
For thou art the man that alone canst   15
   Procure my Liberty.

But if thou wilt harden thy heart still,
   And be deaf to my pitiful moan,
Then I must endure the smart still,
   And tumble in straw alone.   20

Yet still I cry, 'O turn love,'
  And I prithee love turn to me,
For thou art the man that alone art
  The cause of my misery.

(The Rivals, 1668)

EDMUND WALLER
(1606–87)

Song

  Go lovely rose,
Tell her that wastes her time and me
  That now she knows
When I resemble her to thee
  How sweet and fair she seems to be.   5

  Tell her that's young
And shuns to have her graces spied,
  That hadst thou sprung
In deserts where no men abide
  Thou must have uncommended died.   10

  Small is the worth
Of beauty from the light retired;
  Bid her come forth,
Suffer herself to be desired,
  And not blush so to be admired.   15

  Then die that she
The common fate of all things rare
  May read in thee;
How small a part of time they share,
  That are so wond'rous sweet and fair.   20

Puerperium

You gods that have the power,
   To trouble and compose
  All that's beneath your bower,
Calm silence on the seas, on earth impose.

Fair Venus in thy soft arms   5
   The god of rage confine,
  For thy whispers are the charms
Which only can divert his fierce design.

What though he frown and to tumult do incline,
   Thou the flame   10
  Kindled in his breast canst tame,
With that snow which unmelted lies on thine!

Great goddess give this thy sacred island rest;
   Make heaven smile,
  That no storm disturb us while   15
Thy chief care, our halcyon, builds her nest.

  Great Gloriana, fair Gloriana,
Bright as high heaven is, and fertile as earth,
   Whose beauty relieves us,
   Whose royal bed gives us   20
   Both glory and peace,
Our present joy and our hopes increase.
                 (*Poems*, 1645)

From *A Panegyric to My Lord Protector*

While with a strong and yet a gentle hand
You bridle faction and our hearts command,
Protect us from ourselves and from the foe,
Make us unite and make us conquer too.

Let partial spirits still aloud complain,   5
Think themselves injured that they cannot reign,
And own no liberty but where they may
Without control upon their fellows prey.

Above the waves as Neptune showed his face,
To chide the winds and save the Trojan race,   10
So has your highness, raised above the rest,
Storms of ambition tossing us repressed.

Your drooping country, torn with civil hate,
Restored by you is made a glorious state,
The seat of empire where the Irish come,   15
And the unwilling Scotch, to fetch their doom.

The sea's our own, and now all nations greet
With bending sails each vessel of our fleet;
Your power extends as far as winds can blow,
Or swelling sails upon the globe may go.   20

Heaven (that has placed this island to give law,
To balance Europe and her states to awe)
In this conjunction does on Britain smile:
The greatest leader and the greatest isle!

Whether this portion of the world were rent,   25
By the rude ocean, from the continent,
Or thus created, it was sure designed
To be the sacred refuge of mankind.

Hither the oppressed shall henceforth resort,
Justice to crave, and succour, at your court,   30
And then your highness not for ours alone
But for the world's protector shall be known.

Fame, swifter than your winged navy, flies
Through every land that near the ocean lies,
Sounding your name and telling dreadful news   35
To all that piracy and rapine use.

With such a chief the meanest nation blessed
Might hope to lift her head above the rest:
What may be thought impossible to do
By us, embraced by the sea and you?   40

Lords of the world's great waste, the ocean, we
Whole forests send to reign upon the sea,
And every coast may trouble or relieve,
But none can visit us without your leave.

Angels and we have this prerogative   45
That none can at our happy seat arrive,
While we descend at pleasure to invade
The bad with vengeance and the good to aid.

Our little world, the image of the great,
Like that, amidst the boundless ocean set,   50
Of her own growth has all that nature craves,
And all that's rare as tribute from the waves.

As Egypt does not on the clouds rely,
But to the Nile owes more than to the sky,
So what our earth and what our heaven denies   55
Our ever-constant friend, the sea, supplies.

The taste of hot Arabia's spice we know,
Free from the scorching sun that makes it grow;
Without the worm in Persian silks we shine;
And without planting drink of every vine.   60

To dig for wealth we weary not our limbs:
Gold, though the heaviest metal, hither swims.
Ours is the harvest where the Indians mow:
We plough the deep and reap what others sow.

Things of the noblest kind our own soil breeds,   65
Stout are our men and warlike are our steeds:
Rome, though her eagle through the world had flown,
Could never make this island all her own.

Here the third Edward, and the Black Prince too,
France-conquering Henry, flourished, and now you,   70
For whom we stayed as did the Grecian state
Till Alexander came to urge their fate.

                                   (*A Panegyric*, 1655)

SIR JOHN SUCKLING
(1609–42)

Sonnet 3

Oh for some honest lover's ghost,
    Some kind unbodied post
    Sent from the shades below!
    I strangely long to know
Whether the nobler chaplets wear   5
Those that their mistress' scorn did bear,
    Or those that were used kindly.

For whatsoe'er they tell us here
    To make those sufferings dear,
    'Twill there I fear be found   10
    That to the being crowned
T' have loved alone will not suffice,
Unless we also have been wise,
    And have our loves enjoyed.

What posture can we think him in,   15
    That here, unloved again,
    Departs, and's thither gone
    Where each sits by his own?
Or how can that Elysium be
Where I my mistress still must see   20
    Circled in others' arms?

For there the judges all are just,
    And Sophonisba must
    Be his whom she held dear,
    Not his who loved her here;   25
The sweet Philoclea, since she died,
Lies by her Pirocles's side,
    Not by Amphialus.

Some bays (perchance) or myrtle bough
   For difference crowns the brow   30
  Of those kind souls that were
  The noble martyrs here;
And if that be the only odds
(As who can tell), ye kinder gods,
   Give me the woman here.   35

Song

Why so pale and wan, fond lover?
   Prithee why so pale?
Will, when looking well can't move her,
  Looking ill prevail?
   Prithee why so pale?   5

Why so dull and mute, young sinner?
   Prithee why so mute?
Will, when speaking well can't win her,
  Saying nothing do't?
   Prithee why so mute?   10

Quit, quit, for shame, this will not move,
   This cannot take her;
If of herself she will not love,
   Nothing can make her:
   The Devil take her.   15

Love's Siege

'Tis now since I sat down before
 That foolish fort, a heart,
(Time strangely spent) a year, and more,
 And still I did my part:

Made my approaches, from her hand   5
 Unto her lip did rise,
And did already understand
 The language of her eyes;

Proceeded on with no less art,
   My tongue was engineer: 10
I thought to undermine the heart
   By whispering in the ear.

When this did nothing, I brought down
   Great cannon-oaths, and shot
A thousand thousand to the town,   15
   And still it yielded not.

I then resolved to starve the place
   By cutting off all kisses,
Praising and gazing on her face,
   And all such little blisses.   20

To draw her out, and from her strength,
   I drew all batteries in,
And brought myself to lie at length
   As if no siege had been.

When I had done what man could do,   25
   And thought the place mine own,
The enemy lay quiet, too,
   And smiled at all was done.

I sent to know from whence, and where,
   These hopes, and this relief?   30
A spy informed, Honour was there,
   And did command in chief.

'March, march,' quoth I, 'the word straight give,
   Let's lose no time, but leave her:
That Giant upon air will live,   35
   And hold it out for ever.

To such a place our camp remove
   As will no siege abide;
I hate a fool that starves her love
   Only to feed her pride.'   40

A Ballad upon a Wedding

I tell thee, Dick, where I have been,
Where I the rarest things have seen,
   Oh, things without compare!
Such sights again cannot be found
In any place on English ground,   5
   Be it at wake or fair.

At Charing Cross, hard by the way
Where we (thou know'st) do sell our hay
   There is a house with stairs;
And there I did see coming down   10
Such folk as are not in our town,
   Vorty, at least, in pairs.

Amongst the rest, one pestilent fine
(His beard no bigger, though, than thine)
   Walked on before the rest.   15
Our landlord looks like nothing to him;
The King (God bless him!), 'twould undo him
   Should he go still so dressed.

At course-a-park, without all doubt,
He should have been the first taken out   20
   By all the maids i' the town,
Though lusty Roger there had been,
Or little George upon the Green,
   Or Vincent of the Crown.

But wot you what? the youth was going   25
To make an end of all his wooing;
   The parson for him stayed.
Yet by his leave, for all his haste,
He did not so much wish all past,
   Perchance, as did the maid.   30

The maid – and thereby hangs a tale;
For such a maid no Whitsun-ale
   Could ever yet produce;
No grape, that's kindly ripe, could be
So round, so plump, so soft as she,   35
   Nor half so full of juice.

Her finger was so small the ring
Would not stay on, which they did bring;
   It was too wide a peck:
And to say truth (for out it must),   40
It looked like the great collar (just)
   About our young colt's neck.

Her feet beneath her petticoat,
Like little mice stole in and out,
   As if they feared the light;   45
But oh, she dances such a way,
No sun upon an Easter day
   Is half so fine a sight!

He would have kissed her once or twice,
But she would not, she was so nice,   50
   She would not do't in sight;
And then she looked as who should say,
'I will do what I list today,
   And you shall do't at night.'

Her cheeks so rare a white was on,   55
No daisy makes comparison
   (Who sees them is undone),
For streaks of red were mingled there,
Such as are on a Katherine pear
   (The side that's next the sun).   60

Her lips were red, and one was thin
Compared to that was next her chin
   (Some bee had stung it newly);
But, Dick, her eyes so guard her face
I durst no more upon them gaze   65
   Than on the sun in July.

Her mouth so small, when she does speak,
Thou'dst swear her teeth her words did break,
   That they might passage get;
But she so handled still the matter, ·   70
They came as good as ours, or better,
   And are not spent a whit.

If wishing should be any sin,
The parson himself had guilty been
   (She looked that day so purely);   75
And did the youth so oft the feat
At night, as some did in conceit,
   It would have spoiled him, surely.

Passion o' me, how I run on!
There's that that would be thought upon,   80
   I trow, besides the bride.
The business of the kitchen's great,
For it is fit that man should eat,
   Not was it there denied.

Just in the nick the cook knocked thrice,   85
And all the waiters in a trice
   His summons did obey;
Each serving-man, with dish in hand,
Marched boldly up, like our trained band,
   Presented, and away.   90

When all the meat was on the table,
What man of knife or teeth was able
   To stay to be entreated?
And this the very reason was –
Before the parson could say grace,   95
   The company was seated.

Now hats fly off, and youths carouse;
Healths first go round, and then the house;
   The bride's came thick and thick:
And when 'twas named another's health,   100
Perhaps he made it hers by stealth;
   And who could help it, Dick?

O' the sudden up they rise and dance;
Then sit again and sigh and glance;
   Then dance again and kiss;   105
Thus several ways the time did pass,
Whilst every woman wished her place,
   And every man wished his!

By this time all were stolen aside
To counsel and undress the bride,   110
   But that he must not know;
But yet 'twas thought he guessed her mind,
And did not mean to stay behind
   Above an hour or so.

When in he came, Dick, there she lay   115
Like new-fallen snow melting away
   ('Twas time, I trow, to part);
Kisses were now the only stay,
Which soon she gave, as who would say,
   'God be with ye, with all my heart.'   120

But just as heavens would have, to cross it,
In came the bridesmaids with the posset.
   The bridegroom ate in spite,
For had he left the women to't,
It would have cost two hours to do't,   125
   Which were too much that night.

At length the candle's out, and now
All that they had not done, they do.
   What that is, who can tell?
But I believe it was no more   130
Than thou and I have done before
   With Bridget and with Nell.

                           (*Fragmenta Aurea*, 1646)

The Constant Lover

   Out upon it, I have loved
      Three whole days together,
   And am like to love three more,
      If it hold fair weather.

   Time shall moult away his wings   5
      Ere he shall discover
   In the whole wide world again
      Such a constant lover.

But a pox upon 't, no praise
 There is due at all to me: 10
Love with me had made no stay,
 Had it any been but she.

Had it any been but she
 And that very face,
There had been at least ere this   15
 A dozen dozen in her place.
    (*The Last Remains of Sir John Suckling*, 1659)

HENRY HUGHES
(*fl.* 1650–60)

Song

I prithee send me back my heart,
 Since I cannot have thine;
For if from yours you will not part,
 Why then shouldst thou have mine?

Yet now I think on 't, let it lie,   5
 To find it were in vain;
For th' hast a thief in either eye
 Would steal it back again.

Why should two hearts in one breast lie,
 And yet not lodge together?   10
O love, where is thy sympathy,
 If thus our breasts thou sever?

But love is such a mystery
 I cannot find it out;
For when I think I'm best resolved,   15
 I then am most in doubt.

Then farewell care, and farewell woe,
 I will no longer pine;
For I'll believe I have her heart
 As much as she hath mine.   20
    (*The Last Remains of Sir John Suckling*, 1659)

SIDNEY GODOLPHIN
(1610–43)

Song

Or love me less, or love me more,
 And play not with my liberty;
Either take all, or all restore,
 Bind me at least, or set me free.
Let me some nobler torture find   5
 Than of a doubtful wavering mind;
Take all my peace; but you betray
 Mine honour too this cruel way.

'Tis true that I have nursed before
 That hope of which I now complain;   10
And having little, sought no more,
 Fearing to meet with your disdain.
The sparks of favour you did give,
 I gently blew to make them live;
And yet have gained by all this care   15
 No rest in hope nor in despair.

I see you wear that pitying smile
 Which you have still vouchsafed my smart,
Content thus cheaply to beguile
 And entertain an harmless heart;   20
But I no longer can give way
 To hope, which doth so little pay;
And yet I dare no freedom owe
 Whilst you are kind, though but in show.

Then give me more, or give me less,   25
 Do not disdain a mutual sense,
Or your unpitying beauties dress
 In their own free indifference;
But show not a severer eye
 Sooner to give me liberty,   30
For I shall love the very scorn
 Which for my sake you do put on.

Song

'Tis affection but dissembled,
    Or dissembled liberty,
To pretend thy passion changed
    With change of thy mistress' eye,
    Following her inconstancy.   5

Hopes which do from favour flourish,
    May perhaps as soon expire
As the cause which did them nourish,
    And disdained they may retire:
    But love is another fire.   10

For if beauty cause thy passion,
    If a fair resistless eye
Melt thee with its soft impression,
    Then thy hopes will never die,
    Nor be cured by cruelty.   15

'Tis not scorn that can remove thee:
    For thou either wilt not see,
Such loved beauty, not to love thee,
    Or wilt else consent that she
    Judges as she ought of thee.   20

Thus thou either canst not sever
    Hope from what appears so fair,
Or unhappier, thou canst never
    Find contentment in despair,
    Nor make love a trifling care.   25

There are seen but few retiring
    Steps in all the paths of love
Made by such who in aspiring,
    Meeting scorn, their hopes remove:
    Yet even these ne'er change their love.   30

Hymn

Lord, when the wise men came from far,
Led to Thy cradle by a star,

Then did the shepherds too rejoice,
Instructed by Thy Angel's voice:
Blest were the wise men in their skill,   5
And shepherds in their harmless will.

Wise men in tracing Nature's laws
Ascend unto the highest Cause;
Shepherds with humble fearfulness
Walk safely, though their light be less: 10
Though wise men better know the way
It seems no honest heart can stray.

There is no merit in the wise
But Love (the shepherds' sacrifice);
Wise men, all ways of knowledge past,   15
To the shepherds' wonder come at last:
To know can only wonder breed,
And not to know is wonder's seed.

A wise man at the altar bows
And offers up his studied vows,   20
And is received; may not the tears,
Which spring too from a shepherd's fears,
And sighs upon his frailty spent,
Though not distinct, be eloquent?

'Tis true, the object sanctifies   25
All passions which within us rise,
But since no creature comprehends
The Cause of causes, End of ends,
He who himself vouchsafes to know
Best pleases his Creator so.   30

When, then, our sorrows we apply
To our own wants and poverty;
When we look up in all distress
And our own misery confess,
Sending both thanks and prayers above;   35
Then, though we do not know, we love.

Sonnet

Madam, 'tis true, your beauties move
    My heart to a respect,
Too little to be paid with love,
    Too great for your neglect:

I neither love, nor yet am free   5
    For though the flame I find
Be not intense in the degree,
    'Tis of the purest kind:

It little wants of love but pain,
    Your beauties take my sense,   10
And lest you should that pride disdain
    My thoughts feel th' influence;

'Tis not a passion's first access
    Ready to multiply,
But like love's calmest state it is   15
    Possessed with victory:

It is like love to truth reduced,
    All the false values gone,
Which were created and induced
    By fond imagination: 20

'Tis either fancy or 'tis fate
    To love you more than I,
I love you at your beauties' rate,
    Less were an injury.

Like unstamped gold I weigh each grace,   25
    So that you may collect
Th' intrinsic value of your face
    Safely from my respect:

And this respect could merit love,
    Were not so fair a sight   30
Payment enough, for who dares move
    Reward for his delight?

                    (*Poems*, 1931)

WILLIAM CARTWRIGHT
(1611–43)

A Song of Dalliance

Hark, my Flora, Love doth call us
To that strife that must befall us.
He has robbed his mother's myrtles
And hath pulled her downy turtles.
See, our genial posts are crowned,   5
And our beds like billows rise;
Softer combat's nowhere found,
And who loses wins the prize.

Let not dark nor shadows fright thee;
Thy limbs of lustre they will light thee.   10
Fear not any can surprise us;
Love himself doth now disguise us.
From thy waist thy girdle throw;
Night and darkness both dwell here.
Words or actions who can know,   15
Where there's neither eye nor ear?

Show thy bosom and then hide it;
License touching and then chide it.
Give a grant and then forbear it;
Offer something and forswear it.   20
Ask where all our shame is gone;
Call us wicked, wanton men.
Do as turtles, kiss and groan;
Say we ne'er shall meet again.

I can hear thee curse, yet chase thee;   25
Drink thy tears, yet still embrace thee.
Easy riches is no treasure;
She that's willing spoils the pleasure.
Love bids learn the restless fight;
Pull and struggle whilst ye twine;   30
Let me use my force tonight,
The next conquest shall be thine.

No Platonic Love

Tell me no more of minds embracing minds,
 And hearts exchanged for hearts;
That spirits spirits meet, as winds do winds,
 And mix their subtlest parts;
That two unbodied essences may kiss,   5
And then like angels, twist and feel one bliss.

I was that silly thing that once was wrought
 To practise this thin love;
I climbed from sex to soul, from soul to thought;
 But thinking there to move,   10
Headlong I rolled from thought to soul, and then
From soul I lighted at the sex again.

As some strict down-looked men pretend to fast
 Who yet in closets eat,
So lovers who profess they spirits taste,   15
 Feed yet on grosser meat;
I know they boast they souls to souls convey,
Howe'er they meet, the body is the way.

Come, I will undeceive thee: they that tread
 Those vain aerial ways   20
Are like young heirs and alchemists, misled
 To waste their wealth and days;
For searching thus to be forever rich,
They only find a med'cine for the itch.

To Chloe,
Who Wished Herself Young Enough for Me

Chloe, why wish you that your years
 Would backwards run till they meet mine,
That perfect likeness, which endears
 Things unto things, might us combine?
Our ages so in date agree   5
That twins do differ more than we.

There are two births: the one when light
  First strikes the new awakened sense;
The other when two souls unite,
  And we must count our life from thence,   10
When you loved me and I loved you,
Then both of us were born anew.

Love then to us did new souls give,
  And in those souls did plant new powers;
Since when another life we live,   15
  The breath we breathe is his, not ours;
Love makes those young whom age doth chill,
And whom he finds young, keeps young still.

Love, like that angel that shall call
  Our bodies from the silent grave,   20
Unto one age doth raise us all,
  None too much, none too little have;
Nay, that the difference may be none,
He makes two not alike, but one.

And now since you and I are such,   25
  Tell me what's yours and what is mine?
Our eyes, our ears, our taste, smell, touch,
  Do, like our souls, in one combine;
So by this, I as well may be
Too old for you, as you for me.   30
  (*Comedies, Tragi-Comedies, with Other Poems*, 1651)

JAMES GRAHAM,
MARQUIS OF MONTROSE
(1612–50)

¶

My dear and only Love, I pray
  This noble world of thee
Be governed by no other sway
  But purest monarchy;

For if confusion have a part,   5
   Which virtuous souls abhor,
And hold a synod in thy heart,
   I'll never love thee more.

Like Alexander I will reign,
   And I will reign alone: 10
My thoughts shall evermore disdain
   A rival on my throne.
He either fears his fate too much,
   Or his deserts are small,
That puts it not unto the touch   15
   To win or lose it all.

But I must rule and govern still,
   And always give the law,
And have each subject at my will,
   And all to stand in awe.   20
But 'gainst my battery, if I find
   Thou shunn'st the prize so sore
As that thou sett'st me up a blind,
   I'll never love thee more.

Or in the empire of thy heart,   25
   Where I should solely be,
Another do pretend a part
   And dares to vie with me;
Or if committees thou erect,
   And go on such a score,   30
I'll sing and laugh at thy neglect,
   And never love thee more.

But if thou wilt be constant then,
   And faithful of thy word,
I'll make thee glorious by my pen   35
   And famous by my sword:
I'll serve thee in such noble ways
   Was never heard before;
I'll crown and deck thee all with bays,
   And love thee evermore.   40
(*A Choice Collection of Comic and
Serious Scots Poems*, 1711)

JOHN CLEVELAND
(1613–58)

From *The King's Disguise*

And why so coffined in this vile disguise,
Which who but sees blasphemes thee with his eyes?
My twins of light within their pent-house shrink,
And hold it their allegiance to wink.
Oh, for a state-distinction to arraign   5
Charles of high treason 'gainst my sovereign.
What an usurper to his prince is wont –
Cloister and shave him – he himself hath don't.
His muffled fabric speaks him a recluse,
His ruins prove it a religious house.   10
The sun hath mewed his beams from off his lamp,
And majesty defaced the royal stamp.
Is't not enough thy dignity's in thrall,
But thou'lt transcribe it in thy shape and all?
As if thy blacks were of too faint a die   15
Without the tincture of tautology.
Flay an Egyptian for his cassock skin
Spun of his country's darkness, line't within
With Presbyterian budge, that drowsy trance,
The Synod's sable, foggy ignorance: 20
Nor bodily nor ghostly negro could
Rough cast thy figure in a sadder mould.
This Privy Chamber of thy shape would be
But the close mourner to thy royalty.
Then break the circle of thy tailor's spell,   25
A pearl within a rugged oyster's shell.
Heaven, which the minster of thy person owns,
Will fine thee for dilapidations.
Like to a martyred abbey's coarser doom,
Devoutly altered to a pigeon room,   30
Or like the college by the changeling rabble,
Manchester's elves, transformed into a stable,

Or if there be a profanation higher:
Such is the sacrilege of thine attire,
By which th'art half deposed. Thou look'st like one   35
Whose looks are under sequestration,
Whose renegado form at the first glance
Shows like the Self-Denying Ordinance.
Angel of light, and darkness too, I doubt,
Inspired within, and yet possessed without.   40
Majestic twilight in the state of grace,
Yet with an excommunicated face:
Charles and his mask are of a different mint,
A psalm of mercy in a miscreant print.
The sun wears midnight, day is beetle-browed,   45
And lightning is in keldar of a cloud.
Oh the accursed stenography of fate!
The princely eagle shrunk into a bat.

Epitaph on the Earl of Strafford

Here lies wise and valiant dust,
Huddled up 'twixt fit and just:
Strafford, who was hurried hence
'Twixt treason and convenience.
He spent his time here in a mist,   5
A Papist, yet a Calvinist.
His prince's nearest joy, and grief,
He had, yet wanted, all relief.
The prop and ruin of the state,
The people's violent love, and hate.   10
One in extremes loved, and abhorred.
Riddles lie here; or, in a word,
Here lies blood. And let it lie
Speechless still, and never cry.
                    (*The Character of a London-Diurnall*, 1647)

WILLIAM HAMMOND
(1614–?)

Husbandry

When I began my love to sow,
    Because with Venus' doves I ploughed
Fool that I was, I did not know
    That frowns for furrows were allowed.

The broken heart to make clods, torn   5
    By the sharp arrows of disdain,
Crumbled by pressing rolls of scorn,
    Gives issue to the springing grain.

Coyness shuts love into a stove;
    So frost-bound lands their own heat feed: 10
Neglect sits brooding upon love,
    As pregnant snow on winter-seed.

The harvest is not till we two
    Shall into one contracted be;
Love's crop alone doth richer grow,   15
    Decreasing to identity.

All other things not nourished are
    But by assimilation:
Love, in himself and diet spare,
    Grows fat by contradiction.   20

Mutual Love

From our loves, heat and light are taught to twine,
    In their bright nuptial bed of solar beams;
From our loves, Thames and Isis learn to join,
    Losing themselves in one another's streams.
And if fate smile, the fire love's emblem bears,   5
If not, the water represents our tears.

From our loves all magnetic virtue grows,
    Steel to th' obdurate loadstone is inclined.
From our loves all the power of chemists flows,
    Earth by the sun is into gold refined.   10
And if fate smile, this shall love's arrows head,
If not, in those is our hard fortune read.

From our still springing loves the youthful bays
    Is in a robe of lasting verdure drest,
From our firm loves the cypress learns to raise,   15
    Green in despite of storms, her deathless crest.
And if fate smile, with that our temples bound,
If not, with this our hearses shall be crowned.

To Her Questioning His Estate

Prithee, no more, how can love sail?
    Thy providence becalms our seas:
Suspensive care binds up each gale;
    Fear doth the lazy current freeze.

Forecast and love, the lover swears,   5
    Removed as the two poles should be:
But if on them must roll the spheres
    Of our well-tuned felicity:

If sums and terrars I must bring,
    Nor may my inventory hide,   10
Know I am richer than the king,
    Who gilt Pactolus' yellow tide.

For love is our philosopher's stone;
    And whatsoe'er doth please thy sense,
My prizing estimation   15
    Shall elevate to quintessence.

Thy lips each cup to wine shall charm,
    As the sun's kisses do the vine;
Naked embraces keep us warm;
    And stript, than May thou art more fine.   20

And when thou hast me in thy arms,
   (The power of fancy's then most high)
Instate me by those mighty charms
   In some imperial monarchy.

Thus I am thy wealth, thou art mine: 25
   And what to each other we appear,
If love us two in one combine,
   The same then in our selves we are.

                         (*Poems*, 1655)

SIR JOHN DENHAM
(1615–69)

From *Cooper's Hill*

There Faunus and Sylvanus keep their courts,   235
And thither all the horned host resorts
To graze the ranker mead; that noble herd
On whose sublime and shady fronts is reared
Nature's great masterpiece, to show how soon
Great things are made, but sooner are undone.   240
Here have I seen the king, when great affairs
Give leave to slacken and unbend his cares,
Attended to the chase by all the flower
Of youth, whose hopes a nobler prey devour.
Pleasure with praise and danger they would buy,   245
And wish a foe that would not only fly.
The stag now conscious of his fatal growth,
At once indulgent to his fear and sloth,
To some dark covert his retreat had made,
Where no man's eye, nor heaven's, should invade   250
His soft repose; when the unexpected sound
Of dogs and men his wakeful ear doth wound.
Roused with the noise, he scarce believes his ear,
Willing to think the illusions of his fear
Had given this alarm; but straight his view   255
Confirms that more than all he fears is true.

Betrayed in all his strengths, the wood beset,
All instruments, all arts of ruin met,
He calls to mind his strength and then his speed,
His winged heels, and then his armed head;   260
With these to avoid, with that his fate to meet;
But fear prevails and bids him thrust his feet.
So fast he flies that his reviewing eye
Has lost the chasers, and his ear the cry;
Exulting, till he finds their nobler sense   265
Their disproportioned speed does recompense.
Then curses his conspiring feet, whose scent
Betrays that safety which their swiftness lent.
Then tries his friends: among the baser herd,
Where he so lately was obeyed and feared,   270
His safety seeks; the herd, unkindly wise,
Or chases him from thence, or from him flies.
Like a declining statesman left forlorn
To his friends' pity and pursuers' scorn,
With shame remembers, while himself was one   275
Of the same herd, himself the same had done.
Thence to the coverts and the conscious groves,
The scenes of his past triumphs and his loves,
Sadly surveying where he ranged alone,
Prince of the soil and all the herd his own,   280
And like a bold knight errant did proclaim
Combat to all, and bore away the dame,
And taught the woods to echo to the stream
His dreadful challenge and his clashing beam;
Yet faintly now declines the fatal strife,   285
So much his love was dearer than his life.
Now every leaf and every moving breath
Presents a foe, and every foe a death.
Wearied, forsaken, and pursued, at last
All safety in despair of safety placed,   290
Courage he thence resumes, resolved to bear
All their assaults, since 'tis in vain to fear.
And now too late he wishes for the fight
That strength he wasted in ignoble flight.
But when he sees the eager chase renewed,   295
Himself by dogs, the dogs by men pursued,
He straight revokes his bold resolve, and more
Repents his courage than his fear before;

Finds that uncertain ways unsafest are,
And doubt a greater mischief than despair.   300
Then to the stream, when neither friends, nor force,
Nor speed, nor art avail, he shapes his course;
Thinks not their rage so desperate to assay
An element more merciless than they:
But fearless they pursue, nor can the flood   305
Quench their dire thirst; alas, they thirst for blood.
So toward a ship the oarfinned galleys ply,
Which wanting sea to ride, or wind to fly,
Stands but to fall revenged on those that dare
Tempt the last fury of extreme despair.   310
So fares the stag among the enraged hounds,
Repels their force, and wounds returns for wounds.
And as a hero, whom his baser foes
In troops surround, now these assails, now those,
Though prodigal of life, disdains to die,   315
By common hands; but if he can descry
Some nobler foe's approach, to him he calls
And begs his fate, and then contented falls:
So when the king a mortal shaft lets fly
From his unerring hand, then glad to die,   320
Proud of the wound, to it resigns his blood
And stains the crystal with a purple flood.
This is a more innocent and happy chase
Than when of old, but in the self-same place,
Fair liberty pursued, and meant a prey   325
To lawless power, here turned and stood at bay,
When in that remedy all hope was placed
Which was, or should have been at least, the last.
Here was that Charter sealed wherein the crown
All marks of arbitrary power lays down.   330
Tyrant and slave, those names of hate and fear,
The happier style of king and subject bear:
Happy when both to the same centre move
When kings give liberty, and subjects love.
Therefore not long in force this Charter stood;   335
Wanting that seal, it must be sealed in blood.
The subjects armed, the more the princes gave,
The advantage only took the more to crave.
Till kings by giving, give themselves away,
And even that power that should deny, betray.   340

'Who gives constrained, but his own fear reviles,
Not thanked, but scorned; nor are they gifts, but spoils.'
Thus kings, by grasping more than they could hold,
First made their subjects by oppression bold;
And popular sway, by forcing kings to give   345
More than was fit for subjects to receive,
Ran to the same extremes; and one excess
Made both, by striving to be greater, less.
When a calm river, raised with sudden rains,
Or snows dissolved, o'erflows the adjoining plains,   350
The husbandmen with high-raised banks secure
Their greedy hopes, and this he can endure.
But if with bays and dams they strive to force
His channel to a new or narrow course,
No longer then within his banks he dwells;   355
First to a torrent, then a deluge swells;
Stronger and fiercer by restraint he roars,
And knows no bound, but makes his power his shores.

(Poems and Translations, 1668)

JOSEPH BEAUMONT
(1616–99)

The Garden

JUNE 12TH

The garden's quit with me: as yesterday
I walked in that, today that walks in me;
   Through all my memory
It sweetly wanders, and has found a way
    To make me honestly possess   5
     What still another's is.

Yet this gain's dainty sense doth gall my mind
With the remembrance of a bitter loss.
   Alas, how odd and cross
Are earth's delights, in which the soul can find   10
    No honey, but withal some sting
     To check the pleasing thing!

For now I'm haunted with the thought of that
Heaven-planted garden, where felicity
    Flourished on every tree.   15
Lost, lost it is; for at the guarded gate
  A flaming sword forbiddeth sin
    (That's I) to enter in.

O Paradise! when I was turned out
Hadst thou but kept the serpent still within,   20
    My banishment had been
Less sad and dangerous: but round about
  This wide world runneth raging he
    To banish me from me:

I feel that through my soul he death hath shot;   25
And thou, alas, hast locked up life's tree.
    O miserable me,
What help were left, had Jesus's pity not
  Showed me another tree, which can
    Enliven dying man.   30

That tree, made fertile by his own dear blood;
And by his death with quickening virtue fraught.
    I now dread not the thought
Of barracadoed Eden, since as good
  A paradise I planted see   35
    On open Calvary.

                      (Minor Poems, 1914)

THOMAS PHILIPOTT
(*c.* 1616–82)

On the Death of a Prince: A Meditation

In what a silence princes pass away
When they're enfranchised from their shells of clay:
No thunder clap rung out this hero's knell
And in loud accents to the world did tell

He was deceased; no trembling earthquake shook   5
The frame of the world as if 'twere palsy-struck.
There was no bearded comet did arise
To light a torch up at his obsequies,
And though so many men should have deceased
When his great soul was from the flesh released   10
That Charon's vessel should have ceased to float,
And he have cried 'Give me another boat!',
Not any yet resigned their vital breath
Obsequiously to wait on him in death.
Thus we may see, Fate's unrelenting knife   15
Will even cut a prince's thread of life,
Nor can his spreading power enforce its strength,
Or his dominions extend its length.
If from the urn his name first issue forth
Not his tall titles or unfathomed worth   20
Can this prerogative or charter give,
That he his cheap, dull vassal shall outlive;
And though the eyes of the multitude before
Followed his presence, and did even adore
The earth that propped his feet: yet when the rust   25
Of his monument shall mingle with his dust,
Contracted to a span, and the rude wind
Shall his abbreviated ashes find,
They cannot from his blast be so exempt
But that he will disperse them to contempt.   30
So many graves his dust shall (he being dead)
Obtain, yet he be nowhere buried.
Who then in titles, crowns or wealth would trust?
Since he can scarce assure himself his dust
Even in the grave shall so protected be,   35
It shall be freed from foreign injury.

On the Nativity of Our Saviour

Who can forget that ne'er forgotten night,
That sparkled with such unaccustomed light?
Wherein when darkness had shut in the day,
A sun at midnight did his beams display;
And God who man's frail house of earth composed   5
Himself in a frail house of earth enclosed;

Who did control the fire, air, sea and earth,
Was clad with all these four, and had a birth
In time, who was begotten before time
Received a birth, or th'early sun did climb   10
Th'ascent o'th East. Whom the vast air, and main,
And precincts of the earth could not contain,
Is circumscribed now in so brief a room,
He's lodged i'the circuit of a virgin's womb;
Who light to Him, that was all light, did give,   15
And made Him, who was life itself, to live:
Who in her arms bore Him, whose hand controls
The massy globe, and bears up both the poles:
And what improved the miracle begun,
He was at once her father, spouse and son: 20
Who than His mother was by far more old,
Yet equal age, did with His Father hold;
Who was a child, yet with His word did make
The world, and with His voice this world can shake.
Now truth's great oracle itself was come,.   25
The faithless oracles were strucken dumb.
No marvel if the shepherds ran to see
Him that should every shepherd's shepherd be:
Who was the door, through whom a certain way
To find out life for all lost sheep there lay: 30
And though this Sun of Righteousness did lie
Wrapped up in clouds of dark obscurity,
Yet He could such a stock of light allow,
As did the heavens with a new star endow,
Which with its beams did gratefully attend   35
Him, who at first those streams of light did lend,
And by the conduct of its rays did bring
The eastern kings to see their heavenly king.
And though all stars, by nature's laws, do run
A course contrariant to the course o'th sun;   40
Yet lo, her statutes violated were,
For here the sun was followed by a star.

                                          (*Poems*, 1646)

RICHARD LOVELACE
(1618–57/8)

Song. To Lucasta. Going to the Wars

Tell me not, sweet, I am unkind,
   That from the nunnery
Of thy chaste breast and quiet mind
   To war and arms I fly.

True, a new mistress now I chase,   5
   The first foe in the field;
And with a stronger faith embrace
   A sword, a horse, a shield.

Yet this inconstancy is such
   As you too shall adore;   10
I could not love thee, dear, so much,
   Loved I not honour more.

Gratiana Dancing and Singing

See! with what constant motion,
Even and glorious as the sun,
   Gratiana steers that noble frame,
Soft as her breast, sweet as her voice,
That gave each winding law and poise,   5
   And swifter than the wings of fame.

She beat the happy pavement
By such a star made firmament,
   Which now no more the roof envies,
But swells up high with Atlas ev'n,   10
Bearing the brighter, nobler heav'n,
   And in her all the deities.

Each step trod out a lover's thought
And the ambitious hopes he brought,
   Chained to her brave feet with such arts,   15
Such sweet command and gentle awe,
As when she ceased, we sighing saw
   The floor lay paved with broken hearts,

So did she move; so did she sing
Like the harmonious spheres that bring   20
   Unto their rounds their music's aid;
Which she performed such a way
As all th' enamoured world will say
   The Graces danced, and Apollo played.

The Grasshopper
To My Noble Friend, Mr Charles Cotton

ODE

Oh thou that swing'st upon the waving hair
   Of some well-filled oaten beard,
Drunk ev'ry night with a delicious tear
   Dropped thee from heav'n, where now th'art reared;

The joys of earth and air are thine entire,   5
   That with thy feet and wings dost hop and fly;
And, when thy poppy works, thou dost retire
   To thy carved acorn-bed to lie.

Up with the day, the sun thou welcom'st then,
   Sport'st in the gilt plaits of his beams,   10
And all these merry days mak'st merry, men,
   Thyself, and melancholy streams.

But ah, the sickle! Golden ears are cropped;
   Ceres and Bacchus bid good night;
Sharp frosty fingers all your flowers have topped,   15
   And what scythes spared, winds shave off quite.

Poor verdant fool! and now green ice! thy joys
  Large and as lasting as thy perch of grass,
Bid us lay in 'gainst winter, rain, and poise
  Their floods with an o'erflowing glass.   20

Thou best of men and friends! we will create
  A genuine summer in each other's breast,
And spite of this cold time and frozen fate,
  Thaw us a warm seat to our rest.

Our sacred hearths shall burn eternally   25
  As vestal flames; the North Wind, he
Shall strike his frost-stretched wings, dissolve, and fly
  This Ætna in epitome.

Dropping December shall come weeping in,
  Bewail th' usurping of his reign;   30
But when in showers of old Greek we begin,
  Shall cry he hath his crown again.

Night as clear Hesper shall our tapers whip
  From the light casements where we play,
And the dark hag from her black mantle strip,   35
  And stick there everlasting day.

Thus richer than untempted kings are we,
  That asking nothing, nothing need:
Though lord of all what seas embrace, yet he
  That wants himself is poor indeed.   40

                                    (*Lucasta*, 1649)

                To Althea. From Prison

    When Love with unconfined wings
      Hovers within my gates,
    And my divine Althea brings
      To whisper at the grates;
    When I lie tangled in her hair   5
      And fettered to her eye,
    The gods that wanton in the air
      Know no such liberty.

When flowing cups run swiftly round,
   With no allaying Thames,   10
Our careless heads with roses bound,
   Our hearts with loyal flames;
When thirsty grief in wine we steep,
   When healths and draughts go free,
Fishes that tipple in the deep   15
   Know no such liberty.

When, like committed linnets, I
With shriller throat shall sing
The sweetness, mercy, majesty,
   And glories of my King;   20
When I shall voice aloud how good
   He is, how great should be,
Enlarged winds that curl the flood
   Know no such liberty.

Stone walls do not a prison make,   25
   Nor iron bars a cage:
Minds innocent and quiet take
   That for an hermitage.
If I have freedom in my love,
   And in my soul am free,   30
Angels alone, that soar above,
   Enjoy such liberty.

Love Made in the First Age: To Chloris

In the nativity of time,
Chloris, it was not thought a crime
   In direct Hebrew for to woo.
Now we make love as all on fire,
Ring retrograde our loud desire,   5
   And court in English, backward, too.

Thrice happy was that golden age,
When compliment was construed rage,
   And fine words in the centre hid;
When cursed 'No' stained no maid's bliss,   10
And all discourse was summed in 'Yes',
   And nought forbad, but to forbid.

Love, then unstinted, Love did sip,
And cherries plucked fresh from the lip;
   On cheeks and roses free he fed;   15
Lasses like autumn plums did drop,
And lads indifferently did crop
   A flower and a maidenhead.

Then unconfined each did tipple
Wine from the bunch, milk from the nipple;   20
   Paps tractable as udders were;
Then equally the wholesome jellies
Were squeezed from olive-trees and bellies,
   Nor suits of trespass did they fear.

A fragrant bank of strawberries,   25
Diapered with violets' eyes,
   Was table, tablecloth, and fare;
No palace to the clouds did swell:
Each humble princess then did dwell
   In the piazza of her hair.   30

Both broken faith and th' cause of it,
All-damning gold, was damned to th' Pit;
   Their troth, sealed with a clasp and kiss,
Lasted until that extreme day
In which they smiled their souls away,   35
   And in each other breathed new bliss.

Because no fault, there was no tear;
No groan did grate the granting ear,
   No false foul breath their del'cate smell;
No serpent kiss poisoned the taste;   40
Each touch was naturally chaste,
   And their mere sense a miracle.

Naked as their own innocence,
And unembroidered from offence
   They went, above poor riches gay;   45
On softer than the cygnet's down
In beds they tumbled of their own,
   For each within the other lay.

Thus did they live, thus did they love,
Repeating only joys above;   50
   And angels were, but with clothes on,
Which they would put off cheerfully,
To bathe them in the Galaxy,
   Then gird them with the heavenly zone.

Now, Chloris! miserably crave   55
The offered bliss you would not have,
   Which evermore I must deny;
Whilst ravished with these noble dreams,
And crowned with mine own soft beams,
   Enjoying of myself I lie.   60

                  (Lucasta, Posthume Poems, 1659–60)

ABRAHAM COWLEY
(1618–67)

The Spring

Though you be absent here I needs must say
The trees as beauteous are, and flowers as gay,
   As ever they were wont to be:
   Nay, the birds' rural music too
   Is as melodious and free   5
   As if they sung to pleasure you.
I saw a rosebud ope this morn: I'll swear
The blushing morning opened not more fair.

How could it be so fair and you away?
How could the trees be beauteous, flowers so gay?   10
   Could they remember but last year,
   How you did them, they you delight,
   The sprouting leaves which you saw here,
   And called their fellows to the sight,
Would, looking round for the same sight in vain,   15
Creep back into their silent barks again.

Where e'er you walked trees were as reverend made
As when of old gods dwelt in every shade.
 Is't possible they should not know
  What loss of honour they sustain,   20
 That thus they smile and flourish now
  And still their former pride retain?
Dull creatures! 'Tis not without a cause that she
Who fled the god of wit was made a tree.

In ancient times sure they much wiser were   25
When they rejoiced the Thracian verse to hear;
 In vain did nature bid them stay
  When Orpheus had his song begun:
 They called their wond'ring roots away
  And bad them silent to him run.   30
How would those learned trees have followed you?
You would have drawn them and their poet too.

But who can blame them now? For, since you're gone,
They're here the only fair, and shine alone.
 You did their natural rights invade: 35
  Wherever you did walk or sit
 The thickest boughs could make no shade,
  Although the sun had granted it;
The fairest flowers could please no more, near you,
Than painted flowers set next to them could do.   40

Whene'er then you come hither, that shall be
The time which this to others is, to me.
 The little joys which here are now
  The names of punishments do bear,
 When by their sight they let us know   45
  How we deprived of greater are.
'Tis you the best of seasons with you bring:
This is for beasts and that for men the spring.

The Thief

Thou robb'st my days of business and delights;
 Of sleep thou robb'st my nights.
 Ah, lovely thief, what wilt thou do?
 What, rob me of heaven too?

Thou even my prayers dost steal from me,   5
    And I with wild idolatry
Begin to God and end them all to thee.

Is it a sin to love that it should thus
    Like an ill conscience torture us?
    Whate'er I do, where e'er I go –   10
    None guiltless e'er was haunted so –
    Still, still, methinks thy face I view
    And still thy shape does me pursue,
As if not you me but I had murdered you.

From books I strive some remedy to take   15
    But thy name all the letters make:
    Whate'er 'tis writ I find that there,
    Like points and commas everywhere.
    Me blessed for this let no man hold,
    For I, as Midas did of old,   20
Perish by turning everything to gold.

What do I seek, alas, or why do I
    Attempt in vain from thee to fly?
    For making thee my deity
    I gave thee then ubiquity.   25
    My pains resemble hell in this:
    The divine presence there too is
But to torment men, not to give them bliss.

The Prophet

Teach me to love? Go, teach thyself more wit:
    I chief professor am of it.
    Teach craft to Scots and thrift to Jews;
    Teach boldness to the stews;
In tyrants' courts teach supple flattery;   5
Teach Jesuits, that have travelled far, to lie;
    Teach fire to burn and winds to blow;
    Teach restless fountains how to flow;
    Teach the dull earth, fixed, to abide;
Teach womankind inconstancy and pride;   10
See if your diligence here will useful prove:
    But, prithee, teach not me to love.

The god of love, if such a thing there be,
   May learn to love from me.
   He who does boast that he has bin   15
   In every heart since Adam's sin,
I'll lay my life, nay mistress on't (that's more)
I'll teach him things he never knew before.
   I'll teach him a receipt to make
   Words that weep and tears that spark;   20
   I'll teach him sighs like those in death,
At which the souls go out too with the breath:
Still the soul stays, yet still does from me run,
   As light and heat does with the sun.

'Tis I who love's Columbus am; 'tis I   25
   Who must new worlds in it descry:
   Rich worlds that yield of treasure more
   Than all that has been known before.
And yet like his, I fear, my fate must be
To find them out for others, not for me.   30
   Me times to come, I know it, shall
   Love's last and greatest prophet call.
   But, ah, what's that if she refuse
To hear the wholesome doctrines of my muse?
If to my share the prophet's fate must come,   35
   Hereafter fame, here martyrdom.
                   (*The Mistress*, 1647)

From *To the Royal Society*

I

Philosophy, the great and only heir
   Of all that human knowledge which has been
Unforfeited by man's rebellious sin,
   Though full of years he do appear
(Philosophy, I say, and call it 'he',   5
For whatsoe'er the painters' fancy be,
   It a male virtue seems to me),
Has still been kept in nonage till of late,
Nor managed or enjoyed his vast estate:

Three or four thousand years, one would have thought, 10
To ripeness and perfection might have brought
    A science so well bred and nursed,
And of such hopeful parts, too, at the first.
But oh, the guardians and the tutors then,
Some negligent and some ambitious men,   15
    Would ne'er consent to set him free,
Or his own natural powers to let him see,
Lest that should put an end to their authority.

2

That his own business he might quite forget,
They amused him with the sports of wanton wit;   20
With the desserts of poetry they fed him,
Instead of solid meats to increase his force;
Instead of vigorous exercise, they led him
Into the pleasant labyrinths of ever-fresh discourse;
    Instead of carrying him to see   25
The riches which do hoarded for him lie
    In nature's endless treasury,
    They chose his eye to entertain,
    His curious but not covetous eye,
With painted scenes, and pageants of the brain.   30
Some few exalted spirits this latter age has shown,
That laboured to assert the liberty,
From guardians who were now usurpers grown,
Of this old minor still, captived philosophy;
    But 'twas rebellion called to fight   35
    For such a long-oppressed right.
Bacon at last, a mighty man, arose,
    Whom a wise king and nature chose
    Lord Chancellor of both their laws,
And boldly undertook the injured pupil's cause.   40

3

Authority, which did a body boast,
Though 'twas but air condensed, and stalked about
Like some old giant's more gigantic ghost
    To terrify the learned rout,
With the plain magic of true reason's light   45
    He chased out of our sight,

Nor suffered living men to be misled
  By the vain shadows of the dead:
To graves, from whence it rose, the conquered phantom fled.
    He broke that monstrous god which stood   50
In midst of the orchard, and the whole did claim,
    Which, with a useless scythe of wood
    And something else not worth a name –
    Both vast for show, yet neither fit
    Or to defend or to beget;   55
    Ridiculous and senseless terrors! – made
Children and superstitious men afraid.
    The orchard's open now and free;
Bacon has broke that scarecrow deity;
    Come, enter, all that will;   60
Behold the ripened fruit; come gather now your fill.
    Yet still, methinks, we fain would be
    Catching at the forbidden tree;
    We would be like the Deity
When truth and falsehood, good and evil, we   65
Without the senses' aid, within ourselves would see;
    For 'tis God only who can find
    All nature in His mind.

4

From words, which are but pictures of the thought
(Though we our thoughts from them perversely drew),   70
To things, the mind's right object, he it brought:
Like foolish birds to painted grapes we flew;
He sought and gathered for our use the true;
And when on heaps the chosen bunches lay,
He pressed them wisely the mechanic way,   75
Till all their juice did in one vessel join,
Ferment into a nourishment divine,
    The thirsty soul's refreshing wine.
Who to the life an exact piece would make,
Must not from others' work a copy take;   80
    No, not from Rubens or Vandyck;
Much less content himself to make it like
The ideas and the images which lie
In his own fancy or his memory.

No, he before his sight must place   85
The natural and living face;
The real object must command
Each judgement of his eye and motion of his hand.

(Works, 1668)

THOMAS STANLEY
(1625–78)

La Belle Confidente

You earthly souls that court a wanton flame
    Whose pale, weak influence
Can rise no higher than the humble name
    And narrow laws of sense,
    Learn by our friendship to create   5
      An immaterial fire,
    Whose brightness angels may admire,
      But cannot emulate.

Sickness may fright the roses from her cheek,
    Or make the lilies fade,   10
But all the subtle ways that death doth seek
    Cannot my love invade.
    Flames that are kindled by the eye,
      Through time and age expire;
    But ours that boast a reach far higher   15
      Can nor decay nor die.

For when we must resign our vital breath,
    Our loves by fate benighted,
We by this friendship shall survive in death,
    Even in divorce united.   20
    Weak love through fortune or distrust
      In time forgets to burn,
    But this pursues us to the urn,
      And marries either's dust.

(Poems, 1651)

PATRICK CARY
(1623/4–57)

¶

And now a fig for the lower house,
The army I do set at nought;
I care not for them both a louse,
For spent is my last groat boys,
  For spent is my last groat.   5

Delinquent I'd not fear to be,
Though 'gainst the cause and Noll I'd fought,
Since England's now a state most free
For who's not worth a groat boys,
  For who's not worth a groat.   10

I'll boldly talk, and do, as sure
By pursuivants ne'er to be sought;
'Tis a protection most secure
Not to be worth a groat boys,
  Not to be worth a groat.   15

I should be soon let loose again,
By some mistake if I were caught;
For what can any hope to gain
From one not worth a groat boys,
  From one not worth a groat?   20

Nay, if some fool should me accuse,
And I unto the bar were brought,
The judges audience would refuse
I being not worth a groat boys,
  I being not worth a groat.   25

Or if some raw one should be bent
To make me in the air to vault,
The rest would cry 'He's innocent,
He is not worth a groat boys,
  He is not worth a groat.'   30

Ye rich men, that so fear the state,
This privilege is to be bought;
Purchase it then, at any rate,
Leave not yourselves a groat boys,
        Leave not yourselves a groat.   35

The parliament which now does sit
(That all may have it as they ought)
Intends to make them for it fit,
And leave no man a groat boys,
        And leave no man a groat.   40

Who writ this song would little care,
Although at th'end his name were wrought;
Committee men their search may spare,
For spent is his last groat boys,
        For spent is his last groat.   45

¶

The invisible things of Him from the creation of the
world are clearly seen; being understood by the things
that are made.
(ROMANS 1.20)

Whilst I beheld the neck o'th'dove
I spied and read these words:
'This pretty dye
Which takes your eye
Is not at all the bird's.   5
The dusky raven might
Have with these colours pleased your sight,
Had God but chose so to ordain above.'
This label wore the dove.

Whilst I admired the nightingale   10
These notes she warbled o'er:
'No melody
Indeed have I,
Admire me then no more.

God has it in his choice   15
To give the owl or me this voice:
'Tis He, 'tis He that makes me tell my tale.'
Thus sang the nightingale.

I smelt and praised the fragrant rose;
Blushing thus answered she: 20
'The praise you gave,
The scent I have,
Do not belong to me.
This harmless odour none
But only God indeed does own;   25
To be His keepers my poor leaves He chose.'
And thus replied the rose.

I took the honey from the bee;
On the bag these words were seen:
'More sweet than this   30
Perchance nought is,
Yet gall it might have been.
If God it should so please,
He could still make it such with ease;
And as well gall to honey change can He.'   35
This learnt I of the bee.

I touched and liked the down o'th'swan,
But felt these words there writ:
'Bristles, thorns here
I soon should bear,   40
Did God ordain but it.
If my down to thy touch
Seem soft and smooth, God made it such;
Give more, or take all this away He can.'
This was I taught by th'swan.   45
                                        (*Poems*, 1978)

NOTES

MICHAEL DRAYTON

p 12. SONNET 9.   9. *bedlam*] madhouse.

p 13. THE TENTH ECLOGUE.   title] Drayton revised this pastoral considerably to make it not simply a love lament but an attack on 'fortune and time' and his own neglect as a poet;   46. *yean*] give birth.

p 16. THE TENTH NYMPHAL.   1–4.] the woodland 'satyr' was often made to speak 'satire' in Renaissance pastoral;   24. *cambrels*] legs;   26. *staring*] bristling;   32. *silly*] innocent;   34. *hit*] come;   43. *bi-cliffed*] twin cliffs of Parnassus, sacred to Apollo and the Muses;   61. *Sylvanus*] god of fields and forests;   69ff] there are frequent complaints about deforestation at this time, especially in Drayton's own *Poly-Olbion*;   69. *Felicia*] the real world in general, here England in particular;   77. *Cynthia*] the moon, but also a common name for Elizabeth I;   80. *bid the base*] children's game, like 'team tag';   103. *stover*] winter fodder;   134. *Jove's dear daughters*] the Muses;   137. *Delphian god*] Apollo, god of poetry;   151. *vile nation*] France.

JOHN DONNE

p 22. THE GOOD-MORROW.   4. *Seven Sleepers*] seven Christians of Ephesus, immured by the Romans, slept for 200 years and emerged unharmed;   5. *but this*] except for this.

p 23. SONG.   2. *mandrake root*] this resembles the human body, and was used to increase fertility.

p 23. THE SUN RISING.   17. *Indias of spice and mine*] East and West Indies respectively.

p 24. THE CANONIZATION.   8. *approve*] try out;   15. *plaguey bill*] list of deaths from plague;   21. *tapers*] candles;   23–7] as the

Phoenix is self-regenerated from its ashes, so the lovers are united, die, and rise again (with the usual sexual play on 'die' = consummation, and on 'rise');   32] 'stanza' is Italian for room.

p 27. AIR AND ANGELS.   18. *overfraught*] overloaded;   23–5] Aquinas held that angels, bodiless beings, appeared to men by taking on a 'body' of air, the purest form of matter; so the man's love can subsist in the sphere or vehicle of his mistress's love, to which it is related as the angelic intelligence is to the heavenly sphere which it directs.

p 27. THE ANNIVERSARY.   18. *inmates*] lodgers.

p 28. LOVE'S GROWTH.   8. *quintessence*] Paracelsus believed every substance had a pure quintessence, which, if extracted, could be used as a powerful medicine;   13. *elemented*] made of a mixture of elements;   18] various interpretations, most plausible of which is that stars seem larger the nearer they are to the sun, on whose light they depend;   23–4] in the old Ptolemaic astronomy, the heavens were constructed of a series of concentric spheres.

p 30. A NOCTURNAL UPON ST LUCY'S DAY.   title] 13 December, conventionally the shortest day in the old Julian calendar;   3. *flasks*] stars, which store sunlight as powder flasks hold gunpowder;   4. *squibs*] small charges;   7] 'whither' must refer to the earth, into which life has receded as if to the feet of a bed;   14. *express*] distil out;   21. *limbeck*] alchemist's retort;   28. *her death*] probably his wife, who died in 1617;   29] the quintessence of that nothing from which God created the world;   39. *Goat*] Capricorn, but also a symbol of lust.

p 31. A VALEDICTION: FORBIDDING MOURNING.   11–12] unlike earthquakes the supposed oscillation of the spheres is harmless;   25–36] beneath the famous conceit lies an ironic phallic imagery in which male and female attributes are reversed.

p 32. THE ECSTASY.   title] Greek *extasis*, a 'standing out', used in the Greek New Testament, and in neo-Platonism to describe the liberation of soul from body; cf. Marvell's *The Garden* (see p. 179);   27. *concoction*] result of refining minerals by heating;   52] each of the heavenly spheres of the Ptolemaic universe was controlled by a guiding angel or 'intelligence';   56. *allay*] alloy, added to the 'pure' metal to make it stronger;   57–8] Paracelsus held that the influence of the stars worked on man by mixing itself with the air;   61–2] the 'spirits' of the blood serve 'to unite and apply the faculties of the soul to the organs of the body' (Donne, *Sermons* II, 262);   67. *That*] 'in order that'; 1633 text reads 'Which'.

p 35. ELEGY 9: THE AUTUMNAL.   16. *anachorit*] anchorite, a recluse sworn to stay in one place;   29] the Persian King is reported to have admired and honoured a plane tree in Lydia;   41–2] Donne believed that at the Resurrection souls would have to reassemble all the scattered parts of their bodies, with many attendant problems;   47. *lation*] motion.

p 36. ELEGY 19: TO HIS MISTRESS.   11. *busk*] corset.   21. *Mahomet's Paradise*] i.e. a deeply sensual one;   29. *empery*] empire;   32. *seal*] the legal meaning, but also slang for genitals;   36. *Atlanta's balls*] Hippomenes outraced the unbeatable Atlanta by throwing down golden apples to distract her;   42. *imputed grace*] Lutheran theological term for Christ's gift of grace to the elect few who will be saved.

p 37. SATIRE 3.   title] one of a group of five, all probably written between 1593 and 1598;   1. *spleen*] anger;   23. *salamanders*] lizards so cold they could extinguish a fire;   23–4. *divine children*] see Daniel 3.8–30.   24. *fires of Spain, and the line*] the heat of Spain and the equator; also, fires of the Spanish Inquisition;   25. *limbecks*] alchemist's retorts;   34–5] the Devil will gladly give him the whole of hell as payment (to be quit = to pay off a debt);   47–8. *obey / The statecloth*] do obeisance to the canopy over the throne;   50. *Geneva*] home of Calvinism;   62. *pay values*] pay fines; those who did not attend Anglican services were fined;   96–7] Philip II of Spain; one of several possible Popes Gregory; Henry VIII; Martin Luther.

p 40. *From* AN ANATOMY OF THE WORLD. THE FIRST ANNIVERSARY.   title] written to commemorate the death in 1610 of Elizabeth Drury, a girl of 14 whom Donne did not know but whom he believed 'capable of the best praise that I could give'; her death provides both occasion and focal point for a generalized meditation on the decay and corruption of a world that is itself dying;   205–6] the new philosophies of the astronomers, Copernicus, Tycho Brahe, Kepler and Galileo, which threatened to subvert the social and philosophical systems based on the Ptolemaic theory, including the idea that an element of fire surrounded the earth;   256. *down-right . . . overthwarts*] vertical and horizontal lines;   258. *eight and forty shares*] Ptolemy divided the stars into so many constellations, supposedly unchanging;   265. *the Goat and Crab*] the Tropic of Capricorn stands at the winter solstice, that of Cancer at the summer solstice;   376. *illude*] deceive;   390. *Egyptian Mages*] they turned their rods into serpents (Exodus 7.10–12);   391. *artist*] magus (astrologer, alchemist) who claimed such powers.

p 43.   ELEGY ON MISTRESS BOULSTRED.   title] died 1609, aged 25;

17. *rounds*] surrounds;   20. *tenth rank*] there were nine orders of angels;   24. *four monarchies*] of Babylon, Persia, Greece and Rome;   72. *not such*] not as good as her, and not dead like her.

p 45.   HOLY SONNETS] the order is that of 1633, which was probably Donne's own and which suggests a coherent meditative sequence designed to lead to that state of contrition that is a necessary precondition of grace. See H. Gardner, Introduction to *Divine Poems*, and D. L. Peterson, 'J.D.'s *Holy Sonnets* and the Anglican Doctrine of Contrition', *Studies in Philology*, LVI (1959), 504–18.

> *Sonnet 4* 1–2] see Revelation 7.1;   8] see Luke 9.27.
> *Sonnet 5* 13. *them*] referring to sins, not 'some'.
> *Sonnet 7* 11] for Jacob and Esau, see Genesis 27.1–36.
> *Sonnet 8* 4. *further from corruption*] because not unevenly mixed.
> *Sonnet 9* 11–12] beauty is a sign of compassion, ugliness of unbending rigour.
> *Sonnet 11* 6] because it was an event beyond time.
> *Sonnet 12* 7. *two wills*] Old and New Testaments;   11–12] based on II Corinthians 3.6: 'Who also hath made us able ministers of the new testament; not of the letter but of the spirit: for the letter killeth, but the spirit giveth life.'

p 51.   GOOD FRIDAY, 1613.   1–2] see note to *The Ecstasy*, line 52;   17. *must die*] God's words to Moses (Exodus 23.20);   24] high above us, and yet opposite to us.

p 52.   A HYMN TO CHRIST.   12. *Thy sea*] Christ's blood;   17. *control*] inhibit, censure;   21. *loving more*] loving other persons or things than Christ.

p 53.   A HYMN TO GOD THE FATHER.   1. *where I begun*] original sin;   5] the refrain depends on 'Donne' and 'done' having the same pronunciation in Donne's time.

BEN JONSON

No attempt has been made to annotate the numerous echoes of classical poets in Jonson; for this see the editions by Herford and Simpson, Parfitt or Donaldson.

p 55. TO WILLIAM CAMDEN.   title] 1551–1623, historian, herald and Jonson's master at Westminster School; author of *Britannia* (1586) and *Remains of a Greater Work Concerning Britain* (1605).

p 56. ON MY FIRST SON.   title] Benjamin, ·died 1603 of plague; 1] 'Benjamin' is Hebrew for 'child of the right hand'.

p 57. TO FINE GRAND.   13. *partie-per-pale*] heraldic term denoting division into two equal parts;   14. *cobweb-lawn*] fine white linen;   15. *imprese*] (pronounced 'imprease') an *impresa* or personal device and motto for a shield.

p 57. TO JOHN DONNE.   1. *whe'er*] whether;   8. *better stone*] Roman custom; either a white chalk mark (see Horace *Odes* 1.36.10) or a pebble, supposedly placed in an urn to mark a good day (see Pliny *Nat. Hist.* 7.131 and Persius 2.1);   10. *puisnes*] underlings of any kind.

p 58. INVITING A FRIEND TO SUPPER.   36. *Poley or Parrot*] names of government informers; Poley was involved in Marlowe's stabbing.

p 59. TO A WEAK GAMESTER.   4. *rank setting*] putting up extravagant stakes;   18–22] 'pluck', 'encountered', 'colour', 'rest' and 'prime' are all derived from the card game primero.

p 60. SALOMON PAVY.   title] child actor in Jonson's *Cynthia's Revels* and *Poetaster*.

p 60. TO PENSHURST.   title] in Kent, home of Robert Sidney, Earl of Leicester (1563–1626), younger brother of Sir Philip (see lines 13–16); the poem was progenitor of a number of country-house poems by Carew (see p. 126), Herrick, Marvell (see p. 173) and others;   2. *touch*] black stone;   36. *officiously*] dutifully;   41–3] the evidence suggests that these details, as many others in the poem, are factually true;   79. *Penates*] household gods.

p 63. TO THE WORLD.   31. *wull*] will.

p 65. TO CELIA] based on Catullus, *Carmina* V; used in *Volpone* III. vii.

p 66. *From* EPISTLE TO ELIZABETH, COUNTESS OF RUTLAND.   title] daughter of Sir Philip Sidney, and herself a poet;   44. *touch*] black stone;   49. *Argive Queen*] Helen of Troy;

58. *Tyndarides*] Castor and Pollux;   57–62] all refer to constellations.

p 67. TO HEAVEN.   24. *With holy Paul*] see Romans 7.24 and Phillipians 1.23.

p 68. A CELEBRATION OF CHARIS: HER TRIUMPH.   28. *nard*] aromatic ointment.

p 69. MASTER VINCENT CORBETT.   title] died 1619, nurseryman and father of the minor poet Richard Corbett, Bishop of Oxford and Norwich.

p 70. *From* AN EPISTLE TO A FRIEND.   65. *purls*] pleats of a ruff; 67. *pound a prick*] to catch (a) a deer, (b) a penis.

p 71. AN ODE TO HIMSELF.   7–8] The Aonian springs and Thespia were both sacred to the Muses;   9. *Clarius*] Apollo; 27. *Japhet's line*] Prometheus, who stole fire from heaven; 30. *issue of Jove's brain*] Minerva, goddess of wisdom.

p 73. TO MR WILLIAM SHAKESPEARE.   20] all three lie close together in Poets' Corner, where Jonson himself later joined them;   35] all Roman tragedians; 'him of Cordova dead' is Seneca;   36–7. *buskin . . . socks*] the high and low shoes of the classical tragic and comic actors respectively.

ROBERT HERRICK

p 78. TO HIS BOOK.   4] cf. Psalm 78.66: 'And he smote his enemies in the hinder parts.'

p 78. UPON JULIA'S VOICE.   4. *lutes of amber*] lutes inlaid with either the fossil resin amber, or the alloy of gold and silver called amber.

p 79. TO THE REVEREND SHADE OF HIS RELIGIOUS FATHER. title] Herrick's father died in 1592, and suicide was suspected; hence the emphatic title;   1. *seven lustres*] thirty-five years; 4. *justments*] Herrick's coinage from Latin *justa* = things which are right or appropriate; as priest, Herrick may have read the whole burial service over the grave;   9] all plants associated with mourning.

p 80. THE VISION.   6. *glorious form*] Venus (see *Aeneid* I 315–20).

p 81. CORINNA'S GOING A-MAYING.   2. *god unshorn*] Apollo, hence the sun;   14. *May*] hawthorn or whitethorn, symbol of fertility; the May games still retained many characteristics of the pagan fertility cults from which they sprung, including much sexual licence;   25. *Titan*] the sun;   51. *green gown*] from rolling on the grass, hence a common euphemism for sexual intercourse;   59–68] cf. Wisdom of Solomon 2.1–8, Proverbs 7.18, Catullus *Carmina* V, Burton *Anatomy of Melancholy* 3.4.2.1.

p 87. THE HOCK CART.   title] Mildmay Fane, 2nd Earl, patron of poets and himself a minor poet and dramatist;   9. *maukin*] scarecrow;   20. *prank*]   dress;   21. *fill-horse*]   shaft-horse;   34. *frumenty*] spiced pudding;   40. *fanes . . . fats*] winnowing fans. and vats;   45. *neat*] cattle;   54. *pain*] effort, exertions.

p 90. A NUPTIAL SONG.   title] Epithalamie = marriage song; Clipseby Crewe (1599–1649), friend and patron of Herrick, married Jane Pulteney in 1625.   18. *blessed field*] see Genesis 27.27, 'the smell of a field which the lord hath blessed'; 36. *disparkling*] spreading sparks;   61. *coddled*] slowly boiled; 70. *gin*] trap;   80. *points*] laces, ties;   94. *lady-smock*] cuckoo flower;   96. *prick-madam*]   golden stonecrop;   *gentle-heart*] unidentified;   97. *maiden's-blush*]   pink   rose;   128. *conceit*] ingenuity;   154–6] i.e. the influence of the planets.

p 94. UPON PRUDENCE BALDWIN.   title] Herrick's maid, died 1678;   3. *Aesculapius*] god of medicine, to whom a cock was a proper offering.

p 95. UPON GLASS.   2. *predicant*] preacher, here specifically a Protestant.

p 97. CEREMONIES FOR CANDLEMAS EVE.   title] feast of Purification of Virgin Mary on 2 February;   17. *bents*] stiff-stemmed grasses.

p 99. HIS LITANY.   15. *lees*] dregs;   25. *burn blue*] a sign of the presence of evil spirits.

p 100. THE WHITE ISLAND.   11. *candour*] both brilliant whiteness and purity.

GEORGE HERBERT

p 103. THE AGONY.   3. *staff*] a measuring rod (rather than a pilgrim's staff).

p 104. AFFLICTION [1].   9. *household-stuff*] fabric for furnishing;   47. *where*] from the Williams manuscript;   1633 has 'neare';   53. *cross-bias*] a bowl is weighted to give it a bias in one direction; to cross-bias it is to try to force it into the opposite direction.

p 106. PRAYER [1].   5. *Engine*] any weapon or machine, in this case one used in a siege;   11. *in ordinary*] probably here 'regularly'; but there are manifold possible meanings which

Herbert probably wishes to draw on, among them a prayer
book, a meal and a tavern.

p 107. JORDAN [1].   12. *pull for prime*] choose a winning hand at the
card game primero.

p 111. THE PEARL.   1–2. *head and pipes*] presumably of a hydraulic
printing press;   13. *whether*] which;   32. *seeled*] the eyes of
young falcons were 'seeled' by sewing the lids together.

p 114. SUBMISSION.   20. *eyes*] a pun on 'ayes', votes for a motion
in the House of Commons; Herbert was MP for Mont-
gomery in 1624.

p 114. THE QUIP.   2. *trainbands*] militia.

p 118. THE JEWS.   2. *scions*] slips cut for grafting.

p 118. THE COLLAR.   title] not a modern clerical collar, which was
not worn in Herbert's time, but any restraining band or
yoke, with a pun on 'choler';   5. *store*] abundance.

p 121. THE FORERUNNERS.   1. *harbingers*] going ahead of a king,
they made a white mark on doors of houses to be used by the
royal party; here they mark hair white to prepare a lodging
for old age;   9. *pass*] care.

p 123. DOOMSDAY.   11–12] music and dancing were thought to
cure the hysterical condition believed to be caused by the bite
of the tarantula.

THOMAS CAREW

p 126. TO SAXHAM.   title] home of Sir John Crofts, grandfather
of Mary Wentworth (see her epitaph, p. 132); one of sev-
eral poëms inspired by Jonson's 'Penshurst' (see p. 60);
18. *volary*] aviary;   42. *hind*] servant.

p 127. A RAPTURE.   cf. Donne, Elegy 19 (see p. 36);   10. *Swiss*]
a mercenary, especially of the Vatican Guard; Carew may
also be glancing at Calvinist Geneva;   15. *stalking pageant*]
stage giant;   76. *alembic*] alchemist's retort (of phallic
shape);   85. *Cyprian*] Cyprus was the birthplace of Venus;
115–16] Lucretia killed herself after being raped, and was the
pattern of married chastity; Pietro Aretino (1492–1556) was
notorious as a writer of erotica;   117. *Lais*] Greek courte-
san;   125–6] Penelope, wife of Odysseus, whose name was
synonymous with wifely fidelity; Carew may also be pun-
ning on the Greek *pene* = shuttle or bobbin;   131–2] Daphne
was turned into a bay tree to avoid rape by Apollo;   134. *sun*]
Apollo;   156. *maugre*] despite.

p 132. AN ELEGY UPON DOCTOR JOHN DONNE. (text from Donne's *Poems* 1633); 35. *two-edged words*] Latinate puns (as opposed to Carew's own English pun on feat/feet); 87. *engross*] both to write in large letters and to make a list; 97. *flamens*] Roman priests; a 'two-edged word' that refers back to the imagery of fire in the poem.

p 135. TO GEORGE SANDYS. title] see p. 216. 1–2] Carew is punning on quire (of paper) and the choir of a church, and on metric and human feet (cf. line 14); 5. *porch*] the poem was printed at the front of Sandys' book.

JOHN MILTON

p 138. *From* AT A VACATION EXERCISE. 19–20] a 'toy' is a superficial or facetious figure or trope, perhaps fashionably 'metaphysical'; 48–57] see *Odyssey* 8.521–2.

p 140. L'ALLEGRO. title] 'The Cheerful Man' as opposed to 'The Thoughtful Man' of 'Il Penseroso'; 10. *Cimmerian desert*] land of perpetual darkness (*Odyssey* 11.13–22); 17–24] this alternative genealogy for the graces is Milton's own invention.; 27. *cranks*] verbal tricks, conceits; 67. *tale*] tally (of sheep); 80. *cynosure*] guiding star; 104. *friar's lantern*] will-o'-the-wisp; 110. *lubber fiend*] friendly and hardworking goblin; 132. *sock*] light shoe of the comic actor.

p 143. IL PENSEROSO. 12. *Melancholy*] often in Renaissance thought the state of high inspiration and insight; 18. *Memnon*] Ethiopian prince (*Odyssey* 11.552); 19. *Ethiop queen*] Cassiopeia, turned into a constellation by the offended nymphs; 23–4] the pedigree is invented by Milton; 35. *cypress lawn*] light material, here black ('sable'); 55. *hist*] summon; 59. *Cynthia*] the moon, whose chariot is drawn by dragons; 87. *the Bear*] Ursa Major, which never sets; 88. *Hermes*] Hermes Trismegistus, Egyptian mystic mistakenly supposed, like Plato, to have anticipated Christian ideas; 89–96] for the melancholic sage, cf. Donne, 'First Anniversary', 391–5 (see p. 43) and Prospero in *The Tempest;* 99. *Thebes, or Pelops' line*] tragedies of the houses of Oedipus and Agamemnon; 102. *buskined*] the buskin or high shoe of the tragic actor; 109] Chaucer, *The Squire's Tale;* 124. *Attic boy*] Cephalus, loved by Aurora, goddess of the dawn; 156. *pale*] area enclosed by the cloisters.

p 148. LYCIDAS. introduction] the 'friend' was Edward King, aspiring poet and priest, whose death was commemorated in a collection *Justa Eduardo King* ('Rites for Edward King') by his Cambridge contemporaries; Milton's was the last poem in the volume; 15. *sisters*] the Muses; 52–5] slopes and peaks of Anglesey (Mona) and the river Dee (Deva) in Chester; 61–3] Orpheus, son of the Muse Calliope, was torn to pieces by a mob, and his head thrown into the river Hebrus; 73. *guerdon*] reward; 75. *blind Fury*] Atropos, one of the three Fates; 77. *Phoebus*] Apollo, god of poetry; 85–6] spring and river associated with classical pastoral; 96. *Hippotades*] Aeolus, god of the winds; 99. *Panope*] sea nymph; 103. *Camus*] of the river Cam; 106. *sanguine flower*] hyacinth; 109] St Peter; 128. *grim wolf*] Roman Catholic church; 130. *two-handed engine*] an 'engine' is any kind of instrument; most plausible explanation is that it is Christ's sword of judgement (Revelation 1.16); 'at the door' does not support this, but suggests the image may refer us back to the 'two massy keys' of St Peter, with 'smite' in its common Biblical sense of 'punish'; 132. *Alpheus*] pastoral river god; 138. *swart star*] Sirius, the Dog Star; 142–50] the list of flowers is an afterthought, added on a separate sheet in Milton's manuscript draft; 160–3] Bellerium was Land's End, where St Michael's Mount guards England against the Catholic threat symbolized by the Spanish towns of Namancos and Bayona; 175. *nectar*] not honey, but the pure drink of the gods; 176. *unexpressive*] inexpressible.

p 152. SONNET 15. title] in 1655 Catholic soldiers massacred many (perhaps 1700) members of the Vaudois sect, seen by many as the first true Protestants, in Piedmont, northern Italy; 12. *triple Tyrant*] the Pope.

p 153. SONNET 16. 1] Milton became totally blind in 1652.

RICHARD CRASHAW

p 155. LUKE 11. title] see verses 27–8, where a woman calls out these words to Jesus; the epigram is Crashaw's reply to her.

p 155. NEW YEAR'S DAY. 4. *dear drops*] the poem was originally called 'An Himne for the Circumsision day of our Lord'.

p 156. CHARITAS NIMIA. title] 'Love beyond measure'; 8] i.e. of Cupid, god of Love.

p 158. A HYMN TO SAINT TERESA. title] Spanish mystic and saint (1515–82); introduction *discalced*] barefoot; 48. *unvalued*] invaluable;   71. *race*] cut, slash;   79. *dart*] in her autobiography Teresa describes a vision of an angel with a 'long dart of gold' which he thrust into her heart 'and the very inwards of my bowels' causing both pain and a desire that it would not stop;   100. *dies*] playing on the common use of 'die' to mean sexual consummation;   172. *zone*] girdle.

p 164. TO THE COUNTESS OF DENBIGH.   title] Susan Villiers, Crashaw's patron and a follower of Queen Henrietta Maria; 1. *heart*] the 1652 text has an emblem above it of a padlocked heart with a verse asserting that love, not force, can unlock it; 36. *cabinet*] case for safe custody of jewels.

ANDREW MARVELL

p 167. THE DEFINITION OF LOVE.   24. *planisphere*] map showing a sphere projected on to a plane.

p 168. TO HIS COY MISTRESS.   11. *vegetable*] having power of simple life and growth, but no more;   29. *quaint honour*] both words used at the time as slang for the vagina;   34. *dew*] 1681 *Poems* reads 'glew'.

p 169. AN HORATION ODE.   title] Cromwell returned from Ireland in May 1650, and left for Scotland (lines 105–8) in July 1650. Fairfax, whose daughter Marvell was soon to tutor, resigned as commander-in-chief of the Parliamentary forces in June 1650, Cromwell succeeding him. Fairfax opposed the Scottish expedition; in late 1650 or early 1651 Marvell joined the Fairfax family at Appleton House (see note to 'Upon Appleton House');   32. *bergamot*] species of pear; 42. *penetration*] occupation of a space by two bodies at the same time;   60. *edge*] it has been pointed out that this is the middle word of the middle line;   47–54] Cromwell was wrongly thought to have tricked Charles into fleeing from Hampton Court to Carisbrooke, a move which helped convince many parliamentarians that the king's duplicity was such that he had to be executed;   72. *happy fate*] according to Pliny (*Nat. Hist.* 28.2) the discovery of the head was seen as a good omen;   105. *Pict*] Scot.

p 172. THE PICTURE OF LITTLE T.C. IN A PROSPECT OF FLOWERS.   title] possibly Theophila Cornewall, born 1644;   10. *Darling of the Gods*] literal translation of the Greek 'theophila'.

p 173. *From* UPON APPLETON HOUSE. title] home of Thomas, 3rd Baron Fairfax of Cameron (1612–71), for whom see note to 'An Horatian Ode'. The opening verses describe his house as unostentatious, and relate the history of the family; 281. *the hero*] either Sir Thomas Fairfax (died 1599) or the Lord General himself; both had fought on the Continent; 292. *dian*] reveille; 301. *virgin Nymph*] Mary Fairfax, to whom Marvell was tutor. (Verses 46–62 turn to the fields around the garden, described in imagery relating them to the Civil Wars; the wood the speaker then enters is thus a sanctuary by contrast); 532. *throstle*] thrush; 535. *stork-like*] the stork was said to leave one of its young to the owner of the house on which it nested; 537. *hewel*] green wood-pecker; 538. *holtfelster*] woodcutter; 577. *sibyl's leaves*] the Cumaean Sibyl wrote her oracular pronouncements on leaves; 580. *Mexique paintings*] made of feathers; the plumes are here the pens of human writers superseded by 'Nature's mystic book' (584); 582. *light mosaic*] of the trembling leaves, as opposed to the heavier Mosaic books of the Bible; 586. *mask*] costume, disguise.

p 179. THE GARDEN. 2. *the palm, the oak, or bays*] for war, politics and poetry respectively; 44. *its own resemblance*] the ocean was thought to contain a 'kind' or species corresponding to each one on land; 51–4] cf. Donne's 'Ecstasy' (see p. 32) and note; also Donne, *Sermons* VI.101, on 'a belief of *extasie* and *raptures*; That the body remaining upon the floore, or in the bed, the soul may be gone out to the contemplation of heavenly things'; 56. *various light*] of God, shining on the disembodied soul.

p 181. ON A DROP OF DEW. 1. *orient*] used of any high-quality gem stone; 37. *manna*] see Exodus 16.21.

p 182. A DIALOGUE BETWEEN THE SOUL AND BODY. 14] the body is made to walk erect, so that when it looks down it seems on the edge of a precipice; 15. *needless*] the body does not need the soul.

p 184. DAMON THE MOWER. 22. *Phaeton*] son of Helios whose sun-chariot he drove dangerously near the earth; 83. *clown's-all-heal*] marsh woundwort (*stachys palustris*).

p 186. BERMUDAS. 20. *Ormus*] Hormuz, on the Persian Gulf; 23. *apples*] pineapples.

p 188. ON MR MILTON'S 'PARADISE LOST'. 22. *in a play*] Dryden in fact attempted an opera in 1674, the year Marvell wrote this poem; 47. *Town-Bayes*] Dryden; 49. *bushy points*] laces or tags tying hose to doublet (as poets tag verses with rhyme); 52. *praise . . . commend*] presumably because of the exigencies of the 'mode' of rhyming verse.

HENRY VAUGHAN

p 192. REGENERATION. 28. *Jacob's bed*] see Genesis 28.10–22; 31. *He*] i.e. Christ, the new ladder to heaven; 61. *I wondered much*] presumably the stones are the souls of the saved and the damned respectively.

p 194. THE RETREAT. 26. *city of palm trees*] Jericho, seen by Moses (Deuteronomy 34.3); hence, the New Jerusalem.

p 195. SILENCE AND STEALTH OF DAYS. 2. *thou*] Vaughan's brother William, died 1648; 19. *snuff*] wick of a snuffed candle; 29. *pearl*] cf. Herbert's poem, p. 111.

p 196. CORRUPTION. 25. *lieger*] a resident ambassador; 40. '*Thrust in thy sickle*'] see Revelation 14.14–20 for Christ's sickle of death and judgement.

p 197. THE WORLD. 37. *pelf*] riches.

p 199. I WALKED THE OTHER DAY. 33–5] referring to Vaughan's brother William.

p 200. THEY ARE ALL GONE INTO THE WORLD OF LIGHT. 38. *perspective*] telescope.

p 202. THE BOOK. 6. *grass*] flax; 11–12] the boards of the book are of thin wood.

MISCELLANY

p 207. SONNET 40. 13. *he*] the sun.
p 208. SONNET 85. 13. *frame*] structure (see *OED* III.7).
p 208. SONNET 86. 3. *distasted*] offended.
p 211. THE POET QUESTIONS PEACE. 178. *proved*] tested; 211. *win*] persuade.
p 214. ON HIS MISTRESS, THE QUEEN OF BOHEMIA. title] Elizabeth (1596–1662), daughter of James I; exiled from Bohemia, with her husband, during Thirty Years War; 10. *Philomel*] nightingale.
p 215. UPON THE SUDDEN RESTRAINT OF THE EARL OF SOMERSET. title] James Carr, favourite of James I, conspired to murder Sir Thomas Overbury (1613).
p 217. THE DEATH OF EURYDICE. 17. *cur*] Cerberus; 39–43] all

people who had been condemned to perpetual torments in the underworld.

p 219. SONNET . . . NEAR MERLOU CASTLE.   title] in France, home of Henri, duc de Montmorenci;   14. *vegetable*] having the power of simple life and growth.

p 220. AN ODE UPON A QUESTION MOVED.   65] addressing the stars.

p 224. THE ALL-SEEING INTELLECT.   190. *frame*] structure; 191. *Intellect*] the highest faculty of the soul;   *The Purple Island*] a long allegorical poem based on the body of man.

p 229. TO HIS LATE MAJESTY.   title] James I, who had written a treatise on Scottish poetry.

p 231. UPON FRANCIS BEAUMONT.   title] the dramatist, died 1616, younger brother of Sir John.

p 232. From BOSWORTH FIELD.   199. *brother's*] Edward IV; 215–17] the Duke of Somerset, executed after the battle of Tewkesbury, 1471, was grandfather of Henry Tudor, who defeated Richard at Bosworth Field in August 1485.

p 234. SONNET 11.   6. *six signs*] of the Zodiac;   8. *Apelles*] Celebrated Greek painter.

p 234. SONNET 6.   1. *sweet soul*] Mary Cunningham, Drummond's fiancée, died 1615.

p 236. MERCY PLEADS FOR MANKIND.   644. *drieth*] drought; 646. *Cynthian mountains*] the 'Mountains of the Moon', supposed source of the Nile;   652. *sophies*] the three Magi; 657–8] John the Baptist; see Luke 1.41.   659–61] see Luke 2.25–38;   670. *devowed*] disavowed.

p 238. BOOK II, THE SECOND SONG.   1. *Aurora*] goddess of dawn;   8. *stonehorse*] stallion;   21. *Nereus' daughter*] sea nymph;   25. *threw the bar*] a heavy rod of wood or iron was thrown in a trial of strength;   50. *this round*] the world; 63–4. *Oreades . . . Hamadryades*] the nymphs of mountains and of trees;   68. *haydigyes*] a reel, or winding country dance.

p 240. IN OBITUM M.S.   title] 'On the death of M.S.' (M.S. probably = 'Maritae Suae', 'his wife').

p 240. ON THE COUNTESS DOWAGER OF PEMBROKE.   title] Mary Herbert, died 1621, herself a poet and the recipient of Sidney's *Arcadia;*   10. *Niobe*] weeping for her children, she was turned to stone by Zeus, but continued to weep.

p 241. THE EXEQUY.   title] 'funeral rite' for King's wife Anne, died 1624;   22. *preposterous*] punning on the Latin = back to front;   101. *bottom*] hull of a ship.

p 246. 10! title] Greek or Latin cheer of joy.

p 248. THE PASSION. 6. *Tophet*] hell.

p 252. ON THE DUKE OF BUCKINGHAM. title] the powerful and unpopular favourite of James I and Charles I, stabbed by John Felton; 6. *pash*] be smashed, demolished; 7. *giddy train*] the mob; 8–12] Buckingham was accused of being in league with various powers, of favouring Catholics, of misguiding James and Charles, and of bleeding the Exchequer for his own aggrandizement; 33. *the vulgar*] the common opinion.

p 253. A GRATULATORY TO MR BEN JONSON. 11. *Musaeus*] legendary Greek poet; 25. *Perseus*] slayer of the gorgon Medusa; 35–6] for stealing fire from heaven, Prometheus was chained to a rock where each day an eagle consumed his liver, which was restored each night; 44. *Pactolus*] gold-bearing river in Lydia; 45–7] Alcinous, rich king of the Phaeacians, famous for his love of horticulture; 57. *palsy*] Jonson suffered a paralysing stroke in 1628.

p 255. A PARLEY WITH HIS EMPTY PURSE. 28. *cross*] coin.

p 256. ON A MAID OF HONOUR. 6. *Priapus*] Phallic god of fruit-fulness.

p 258. AGAINST THEM WHO LAY UNCHASTITY TO THE SEX OF WOMAN. title] an answer to Donne's 'Go and catch a falling star' (see p. 23); 10. *the West*] the gold mines of America and the West Indies; 12] alchemists tried to make gold from copper.

p 259. NOX NOCTI. title] 'night unto night showeth knowledge' (Psalms 19.2).

p 260. FOR THE LADY OLIVIA PORTER. title] Olivia Boteler (died 1663), wife of Endymion Porter, one of the leading patrons of the period.

p 264. PUERPERIUM. title] 'Confinement' (for the birth of Charles I's fourth son, Henry); 16. *halcyon*] the kingfisher, bird of peace.

p 264. *From* A PANEGYRIC TO MY LORD PROTECTOR. 9–10] Neptune quieted a storm raised by Juno to drown Aeneas and his followers.

p 267. SONNET 3. 2. *post*] messenger; 5. *whether*] which; 23. *Sophonisba*] Carthaginian lady who committed suicide for the sake of her lover Masinissa, whom she preferred to her husband Syphax; 26–8] characters in Sidney's *Arcadia*.

p 270. A BALLAD UPON A WEDDING. 6. *wake*] parish festival; 7–8] Charing Cross is 'hard by' the modern Haymarket;

12. *Vorty*] rustic dialect for 'forty'; 19. *course-a-park*] country game in which girl called out one of the other sex to chase her (*OED*); 32. *Whitsun-ale*] country festival associated with both Whit Sunday and sheep-shearing; 47–8] the sun was supposed to dance on Easter Day; 89. *trained band*] militia; 122. *posset*] spiced drink.

p 279. A SONG OF DALLIANCE. 5. *genial*] nuptial.

p 281. MY DEAR AND ONLY LOVE. 15. *touch*] touchstone, hence test; 23. *blind*] siege fortification.

p 283. *From* THE KING'S DISGUISE. title] Charles I left Oxford in secret in April 1646, and gave himself up to the Scots at Newark in May; 11. *mewed*] shed; 15. *blacks*] ink was made of lampblack; 18. *darkness*] see Exodus 10.21–23 for the ninth of the Ten Plagues of Egypt; 19. *budge*] fur; 21] 'neither Egyptian nor Presbyterian could'; 31–2] the Earl of Manchester 'purified' Cambridge University for Parliament; 37. *renegado*] traitor, turncoat; 38] this Ordinance was pressed by Cromwell; it stopped anyone holding a command in the army and a seat in Parliament simultaneously; 46. *keldar*] womb.

p 284. ON THE EARL OF STRAFFORD. title] Thomas Wentworth (1593–1641), Charles I's most able and most feared minister, impeached and executed on a spurious charge of treason; 1–4] the charge was never proved, and Charles signed the death warrant through fear of the mob; 6] accused of being a Papist, he was in fact a Calvinist.

p 285. HUSBANDRY. 5–6] 'to make the broken heart into clods, it is torn by the sharp arrows of disdain'; 18. *assimilation*] 'absorption of nutriment into the system' (*OED*).

p 286. TO HER QUESTIONING HIS ESTATE. 9. *terrars*] terriers or rent-rolls; 11–12] Croesus' wealth came from the gold-bearing sands of the Pactolus; 16. *quintessence*] the elixir for which alchemists searched.

p 287. *From* COOPER'S HILL. title] near Windsor; 235. *Faunus and Sylvanus*] Latin gods of field and woodland, both identified with the Greek Pan; 273–6] it has been suggested that the stag is Strafford; 325–30] Magna Carta, signed at Runnymede.

p 290. THE GARDEN. 1. *quit*] even.

p 291. ON THE DEATH OF A PRINCE. 17] i.e. make the thread of life stronger; 19. *urn*] the urn of Fate, from which the names of those to die are chosen.

p 295. THE GRASSHOPPER.   14. *Ceres*] goddess of corn; *Bacchus*] god of wine;   25–6] a fire was kept burning by the Vestal Virgins; Vesta was goddess of the hearth, and thus every house her temple;   31. *old Greek*] possibly the reading of classical writers, but a 'greek' was a card-sharper, and line 34 suggests a game of cards;   33. *Hesper*] the evening star.

p 296. TO ALTHEA. FROM PRISON.   title] the royalist Lovelace was imprisoned twice by the parliamentarians, in 1642 and 1648.

p 297. LOVE MADE IN THE FIRST AGE.   8] Lovelace is playing on 'to comply'; thus 'complying' was construed as 'rage' or passion.

p 299. THE SPRING.   23–4] Daphne fled from Apollo, god of poetry, and was turned into a tree to avoid rape;   25–32] Orpheus (from Thrace) charmed the trees and rocks from Olympus with his music.

p 302. *From* TO THE ROYAL SOCIETY.   title] founded 1660; this poem written for Thomas Sprat's *History* of the Society, 1667. There are 184 lines in all;   63. *forbidden tree*] both abstract reasoning and mystical insight as ways to knowledge;   79. *piece*] picture.

p 306. AND NOW A FIG FOR THE LOWER HOUSE.   5. *groat*] rhymes with 'nought', etc;   6. *Delinquent*] royalist;   12. *pursuivants*] officers of the state.

FURTHER READING

JOHN AUBREY, *Aubrey's Brief Lives*, ed. Oliver Lawson Dick, 3rd edn, London, 1958.

HERSCHEL BAKER, *The Wars of Truth: Studies in the Decay of Christian Humanism in the Earlier 17th Century*, Cambridge, Mass., 1952.

JOAN BENNETT, *Five Metaphysical Poets*, 3rd edn, Cambridge, 1964.

S. L. BETHELL, *The Cultural Revolution of the 17th Century*, London, 1951.

MALCOLM BRADBURY AND DAVID PALMER (eds), *Metaphysical Poetry*, Stratford-upon-Avon Studies, XI, London, 1970.

DOUGLAS BUSH, *English Literature in the Earlier 17th Century*, 2nd edn, Oxford, 1962.

PATRICK CRUTWELL, *The Shakespearean Moment and Its Place in the Poetry of the 17th Century*, London, 1954.

GODFREY DAVIES, *The Early Stuarts 1603–1660*, 2nd edn, Oxford, 1959.

T. S. ELIOT, 'The Metaphysical Poets', in *Selected Essays*, 3rd edn, London, 1951.

BORIS FORD (ed.), *From Donne to Marvell*, Harmondsworth, 1956.

ROSEMARY FREEMAN, *English Emblem Books*, London, 1948.

WILLIAM E. HALEWOOD, *The Poetry of Grace: Reformation Themes and Structures in English 17th-Century Poetry*, New Haven, 1970.

HIRAM HAYDN, *The Counter-Renaissance*, New York, 1950.

CHRISTOPHER HILL, *Puritanism and Revolution: Studies in Interpretation of the English Revolution of the 17th Century*, London, 1958.

CHRISTOPHER HILL, *Society and Puritanism in Pre-Revolutionary England*, London, 1964.

JOHN HOLLANDER, *The Untuning of the Sky: Ideas of Music in English Poetry 1500–1700*, Princeton, 1961.

B. L. JOSEPH, *Shakespeare's Eden: The Commonwealth of England 1558–1629*, London, 1971.

WILLIAM R. KEAST (ed.), *Seventeenth-Century English Poetry: Modern Essays in Criticism*, New York, 1962.

J. P. KENYON, *Stuart England*, London, 1978.

FRANK KERMODE (ed.), *The Metaphysical Poets*, Greenwich, Conn., 1969.

L. C. KNIGHTS, *Drama and Society in the Age of Jonson*, London, 1937.

WILLIAM M. LAMONT, *Godly Rule: Politics and Religion, 1603–1660*, London, 1969.

ARTHUR O. LOVEJOY, *The Great Chain of Being: A Study of the History of an Idea*, Cambridge, Mass., 1936.

MOLLY M. MAHOOD, *Poetry and Humanism*, London, 1950.

LOUIS L. MARTZ, *The Poetry of Meditation: A Study in English Religious Literature of the 17th century*, New Haven, 1954.

JOSEPH A. MAZZEO, *Renaissance and Revolution: Backgrounds to 17th-Century English Literature*, New York, 1965.

JOSEPH A. MAZZEO, *Renaissance and 17th-Century Studies*, New York, 1964.

EARL MINER, *The Cavalier Mode from Jonson to Cotton*, Princeton, 1971.

EARL MINER, *The Metaphysical Mode from Donne to Cowley*, Princeton, 1969.

PAUL E. MORE AND FRANK L. CROSS (eds), *Anglicanism: The Thought and Practice of the Church of England, illustrated from the Religious Literature of the 17th Century*, London, 1935.

JOHN R. MULDER, *The Temple of the Mind: Education and Literary Taste in 17th-Century England*, New York, 1969.

C. A. PATRIDES AND RAYMOND B. WADDINGTON (eds), *The Age of Milton: Backgrounds to 17th-Century Literature*, Manchester, 1980.

MARIO PRAZ, *Studies in 17th-Century Imagery*, 2nd edn, Rome, 1964.

CHRISTOPHER RICKS (ed.), *English Poetry and Prose 1540–1674*, London, 1970.

ISABEL RIVERS, *Classical and Christian Ideas in English Renaissance Poetry*, London, 1979.

MALCOLM M. ROSS, *Poetry and Dogma: The Transformation of Eucharistic Symbols in 17th-Century English Poetry*, New Brunswick, 1954.

MAREN-SOFIE ROSTVIG, *The Happy Man: Studies in the Metamorphoses of a Classical Ideal, 1600–1700*, Oslo, 1954.

ROBERT L. SHARP, *From Donne to Dryden: The Revolt against Metaphysical Poetry*, Chapel Hill, 1940.

JAMES SMITH, 'On Metaphysical Poetry', *Scrutiny*, II (1933), 222–39.

LEO SPITZER, *Classical and Christian Ideas of World Harmony*, Baltimore, 1963.

STANLEY STEWART, *The Enclosed Garden: The Tradition and the Image in 17th-Century Poetry*, Madison, 1966.

LAURENCE STONE, *The Causes of the English Revolution 1529–1642*, London, 1972.

JOSEPH H. SUMMERS, *The Heirs of Donne and Jonson*, New York and London, 1970.

H. R. SWARDSON, *Poetry and the Fountain of Light*, London, 1962.

ROSAMOND TUVE, *Elizabethan and Metaphysical Imagery*, Chicago, 1947.

BRIAN VICKERS, *Classical Rhetoric in English Poetry*, London, 1970.

GEOFFREY WALTON, *Metaphysical to Augustan*, London, 1955.

BASIL WILLEY, *The Seventeenth-Century Background*, London, 1934.

INDEX OF FIRST LINES